D1445708

PITT SERIES IN

POLICY AND

INSTITUTIONAL

STUDIES

GLOBAL

■

COMPETITIVENESS

■

AND INDUSTRIAL

■

GROWTH IN

■

TAIWAN AND

■

THE PHILIPPINES

Cheng-Tian Kuo

University of Pittsburgh Press
Pittsburgh and London

Published by the University of Pittsburgh Press, Pittsburgh, Pa., 15260
Copyright © 1995, University of Pittsburgh Press
All rights reserved
Manufactured in the United States of America
Printed on acid-free paper

Library of Congress Cataloging-in-Publication Data
Kuo, Cheng-Tian, 1957–
    Global competitiveness and industrial growth in Taiwan and the
Philippines / Cheng-Tian Kuo.
        p.   cm. — (Pitt series in policy and institutional studies)
    Includes bibliographical references and index.
    ISBN 0-8229-3860-X (alk. paper)
    1. Industries—Taiwan.   2. Industries—Philippines.   3. Industrial
policy—Taiwan.   4. Industrial policy—Philippines.   I. Title.
II. Series.
HC430.5.K8815   1995
338.095124′9—dc20   94-39789
                                                              CIP
            A CIP catalogue record for this book is available from
                          the British Library.
                          Eurospan, London

To Darwen Tsao
who sacrificed so much for this book

Contents

Tables

Figures

Preface

On the relationship between the social sciences and society, Samuel Huntington made a laudable statement: "works in the social sciences should be judged not only on their intellectual merit but also by the contributions they make to achieving moral purposes" (1988, 4). Ironically it was Huntington's writing on one-party rule (1968) that has been most often cited and abused by politicians and coopted scholars of authoritarian regimes to justify their suppression of human rights and democratic values in the name of social order and economic development.

Unfortunately, the academic response to such a justification of authoritarianism has been one of uneasy complacence. Many economists, sociologists, and political scientists accept authoritarianism as a necessary evil for revamping Third World economies. Even scholars of the left concede that authoritarian rule may actually create "dependent development" in developing countries. Those developing countries and former socialist countries which recently transformed from authoritarian rule but failed to achieve the expected level of economic prosperity have begun to loose confidence in democracy. It is unfortunate that these people have overlooked the tremendous human price paid for authoritarianism. It is a tragedy, however, that the academic community has not been able to resolve the dilemma between authoritarianism and economic development and is leaving the issue behind.

By exposing the misconstrued Taiwan miracle and analyzing the Philippines's disastrous experimentation with the Taiwanese and Korean models, I hope to destroy the popular myth that authoritarianism, despite its political defects, is the cure for economic backwardness. "Whatever may have been the benefits relative to the costs of authoritarianism in the past," Raymond Vernon cautioned two decades ago, "the costs appear to be greater than the benefits now" (1971, 354). His warning still holds true today.

In this lengthy and strenuous academic journey, Darwen Tsao gave me unreserved support to overcome numerous psychological and material hardships. Without her encouragement and sacrifice, this journey would have been an endlessly long march. That this research is devoted to her expresses only a small fraction of my appreciation and apology to her.

During my research I have benefitted from the guidance, assistance, and comments by the following people: Ruping Alonzo, Shiping Cai, Dante Canlas, Steve Chan, Cuengon Chen, Mingtong Chen, T.J. Chen, Yenliang Chen, Cal Clark, Bruce Cumings, Emmanuel de Dios, Richard Doner, Raul Fabella, Ricardo Ferrer, Barbara Geddes, Stephen Haggard, Linxu He, Christopher Holoman, Fu Hu, Paul Hutchcroft, D. Gale Johnson, Peter Katzenstein, Chikeung Ko, Danny Lam, Zhizhen Liang, Leo Lee, Charles Lipson, Manuel Montes, James Nolt, David O'Connor, John Padgett, William Parish, Rongju Qu, Philippe C. Schmitter, Duncan Snidal, Tang Tsou, Daniel Verdier, Robert Wade, Tiwu Wang, Edwin Winckler, Quanzhen Xiao, Olive Yabut, Yufa Zhang, Hongyuan Zhu, Yunhan Zhu, and former Philippine President Diosdado Macapagal. Particularly, I appreciate the careful reading and detailed comments on the entire manuscript by Steve Chan, T.J. Chen, Cal Clark, Richard Doner, and Edwin Winckler.

I wish to thank and pay my respect to those Taiwanese and Philippine officials, staff of industry associations, and business leaders who granted my interviews and provided me with vital documents but who wished to remain anonymous because of post-authoritarianism blues. For the first time in decades, they had the opportunity to tell the true story (though not a pretty one) about what really happened under the "enlightened despotism."

Finally, I am grateful to the financial support of my relatives, the *China Times*, and the Center for East Asian Studies at the University of Chicago. The opinions and errors in this research, however, are my responsibility and should not be regarded as those of the above-mentioned institutions and persons.

GLOBAL

COMPETITIVENESS

AND INDUSTRIAL

GROWTH IN

TAIWAN AND

THE PHILIPPINES

1

INTRODUCTION

Theoretical and Empirical Questions

The economic achievements of Asian Newly Industrializing Countries (NICs)[1] in the past thirty years have impressed scholars, journalists, and decision makers all over the world. During the 1950s the economic conditions of these NICs were not much different from other developing countries: per capita income was low, the industrial sector was small and weak, export products were not competitive, balance-of-payments problems were serious, and workers were unemployed or underemployed. In the 1960s, however, these countries embarked on a rapid pace of economic development. Two-digit growth rates were frequently registered by these countries in the 1960s and 1970s, despite the turbulence in the world economy caused by the two oil crises. At the beginning of the 1990s, while Latin American NICs are suffering from chronic debt crises, Asian NICs continue their industrial adjustment and are ready to join the club of developed countries.

What has caused the success of the Asian NICs? Social scientists have offered several plausible explanations: the adoption of liberal economic policies, the ideology of Confucianism, the history of colonialism, land reforms, Cold War politics, and the absence of serious class conflicts. These explanations have provided only partial, and sometimes incorrect, answers to this development question.

In recent years, these explanations have been modified and incorporated into a powerful theory of political economy, the theory of the developmental state. A developmental state contributes to rapid economic growth in several ways. It can resist political pressure from antigrowth interest groups such as landlords and inefficient producers. It can formulate long-term development strategies without the distortions of short-term political concerns. It can mobilize and utilize social resources more efficiently. It can also implement development policies more consistently and effectively.

Since Taiwan, Singapore, and South Korea have all been authoritarian states, several theorists of the developmental state have concluded that an authoritarian state is *the* major contributor to the economic miracle in these countries. Therefore, to the dismay of believers in democracy, the experiences of Asian NICs seem to suggest an inevitable trade-off between democratic freedom and economic development.

This trade-off thesis, along with the Asian development models, has had an impact on some countries that face critical economic decisions. China's reformers learned from the Korean model and formulated "neo-authoritarianism" in order to promulgate their program. In the former Soviet republics, leaders have asked for dictatorial power to cope with deteriorating economic conditions. Even in newborn democracies such as Poland and the Philippines, there have been demands and efforts to rebuild "strong leadership" in order to salvage their economies.

A reexamination of the Asian development models, therefore, has significant academic and policy implications for the 1990s. First, if the autonomous state thesis is correct in explaining the development experiences of the NICs in the past few decades, then the same theory can be used to explain the unsuccessful experiences of other developing countries. Furthermore, if the thesis is correct, other

Third World nations and newborn democracies should accept the trade-off between political democracy and economic welfare. A "benevolent despot" might be a necessary evil for all late developers.

In this book I will argue, first, that the theory of the developmental state has serious logical flaws: either the definition of the developmental state is ambiguous or its components have no theoretical relationship to rapid economic performance. Second, by carefully reexamining historical records and doing a stratified comparative study of a successful case (Taiwan) and a failed case (the Philippines), I will empirically refute the developmental state theory.

Third, and most important, I will demonstrate that three types of economic institutions (laissez-faire, clientelism, and corporatism) are the major explanations for the success or failure of economic development in Third World countries. The institution of laissez-faire is associated with rapid growth and with decline, since it does not obstruct or protect the domestic economy from international market fluctuations. A clientelist institution may stimulate short-term, superficial growth. But it encourages the expansion of rent-seeking behavior that retards economic growth in the long run. Finally, a corporatist institution tends to promote growth through strong cooperation within the business sector and between the government and business.

Current Explanations

In addition to the developmental state theory, current explanations for Asian economic performance include the liberal economics approach and the Marxist approach. This section gives a brief overview of these explanations.

Liberal Economics

The most direct causes affecting economic development are economic: for example, the supply of capital, labor, technology, and infrastructure. The prices and quantities of these factors are in turn determined by consumption patterns, investment rates, savings rates, interest rates, wage rates, and money supply, among other variables. Exchange rates, foreign borrowing, and comparative advantages, in adding an international dimension to economic development, further complicate the relationships among these factors. Neoclassical economics has presented an enormous amount of theoretical and statistical work on the relationships among these variables; this body of knowledge explains well the difference in economic performance among countries. The controversy, however, lies in which development policy or strategy best generates or strengthens these economic causes of development in the Third World, and which political factors may affect the choice of development policies and strategies.

The liberal economic view, which has been supported by most international development agencies, argues that free trade will facilitate economic growth because it encourages specialization and efficiency. The free trade strategy is composed of two parts: export promotion and import liberalization. The export promotion policy postulates that since the comparative advantage of the less-developed countries (LDCs) lies in their rich natural resources and abundant labor, such countries should develop these advantages and trade with industrialized countries for their manufactured or high-capital, high-technology goods, since industrialized countries have a comparative advantage in this area. Both trading parties benefit from trade and reach so-called Pareto outcomes. (A Pareto outcome is an efficient outcome with respect to both production and distribution.) Standard policy prescriptions include the development of labor-intensive industries (such as garments, textiles, handicrafts, shoes, and electronics assembly) and agriculture production and processing (such as sugar, rice, coffee, rubber, tobacco, and logs).

The import liberalization policy of the free trade strategy postulates that liberalization will encourage competition. Liberal economists abhor import controls derived from the inward-looking development strategy which, they argue, will result in inefficiency, inflation, and stagnation. Furthermore, the import-substitution industrialization (ISI) strategy is associated with the worst evil in liberal economics, government intervention in the market. Price distortion, corruption, waste of resources, and inefficiency will all ensue from government intervention. Therefore, standard policy prescriptions by liberal economists include the devaluation of currency, establishment of export processing zones, tax incentives for export industries, reduction of tariffs, and removal of quantitative import controls.

Cross-national studies conducted by liberal economists seem to confirm the relationship between development strategies and economic growth.[2] Representing the liberal economic view, Bela Balassa observes:

Continued outward orientation . . . led to increases in export market shares. . . . By contrast, the largest losses in market shares were experienced in [countries] where government interventions in the market mechanism in general, and protectionist measures in particular, were the most far-reaching. In turn, increases in export market shares had favorable effects on the rate of economic growth whereas reliance on import substitution had the opposite effects. (Balassa 1984, 119)

Although derived from sophisticated equations and supported by some empirical evidence, the liberal economic view has a number of weaknesses. First, theoretical debates with regard to the beneficial impact of export promotion and import liberalization remain. Bello, Kinley, and Elinson argue that an export-led industrialization (ELI) strategy may aggravate problems of balance of payments, unbalanced development, fiscal crises, and labor resistance (1982, 151). International competition may encourage efficiency, but it may also deter investment when financial and technological gaps between local and foreign producers are overwhelming. Although protection may result in inefficiency, it may encourage investment as well. Furthermore, the concept of comparative advantage is antithetical to innovation and industrial adjustment. If developing countries specialize in labor-intensive industries and agriculture production, how do they ever become advanced industrial nations? In response to these theoretical problems, some liberal economists concede that liberalization policies should be preceded by investment rehabilitation measures with certain limited protection (World Bank 1980, 1, 37).

The second weakness lies in the empirical evidence. "With the exception of Switzerland and the Netherlands," economic historian

Dieter Senghaas observes, "none of the present highly industrialized countries has developed in conditions of continuous free trade; not even England did so during her take-off phase up to the middle of the last century" (1985, 23). In the most cherished case of the triumph of liberal economics—the Asian "four little tigers"—researchers have found evidence that the import-substitution strategy has been an important element in the four tigers' development processes (Bradford 1986, 121; Chou 1985, 138; Lau 1986, 78; Rhee 1985, 181; Wade 1988, 35). Even staunch supporter of liberal economics Bela Balassa was embarrassed to discover that Taiwan's exports during the 1960s and 1970s "were discriminated against in the manufacturing sector as the average rate of import protection exceeded subsidies to exports" (1978, 37). Furthermore, the experiment of economic liberalism in Brazil from 1964 to 1967 resulted in a disastrous outcome instead of an economic miracle (Evans 1979, 217). In the Philippines, currency devaluation and export incentives in the 1970s had little effect on industrial production (Bautista, Power, and Associates 1979, 24). And the "emperor's new clothes" have not materialized in Columbia despite its ELI policies that encouraged textile and garment exports (Morawetz 1981).

The major weakness of the liberal economics view is that it is apolitical. Even if the ELI strategy works as liberal economists describe, why have so few countries followed the prescription? More important, why have those countries that experimented with the strategy failed to achieve the expected outcome? As Frederic C. Deyo suggests, development strategies in Third World countries may be "little more than vague pronouncements" because ISI interests may be so strong that the government adopts only cosmetic ELI policies to appease international lending agencies (1987a, 16).[3] Even if the political leadership is committed to the ELI strategy, there may be misunderstanding, distortion, or lack of capability in the implementation process (Jones and Sakong 1980, 2–3; Rhee 1985, 178). In the Philippines, for instance, Marcos established the Do Tank to supervise the implementation of "New Society" programs in the countryside. Several coordination and control groups also assisted in the work. The implementation, however, was "all noise but ultimately [meant] nothing" (Rodriguez 1986, 119–20).

The apolitical nature of the liberal economic view inspired two political explanations for Third World economic problems, the dependency theory and the developmental state theory.

The Dependency Theory

Applying the Marxist theory of class conflict to international economic relations, dependency theorists argue that the global capitalist system has enabled the "center countries" (i.e., industrial nations) to exploit the "peripheral countries" (i.e., developing countries) the same way that the capitalist class has exploited the labor class in all capitalist societies. Industrial nations—by means of trade, multinational corporations (MNCs), and international lending institutions—dominate Third World economies and control their production profits. As a consequence, most developing economies suffer from stagnation, deteriorating balance-of-payments problems, chronic debt crises, the enclave economy syndrome, destruction of local industries, unstable economic performance, and increasing income inequality.[4]

Critics of the dependency theory, however, suggest that the theoretical relation between external dependence and economic development is more complicated than the dependency theorists have suggested. The effects of international factors on economic development are determined more by the timing of industrialization, the type of MNCs, state capacities, state policies, the economic policies of trading partners, and local socioeconomic conditions than by the simple presence of international factors.[5]

Early dependency theorists also downplayed the role of the state. A capitalist state is either structurally dependent on capital or merely an executive committee of local and international capital. State policies, therefore, always favor capital at the expense of labor. Recent dependency theorists have incorporated the role of an autonomous state into their theoretical framework to explain the economic miracles of the Asian NICs (e.g., Evans 1987; Hamilton 1986; Kim 1987; Koo 1986; Lim 1985). One can argue, however, that the new emphasis on the developmental state may have seriously undermined the theoretical status of class conflict in dependency theories.

A more fundamental theoretical problem with the dependency theory is whether the class analysis can be applied to Third World countries at all (Rudolph and Rudolph 1988; Scott 1972; Wolters 1984). As James C. Scott explains,

[Class analysis's] overall value is dubious in the typical nonindustrial situation where most political groupings cut vertically across class lines and where even nominally class-based organizations like trade unions operate within parochial boundaries of ethnicity or religion or are simply personal vehicles. In a wider sense, too, the fact that class categories are not prominent in either oral or written political discourse in the Third World damages their *a priori* explanatory value (1972, 91).

The Developmental State Theory

THE THEORY AND ITS COMPONENTS

The developmental state theory considers the existence of a developmental state a necessary, if not a sufficient, condition for rapid economic growth in developing countries.[6] But what is a developmental state? Why is it able to contribute to economic development? Although various theorists of the developmental state (hereafter called statists) have offered different definitions, a developmental state usually includes the following core components that contribute to rapid growth: state autonomy, strong capacity, and a committed leadership.[7]

The first component of a developmental state is its autonomy. The developmental state makes national policies free from the influence of capitalists, landlords, workers, and politicians. Why should the state be autonomous from these interest groups? The statists explain that these groups are concerned only with their short-term self-interest and therefore represent obstacles to the development of long-term, collective interests.

Capitalists (both domestic and foreign) are interested only in company profit, monopoly rent, and protection from the government against domestic and foreign competitors. Olson's *The Rise and Decline of Nations* offers theoretical support for this argument. Landlords are opposed to industrialization because they would be forced to compete with industrialists for workers, capital, and political influence. The Marxist theory provides a theoretical base for this analysis of feudal political economy. Workers are concerned only with raising wages and benefits, which will undermine the competitiveness of company products. A simple cost-benefit function would suffice to demonstrate this point. Finally, theories and documentation of log-rolling and pork barrels in democratic societies have strengthened the argument that politicians are devoted to the protection of local, narrow, short-term interests, often at the expense of national, long-term developmental interests.

The second component of a developmental state is its strong capacity. Once the state is autonomous from the above-mentioned social groups, it needs a planning agency, a centralized bureaucracy, and well-educated bureaucrats to implement developmental policies effectively.

A planning agency formulates long-term economic development programs, coordinates different government departments, and provides timely advice about market conditions to both political and business leaders. A centralized bureaucracy is able to implement government policies consistently and effectively. This bureaucracy is staffed by well-educated technocrats who have expertise in economic affairs and who are concerned only with economic efficiency, not with political patronage.

The developmental state's autonomy and strong capacity reinforce each other. Since it is autonomous from interest groups, the state's implementation of national policies is more effective. Having a centralized state and a planning agency staffed with well-educated officials makes social groups less likely to exert strong influence over state policies.

Finally, the third component of a developmental state is a strong-willed, powerful, political leadership committed to economic development. A committed leadership initiates groundbreaking programs, recruits and supervises technocrats, and persistently reallocates scarce resources to support economic development. The term "enlightened despot" is often used or implied in the works of statists to describe such leadership.[8] Although this component of developmental leadership is not as widely cited by the statists as the components of state autonomy and capacity, it is a crucial theoretical element that prevents the developmental state from being a "rent-seeking" state.

The statists have cited the experiences of Singapore, Taiwan, and South Korea as their exemplars of rapid growth led by a developmental state. In these countries authoritarian states dominate all social groups. They all have planning agencies and centralized bureaucracies staffed by well-educated bureaucrats. The statists have quoted from the writings of and stories about Presidents Lee Kuanyew (Singapore), Park Chunghee (South Korea), and Jiang Jingguo (Taiwan) to demonstrate these leaders' commitment to economic development.

CRITICISMS OF THE DEVELOPMENTAL STATE THEORY

As rigorous as it is, the theory of the developmental state contains many controversial arguments. First, state autonomy is not a well-defined concept, and its causal relationship to economic development is not clear.[9] Most statists would admit that the state cannot be totally autonomous from society, and they correctly use the term "relative autonomy" to describe the developmental state. But the attempt to make relative autonomy operative as a base for meaningful comparison has not been successful. Furthermore, some statists have equated "autonomous state" with "authoritarian state," a connection that has not been confirmed by existing social science theories of economic development.[10]

Even if this definitional problem is resolved, an autonomous state may not be congenial to or necessary for rapid growth. The literature on the "rent-seeking state" or the "predatory rule of the state" suggests that state elites have an incentive to maximize their rents at the expense of society.[11] Because they are autonomous from society, as David A. Lake points out (1992, 24–37), autocratic states tend to generate more rent-seeking behavior, and hence, more inefficiency in society than do democratic states. From the perspective of organization theory, an autonomous state may refuse to change due to its organizational inertia and may formulate incorrect economic strategies out of a lack of information, as do most communist states. Furthermore, the assumption that social groups tend to be against economic development is debatable. Capitalists usually follow market signals more closely than state officials do because of the capitalists' sole attention to profit maximization. Their policy suggestions, therefore, may be more realistic and more in favor of economic development than those state policies that are made without prior consultation with capitalists. Landlords in developing countries are usually the capital owners. As rational economic actors, they have the capacity and the same incentive as industrialists to invest in lucrative industries. Workers' demands for higher wages need not hurt product competitiveness if their productivity increases as fast or faster than wage increases. Finally, politicians have no reason to oppose long-term economic development programs that are consistent with their constituents' interests, for example, the encouragement of labor-intensive industries.

Second, the strong capacity argument is debatable because, according to liberal economists, a state can contribute to rapid economic growth without being strong. A strong state may have the organizational tendency to intervene too much in the market, thus obstructing economic development.[12] Recent scholars have also shown that it makes little difference in economic policies and performance whether the state is strong or weak.[13] As Moon correctly argues,

state strength guarantees neither the choice and implementation of efficient, coherent, and consistent policies, nor good economic performance. State intervention has often proved to be market-distorting and counter-productive. The failure to establish causal connections between state strength and economic performance significantly undermines the relevancy and validity of the statist perspective. (1990, 25)

Furthermore, how do we explain the sudden rise of a strong state in developing countries where the modernization of social institutions is always a serious question?

Examining the three ingredients of a strong state (planning agency, centralization, and well-educated bureaucrats) leads to more debates. First, planning agencies and their economic development plans may exist only on paper—as is the case in most developing countries (Deyo 1987a, 16). But these agencies may be so intrusive that the market cannot function well, as has been the case in central-planning economies. Second, the positive relationship between centralization and efficiency has not found conclusive theoretical or empirical support in economics, organization theory, or administration theory. Decentralization may be more effective than centralization when local environments vary wildly and require immediate responses. Market conditions often fit such a description. Third, although educated bureaucrats are a prerequisite for policy making and implementation, other factors, such as the quality of information sources, the bureaucrats' sincerity in implementing national policies, and their competence in coordinating official and private resources, are more important. High educational level may not guarantee these qualities of an efficient bureaucrat.

Finally, the relationship between a developmental leadership and economic development may constitute a tautology. The statists have not been able to demonstrate this relationship with evidence other than the leaders' writings and stories. These data sources are very likely the propaganda of authoritarian governments and can be found in other nondevelopmental states. To assume that only in a few fast-growing economies are the leaders committed developmentalists is to infer that political leaders in other developing countries are not as rational.

In addition to the respective problems of its components, the developmental state theory as a whole engages two more controversies. First, a strong state may soon become a nonautonomous or self-destructing state. The very existence of a strong state that dominates the allocation of social resources constitutes a lucrative target for appropriation. Individuals, social groups, and state officials themselves will soon turn the developmental state into a rent-seeking machine, and no other institutional forces will have effective means to control the state.[14]

Second, the developmental state theory has little support from organization theories. Ordinary problems with social organizations, such as inertia, displacement of goals, departmental conflicts, and information distortion seem to suddenly disappear in a developmental state. As the monopoly of political power in a nation, the state is usually regarded by organization theorists as one of the most inert organizations, one of the least likely to initiate changes and support efficiency goals. How, then, does the developmental state solve all these problems once and for all in a short period of time? Can a committed new leadership disrupt a large-scale state's organizational continuity of norms, behavior, and rules?[15]

A social organization, or a state, can be developmental if self-adaptation routines are institutionalized within the organization (Nelson and Winter 1982). These self-adaptation routines do exist in the Asian "developmental states," but these routines are connected to actors outside the states. Chapter 2 will explore how different institutions contribute to its becoming a developmental state or prevent it from doing so.

Dissatisfaction with the developmental state theory in its original form has prompted the emergence of two alternative theoretical orientations: the competitive advantage school and the policy network school. The first focuses on the "competitive advantages" (Porter 1990) or "X-efficiency" (Leibenstein 1976) of firms as a source of economic development. Most of these works, written by business scientists, agree with the liberal economists' insistence on a small state and free market but refuse to treat firms or industries equally. Michael Porter argues that the major determinants of a country's competitiveness are: (1) factor conditions, (2) demand conditions, (3) related and supporting industries, and (4) firm strategy, structure, and rivalry. None of these factors can be directly manufactured by the government. "Government cannot create competitive industries, only companies can do that" (1990, 86). Porter's research on Japan's economic development, Friedman's research (1988) on Japan's machine tool industry, and Lam's work (1990) on Taiwan's high-tech industries exemplify this emphasis on firms rather than the state.

One can even include in this theoretical orientation the work of Gerschenkron, which has been regarded by the statists as the prelude to the developmental state theory. In his work, however, Gerschenkron describes how German banks, with little state assistance, mobilized investment capital in the society to create modern industries, and how the banks helped the industries organize production cartels in order to regulate vicious competition (1962, 13–17).

Also related to this theoretical orientation are sociological studies on the impact of Asian family systems on economic growth. For instance, Greenhalgh (1988) has systematically explored how Taiwan's family enterprises overcame the encroachment of the state and of multinational corporations and became dominant in the vibrant economy. Siu-lun Wong explained the lack of working-class consciousness in Hong Kong's textile industry as a result of pervasive familism (1989).

The virtue of this "competitive advantage" school is the short theoretical distance between its explanatory variables and its dependent variables. After all, what better explains the productive activity of an economy than firms' performance? To avoid the apolitical nature of the liberal economic analyses, however, we need to integrate this approach with either the statist or the policy network approach.

The second theoretical orientation is to study the policy networks between the state and producers.[16] Within this orientation the state remains an important factor in determining economic development. But effective policy making and implementation require the existence of a complementary policy network that provides accurate information to state policy makers and resolves collective action problems among producers. Within this orientation scholars disagree on the theoretical role of the developmental state. The statists continue to emphasize the pivotal role of the developmental state but are beginning to consider the complementary role of policy networks. For instance, Wade's governed market theory "emphasizes the developmental virtues of a hard or soft authoritarian state in corporatist relations with the private sector" (1990b, 29). He does not, however, provide detailed analyses of the internal and external functioning of corporatist associations. Nor does he regard them as a significant source of policy input to the state (1990b, 280–84).

Evans's "embedded state" constitutes a significant departure from the developmental state theory. He takes policy networks more seriously and adds to the developmental state the dimension of "institutionalized links" between the state and producers. But he argues that the effective functioning of institutionalized links still depends on the existence of a developmental state (Evans 1989, 574).[17] Several other statists have argued along a similar line, with a timely and persuasive emphasis on the dynamics of state strength, in order to explain the complex transformation of state-society relationships in the post-authoritarian regimes of South Korea and Taiwan (Kim and Huang 1991; Moon 1990; Haggard, Kim, and Moon 1991). Nevertheless, the developmental state theory's applicability to the initial economic take-off periods (Taiwan in the early 1960s and South Korea from the mid-1960s to the early 1970s) is not directly challenged by these new improved statist theories. Nor do these new theories make a strong argument for the contribution of post-authoritarian states to the still-impressive economic growth records of the Asian NICs.

In contrast to these statists' continued emphasis on the developmental state, Daniel Okimoto, in his account of Japan's economic development, suggests that policy networks have at least the same, if not more, causal importance as a developmental state in effective policy making and implementation. The success of the Japanese state's intervention is a result of Japan's complementary market structure, which provides multiple points of entry for the intervention. These multiple points of entry are the networks of keiretsu (industrial grouping), intercorporate stockholding, banking-business ties, subcontracting networks, trading companies, and industrial associations. Also included are amakudari (exchange of official and private positions), personal networks, and institutionalized consultation forums (Okimoto 1989, 160–65). Both the state and producers have utilized these networks to influence each other, and the result is often a consensus-building process instead of the state dominance described by the statists.[18]

Consistent with Okimoto's network arguments is Laothamatas's study (1992) on the vital role of business associations in Thailand's successful economic development in the last decade. He argues that Thailand's transformation to export-led industrialization and the rapid growth of the Thai economy since the early 1980s can be attributed to the rise of active and powerful business associations. In the late 1970s the Thai government began to encourage the creation of business associations and government-business dialogue. In 1981 the government established the Joint Public-Private Consultative Committee on Economic Problems (JPPCC), which consists of the prime minister, economic officials, and representatives of business associations. Since then, JPPCC has routinely submitted policy proposals on national economic issues to the government, and the government has been responsive to these proposals.

Richard F. Doner (1991; 1992) and Michael D. Shafer (1990) have each proposed very sophisticated theories of political economy combining both the statist and policy network analyses. Doner's institutional theory of political economy suggests that the state is only one of the institutions that may contribute to economic growth. Among other factors, the existence or absence of production networks, business associations, ethnic ties, and ruling coalitions will affect economic performance. Shafer's "sectoral analysis" focuses our attention on the varying economic consequences of state-society relations and coalition formation in different sectors.[19] Although their theories are somewhat compromised by parsimony and generality, Doner and Shafer have successfully integrated existing theories of political economy without the weaknesses of the developmental state theory.

This study will build on these network and institutional analyses to construct an institutional theory that explains both the success and failure of economic development in Third World countries. The state remains the single most important actor in the economy. Yet its impact on economic development is determined not simply by the characteristics within the state, as the statists have argued, but ultimately by the networks and institutions that link the state to other actors in the economy.

Research Methodology

Scope of Research

Economic development is too complicated a subject to be covered in one book. This study has had to make a hard choice among issues and variables in the development process of Taiwan and the Philippines. First of all, this study is primarily about the politics of *industrial* policies. The politics of macroeconomic policies, despite the vital importance of these policies for economic development, is discussed only as a supplement.

Second, the main typology used in this study (clientelism, laissez-faire, and state corporatism) might be criticized for being both too broad (because it does not differentiate among more subcategories) and too narrow (because it does not cover other institutions such as the military and political parties). Given the small number of cases in this study, however, this typology seems to provide an optimal level of testable explanations without causing the statistical problem associated with the degree of freedom. When the number of cases increases, this typology can easily be differentiated or connected to other institutions.

Finally, this research focuses on the economic and industrial development in Taiwan and the Philippines from the 1950s to the mid-1980s. Since the mid-1980s both Taiwan and the Philippines have been in a chaotic process of democratic transition. In Taiwan the vast outflow of investments to China and other countries after 1987 adds additional uncertainty to state-business interactions. One can argue that clientelism is reemerging in Taiwan while the Philippines remains a "changeless land" (Timberman 1991). But this will be the subject of further research.

Research Design

This research adopts a modified version of the "most similar systems" research design (Przeworski and Teune 1970, 34). Taiwan and the Philippines are selected for comparison because they share a number of important attributes (though not their types of institutions) that may affect their economic performance. Since Taiwan and the Philippines are not exactly alike, a third country is introduced intermittently as a control case in order to reduce the methodological importance of their differences.

The second step is to select a few representative industries for comparison within each country and across countries. These industries should be very important to both economies and representative of the entire industrial sector of the respective country so that a strong link between macro and "meso" levels of analysis is established (Cawson 1985). The selection of these important industries, however, does not guarantee that the political economy at the industry level is consistent with that at the national level. Thus, in addition to the national-level theories already discussed, further explanations and revisions are needed. A combination of both national- and industry-level analyses allows us to maximize the use of data with a more careful experimental control than single-case and two-country studies would allow.

The major differences and similarities between Taiwan and the Philippines are summarized in Table 1–1. Data from South Korea are provided to control for the differences between Taiwan and the Philippines.[20] Whenever appropriate, the statistics reported in Table 1–1 date from the 1960s and 1970s to demonstrate the two countries' similarities in initial conditions.

This study selects the textile, plywood, and electronics industries in Taiwan and the Philippines for further comparison. The textile industry has contributed enormously to the industrialization of developing countries (e.g., Taiwan, South Korea, and Hong Kong) as well as developed countries (e.g., Britain and Japan). It is labor-intensive, requires a relatively modest amount of capital, and has a short period of investment return. Since these attributes are well suited to the capital-short, labor-abundant conditions of most developing countries, the textile industry has almost become a standard prescription item in World Bank development programs.

The electronics industry is another common prescription item from World Bank economists. The electronics industry in most developing countries specializes in assembly and packaging, not in design and manufacturing, which are more technology- and capital-intensive. Therefore, it is similar to the textile industry in terms of labor-intensiveness, capital requirement, and investment return.

The plywood industry is also a labor-intensive industry with modest start-up costs and a short investment return period. Although not the most important industry in Taiwan and the Philippines, the plywood industry was a rising star in both economies around 1960. Interestingly enough, Japan, South Korea, and Taiwan all produced competitive plywood products for the international market, while the Philippines, which supplied most of the logs to these three countries, was not able to compete in the international market. By studying the plywood industries of Taiwan and the Philippines we will be able to

Table 1–1

Similarities Among Taiwan, the Philippines, and South Korea in 1960

	Taiwan	Philippines	South Korea
Socioeconomic			
Area (in thousands of km²)	36	300	99
Population (in millions)	16.3	43.3	36
Adult literacy rate (%)	54[a]	72	71
Family ties	Strong	Strong	Strong
Local clientelism	Strong	Strong	?
Date of market saturation	Late 1950s	Late 1950s	Late 1950s
Working population (% of total)	52	52	54
Agro population (% of total)	56	61	66
Agro productivity	High[b]	High[b]	Medium[b]
GNP growth rate (%)	7.9[c]	6.0[c]	5.0[c]
GNP growth rate (per capita)	4.2	2.7	2.1
Government			
Stability	High	High	High
Authoritarianism	Strong	Strong[d]	Strong
Labor suppression	Strong	Strong[d]	Strong
Land reforms in	1949, 1951, 1953	1954, 1955, 1963, 1972	1946, 1948, 1950
Agro investment	Large[e]	Large[e]	Large[e]
Public expenditure	Large	Large	Large
Military spending	Large	Small	Large
ISI experience	Successful	Successful	Successful
EOI policies	Yes	Yes[f]	Yes
International			
Colonial rule by	Japan	United States	Japan
War damages	Extensive	Extensive	Extensive[g]
Level of foreign aid	High[h]	Medium	High
Anticommunist	Yes	Yes	Yes
U.S. tarriff privilege	Yes	Yes	Yes
Service of debt (% of GNP)	1.4[i]	1.5[i]	3.7[i]
Public loans (in millions)			
1970	100	123	462
1976	581	890	1,701
Net FDI (in millions)			
1970	61	−29	38
1976	69	127	173

Sources: World Bank (1978, 76–111) and ECAFE (1962, 11–12).

Note: Although Taiwan and the Philippines differ in some important aspects, a comparison to other countries such as South Korea can reduce the importance of such differences. The purpose of choosing 1960 and 1970 data is to compare the initial conditions of the three countries before they embarked on ELI.

[a] CEPD (1987, 7) lists this figure as 73 percent.

[b] 1950–1970.

[c] 1950–1959.

[d] 1972–1986.

[e] Before 1973.

[f] Especially during the 1970s.

[g] Korean damage was primarily the result of the Korean War, not World War II.

[h] Before 1964.

[i] 1970.

understand how state-business relationships affected industrial performance.

The selection of comparable industries prevents the disturbing effect of industry-specific technology on political institutions (Woodward 1980). Since Taiwan and the Philippines utilized similar technology in similar industries, their differences in institutions and economic performance have to be explained by factors other than technology or industries. Other important industries such as cement, coconut, and plastics exist in Taiwan or the Philippines, but these industries are not comparable due to their idiosyncrasies in each country.

Data

Most of the current research on Taiwan's economic development relies on macroeconomic data, lists of public policies, and (quasi-) official stories. Unfortunately, the publication of these sources has often been politically manipulated to justify authoritarian rule. It is not difficult, therefore, to arrive at a "developmental state" argument from these sources. For instance, if we examine the writings of Park Chunghee, Jiang Jieshi, and Jiang Jingguo, we may conclude that the foresight and commitment of the leadership to economic development is important. Nevertheless, we can find the same degree or even a higher degree of foresight and commitment in Marcos's *Notes on the New Society of the Philippines*, which was actually a commissioned work written by a group of scholars at the University of the Philippines. The entirety of the "success" story can be told only by referring to alternative sources.

Newspaper clippings constitute one source for these stories. Although there are "voluntary restraints" on the part of publishers, economic news in Taiwan is relatively free of "state intervention." I examined such a data source in the archive department of the *United Daily News* (Taibei), which filed economic news of all major Taiwanese newspapers from the 1940s.

The second data source is the proceedings of industrial associations: the Taiwan Electrical Appliance Manufacturers Association, the Taiwan Plywood Manufacturers and Exporters Association, and the Taiwan Cotton Spinners Association. Taiwan's business associations are semiofficial organizations regulated by the government and partly staffed by Guomingdang cadres (GMD; the Nationalist party). Hence, they are required to report their budget, activities, and meetings in detail.

For study of the Philippines, newspaper clippings are a high-quality source because the Philippines, as one Filipino journalist boasts, has "the freest free press" in the world. Even during Marcos's rule, reports on Marcos's cronism were quite common, and more detailed reports of it have been disclosed since 1986. The major newspapers I carefully examined are the *Manila Bulletin* and its predecessors: the *Manila Daily Bulletin* (from 1938 to September 1972) and the *Bulletin Today* (from October 1972 to April 1986). The fact that *Bulletin Today* was politically pro-Marcos did not have much effect on the quality and neutrality of the economic news I used.

Academic and nonacademic journals stored in the University of the Philippines Library and the Economic School Library are rich in detail and variety. Some of the data date back to the 1940s, which improves the depth and breadth of this research.

In addition to these written documents, I have conducted numerous interviews with government officials, association officials, and business leaders to understand state-business relationships in the Philippines. Although most of the respondents were willing to speak out, they were not eager to share written documents such as association proceedings or meeting minutes. With the exception of the plywood association, most groups would not make these documents public. Some simply did not keep such documents. These associations are private organizations not regulated by the government. They are not required to submit copies of their proceedings or meeting records to the government or to other public organizations, as their Taiwanese and Korean counterparts are. Therefore, my analysis of the Philippines's case relies more on newspaper clippings, journals, and interviews.

The next chapter introduces the institutional approach as a competing explanation for the developmental state theory. The institutional approach follows the bounded rationality school and organization theories to address two major problems in economic development: policy and collective action. Then, it identifies three types of institutions (clientelism, laissez-faire, and state corporatism) that have different capabilities for resolving the policy and collective action problems. Microeconomic relationships among institutions and their interactions with international economic factors are also examined.

Chapter 3 compares state-business relationships in Taiwan and the Philippines at the national level. A careful examination of historical data in both countries reveals that the developmental state bears an ambiguous relationship to economic development. State corporatism in Taiwan and clientelism in the Philippines are the major cause for the difference in their economic performance. Chapters 4 through 6 examine state-business relationships at the industry level. Empirical evidence from the textile, plywood, and electronics industries in both countries demonstrates again that a developmental state had little positive impact on industrial growth, and may even have had a negative impact. Different institutions provide a better explanation for the variation in industrial performance. Each of these chapters begins with a comparison of growth records, an assessment of the business organization in the industry, an analysis of the state's responsiveness to the industry, and a summary that compares the applicability of the developmental state and institutional theories. The last chapter draws conclusions from the findings of this research. Appendix 1 provides statistical tests of the theses of market fluctuations and product cycles that might explain the differences in industrial performance across nations.

2

INSTITUTIONS AND GLOBAL COMPETITIVENESS

The evolution of institutions that create an hospitable environment for cooperative solutions to complex exchange provides for economic growth.
—Douglass C. North, *Institutions, Institutional Change and Economic Performance*

The central thesis of this study is that the impact of an institution on the performance of an economy varies according to the type of institution concerned. Some institutions tend to promote growth, others to produce stagnation, and still others to have little impact on an economy. In this chapter I will discuss three ideal types of institutions (laissez-faire, clientelism, and corporatism) and their theoretical relationship to economic performance.

The first section explains the two major obstacles to economic growth: policy problems and collective action problems. The second section elaborates why and how the three institutions have different capabilities for resolving these growth problems, and therefore, why they have varying degrees of impact on economic performance. The third section provides a microfoundation for these institutions as a way of understanding how individual actors (state officials and business people) behave under institutional constraints and of analyzing the dynamics of institutional transformation. The last section summarizes the theoretical arguments of this chapter.

Policy and Collective Action Problems

This study focuses on the state and on business as the two major actors in the growth or decline of an economy. Each actor, however, has a set of distinctive problems to face. The state needs to resolve policy-making and policy implementation problems, while business is struggling with collective action problems.

Policy Problems

Liberal economists have discovered a relationship between certain economic policies and economic performance. For example, encouraging saving and investment, controlling inflation, promoting exports, supporting research and development, reducing trade barriers, and removing bureaucratic red tape are some of the "correct policies" nations should pursue. Assume that the liberal economists' arguments are all true and beyond debate, the problem of economic development, then, can be dramatically reduced to a choice between turning national leaders into liberal economists or hiring a group of competent liberal economists to make these development decisions. Either way, economic development should not be a costly and frustrating experience for any country.

Unfortunately, the theoretical conciseness of these liberal economic policies is achieved at the expense of ignoring a plethora of policy problems analyzed by organization theorists. First, in the policy-making process, national decision makers may not know what the correct policies are, given their nation's particular natural and human resources. The lack of reliable economic data is a common problem for developing countries. Without the data, economic models cannot function. After the national data are collected, the analysts need to process an enormous amount of international data as well to assess the impact of the international market on the effect of national policies. In the process of data collection, however, there is room for distortion and misperception. Although the government can contract with economists or consulting firms to collect and analyze the data, there is no guarantee that two economists or consulting firms will arrive at the same conclusions.

Even if the policy makers know the correct policies, they may reject them for political reasons. The leaders and their allies might, for example, have established interests in some business that would be hurt by the "correct policies." Or, proposed policies might strengthen the economic base of political enemies. Economic bureaucrats might resist foreign ideas for fear of losing reputation, prestige, and influence.[1]

After the "correct policies" are established, another set of policy problems follow—those of implementation. The gap between policy making and policy implementation is a common theme in organizational studies. "Public policies are rarely self-executing," George Edwards (1980, 1) explains, "since the people who originally determine public policies are usually not the same people who implement them, there is considerable room for misunderstanding and distortion of decision makers' intentions." Graham Allison (1971), in his classic book on *The Essence of Decision*, points out the problems of policy implementation that result from organizational and bureaucratic politics. In addition to internal constraints, such as the sunk costs of investment and structural, political, and historical factors, an organization's failure to adapt to a changing environment results from a set of external constraints such as legal and fiscal barriers, availability of information, and legitimacy problems (Hanan 1977).[2]

Collective Action Problems

While the state is immersed in these decision-making and implementation problems, business is often plagued by collective action problems. How to avoid vicious price wars among themselves? How to reduce the collective costs of production for a particular industry or business? How to ensure the supply of key inputs to an industry? And how to stabilize supply and sales relations in a competitive market? In a world economy where nations practice mercantilist policies, how to prevent unfair foreign competition and expand foreign markets? When technology is not available at home, how to acquire inexpensive and appropriate technology from abroad?

Collective action problems also occur when business interacts with the state. Because of the problems of policy making and implementation within the state, businesses have a collective interest in improving the quality of policies and monitoring their implementation. From the policy-making process (providing policy information, drafting bills, lobbying decision makers, campaigning for bills) to the implementation process (monitoring policy implementation, getting and giving feedback on the results of policies, and adjusting policy deviations), many activities require substantial investments of time, energy, and money by business.

Furthermore, business needs to watch out for individuals and companies that seek favors and privileges from state officials at the expense of other competitors. These individuals may provide decision makers with incorrect information about business or interfere with the implementation of policies.

Policy and Collective Action Problems in Developing Countries

Although these policy and collective action problems are universal, they are more acute in developing countries.[3] Compared to industrialized countries, Third World bureaucracies have a short history of development. When their colonial masters left after World War II, local elites hastily took control of government machinery. But it took time to develop decision-making and implementation routines. The quality of bureaucrats in developing countries is typically low due to the lack of education of the masses from which they are recruited. Also, the civil servant ethic competes with traditional family and clientelist values.

Surrounded by an increasingly interdependent world, a developing country's economic relationships with other nations impose extra burdens on the bureaucracy. Money supply, exchange rates, inflation, interest rates, and stock market fluctuations are not determined by domestic policies alone but also, or more often, by international market conditions. And it is more difficult to gather accurate and timely information about foreign market conditions than about the domestic market. Furthermore, the number of actors in the decision-making and implementation process continues to increase as a result of the internationalization of economies. The bureaucracy needs to deal with both domestic and foreign actors, such as multinational corporations and international organizations (the World Bank, International Monetary Fund, General Agreement on Tariffs and Trade, etc.). New routines need to be developed in the bureaucracy so that it can interact with these foreign actors.

Businesses in the developing countries also have more serious collective action problems than their counterparts in industrial countries. Their domestic markets are either small or lacking in purchasing power, making cutthroat competition more likely. The underdevelopment of the economy makes the supply of quality inputs more problematic. Third World companies are in general smaller in size, weaker in mobilizing capital, backward in technological development, and less experienced in establishing international sales networks. But they still need to continually find market niches to compete with multinational corporations and with competitors from other developing countries.

Similarly, The relationships of Third World companies with the state are more difficult as a result of internationalization. Their governments tend to give preferences to MNCs as a way of attracting capital and technology inflow. The attention given to MNCs by the host government, in the form of tax breaks, electricity supply, labor control, infrastructure support, and local loans, may indirectly hurt domestic companies. The business community, therefore, is divided between foreign companies and domestic companies.[4]

Institutional Sources of Global Competitiveness

Current theories of economic development provide some answers to these policy and collective action problems. Liberal economists recommend a small government to reduce the distorting impact of state policies on the economy. Since state intervention is reduced, policy-making and implementation problems are trimmed. Collective action problems within businesses are left to each company to cope with. Through perfect competition, liberal economists argue, companies will rapidly improve their efficiency and capabilities. Those who do not will simply be driven out of the market. As a consequence, the potential of an economy will be fully unleashed. The institutional source of global competitiveness, therefore, lies in the free market system.

For the dependency theorists, the institutional source of global competitiveness lies in reforming the world capitalist system. Once the feudal, exploitative economic relationships between industrial and developing countries are abolished, developing countries will achieve rapid growth. Until that time, the de-linkage school of the dependency theory proposes, international economic relations should be totally or selectively terminated, thus alleviating the complexity of policy and collective action problems.

Neither liberal economics nor the dependency theory, however, offers a satisfactory solution to policy and collective action problems. Liberal economics assumes these problems will go away with the adoption of a free market. As Rhee correctly points out: "In a stagnant and depressed economy, neither rational incentives nor anything else will be sufficient to bring about immediate change unless the institutional mechanisms that generate vitality are in operation" (1985, 181). The dependency theory subsumes policy and collective action problems under the problem of the exploitative world capitalist system.

The developmental state theory cannot provide more direct solutions to the problems either. This theory distrusts the power of the free market to resolve problems of economic development. The existence of a developmental state, the theory suggests, will provide an answer to policy and collective action problems. The state may establish agencies (e.g., a central planning agency) that improve the quality of decision making and implementation. It may help businesses resolve their collective action problems by providing technology, coordinating market behavior, gathering world market information, and rejecting clientelistic influence.

Many governments of the Third World, developmental or not, have performed these functions with varying degrees of success. The question, then, becomes: Why do developmental states exist in some countries but not others? How do these developmental states in developing countries avoid the organizational and bureaucratic problems that even well-developed governments in industrial countries are forced to live with? Since "there are limits to the competence of even the best-run and best-intentioned bureaucracy to pass judgement on economic and engineering details submitted by individual (or groups of) entrepreneurs" (ILO 1974, 32), what is needed is an institutional explanation that goes beyond the state to account for these puzzles.

The institutional explanation proposed here builds on Douglass C. North's institutionalism, which integrates theories of bounded rationality, transaction costs, and property rights to explain economic performance (1990). In the rest of this study, the word "institution" refers to the formal and informal relationships between the state and business with regard to economic development.[5] This research focuses on three ideal types of institutions, which cover the major types of state-business relations in developing countries. These are clientelism, laissez-faire, and state corporatism.

Laissez-Faire

A logical place to begin the study of the economic impact of institutions is with the absence of any institutions. The discussions of the free market by Adam Smith (1976 [1904]), F. A. Hayek (1933), and Milton Friedman (1982) provide examples of this situation. The business community is totally disorganized. Business associations, if any, do not assume meaningful economic functions. Firms compete with one another in the free market with no collusion or collective bargaining. The government's role in the economy is restricted to making rules, mediating disputes, and mitigating market imperfections and negative externalities. There is little interaction between business and the government except for regular transactions such as collecting taxes, issuing patents, and setting standards, which do not distort normal market functioning. Thus, firms are totally exposed to the whim of market forces without government intervention and private collective measures.

Since the government plays a minimal role in the economy, policy problems are reduced to a minimum. Fewer policies mean fewer distortions in the policy-making and implementation process. Thus, under perfect market competition, laissez-faire encourages efficiency. The economy as a whole benefits from the elimination of market distortions and the improvement of efficiency.

As discussed in the previous chapter, the weakness of the laissez-faire solution is its tendency to assume problems will go away in an ideal world. In the real world, state officials have a strong tendency to intervene in the economy for political purposes. Organizational problems of policy making and implementation will be omnipresent as long as organizations exist. Even in Smith's and Friedman's world of perfect competition, the government still needs to maintain appropriate levels of money supply, engage in infrastructure construction, provide public goods, levy taxes, prevent market failures and imperfections, and enforce contract and property rights.[6] These economic functions require more than a modest level of policy making and implementation; or, in the words of the statists, these functions require certain levels of state autonomy and capacity. Hence, there is no escape from policy problems. Furthermore, as the idea of the welfare state becomes popular, the state assumes more and more economic and social functions. Simply assuming policy problems will go away is not a realistic solution.

Under the laissez-faire institution, the state encounters particular policy problems. On the policy input side, the state is overburdened with the numerous, conflicting, and redundant demands of individual firms. On the implementation side, the state is again overstretched in dealing with the idiosyncratic problems of each firm. Policy feedback is so diffuse that the state does not know how to adjust or improve its policies.

Collective action problems also arise in laissez-faire. Although market competition may encourage efficiency, severe recessions may drive out even the most efficient firms, whose capital and labor must then be reallocated.[7] Market uncertainties deter innovative investments and expansionary plans based on scale-economy considerations. Free-rider problems and opportunism further increase the costs of rule enforcement (North 1981, 18). Because business is disorganized, no collective solutions can be negotiated to reduce the severity of these problems.

Since the laissez-faire institution generates both efficiency gains and policy and collective action problems, its impact on economic growth is mixed. Most of the developing countries, loaded with market-distorting policies, would immediately benefit from the adoption of the laissez-faire institution. Given the corruption and low quality of bureaucrats in some developing countries, it is even more advisable to reduce government intervention in the market in order to reduce policy-making and implementation problems. With a reduced role for government, business will also shift its investments in political patrons to more productive areas.

But where and how should the government reduce its intervention? It has made mistakes by introducing the distorting policies in the first place. What mechanisms can guarantee that it can correctly reduce distorting policies or expand government activities when necessary? Furthermore, it takes time to restore or create business confidence after a long period of arbitrary state controls. Without proper mechanisms to ensure the stability and quality of government policies and to overcome collective action problems within business, business confidence may not emerge rapidly.

Clientelism

As commonly defined by the theorists of clientelism, a patron-client relationship is "*a vertical dyadic alliance, i.e., an alliance between two persons of unequal status, power or resources each of whom finds it useful to have as an ally someone superior or inferior to himself*" (Lande 1977, xx; emphasis in original).[8] In this study, "patrons" refers to individual state officials and "clients" to individual business people. The business community is disorganized, and business associations resemble loose social clubs devoid of strong control over their members. Within one particular sector, a number of associations engage in factional struggles. Membership in these associations is selective and representative of merely a fraction of the entire sector. Official patrons are responsive only to the needs of their clients.

Clientelism exacerbates policy problems in several ways. First, policy inputs tend to reflect the interests of well-connected firms more than the collective welfare of business. Second, because of factional turnovers or deadlocks, economic policies may become inconsistent or impractical. Third, clientelism erodes state capacity.

State officials treat their offices as personal property where favors are exchanged with clients. These officials can be very efficient in one sense: they do not delay in handling the demands of their clients. Yet this efficiency comes at the expense of long delays in handling non-client demands. Officials express little interest in implementing economic directives from above, with the exception of those from their political patrons (superpatrons). Nor do they have any incentive to implement economic policies without bias, which would only undermine their own power base. Thus, problems of inertia and goal displacement are exacerbated under clientelism.[9]

Fourth, clientelism undermines the normal functioning of party politics. Party members are loyal only to their patrons and not necessarily to the party leader. They may oppose the party's decisions or even switch party membership when their factional leaders ask them to do so. Hence, political parties cannot provide consistent guidelines for and supervision over economic bureaucracy.

Fifth, a clientelist state tends to be inflationary (Scott 1972, 111–13) and is a very "expensive state" (Di Palma 1980, 156). On the one hand, the state needs to support an ever-growing state bureaucracy filled with the political appointees of new superpatrons. On the other hand, it needs to finance unnecessary projects to appease business clients. How does the state generate the revenue? It can raise taxes, expand money supply, or borrow from abroad. Since business clients can always avoid heavy taxes through their political connections, and since there are economic and political limits to the use of fiscal and monetary instruments,[10] most developing countries resort to foreign loans to finance domestic clientelism. These practices ultimately lead to a "fiscal crisis" of the state (O'Connor 1973).

In addition to its policy problems, clientelism also exacerbates collective action problems among business people. Business factions are more interested in dividing the existing economic pie than in increasing the size of the pie. Profits are merely transferred from one faction to another, with transaction costs continually lost in the process. More often, in the name of rationalization, profits are taken from a large group of efficient producers and transferred to a small group of inefficient clients. Because of repetitive transfers of revenue shares, all business people suffer greater risks and are forced to make higher political contributions. To cover such risks and political costs, business people move their investments from production to real estate and other speculative activities (e.g., smuggling) that can generate windfall profits through political connections. Those who remain in production activities opt for short-term maximization of profits to hedge against the risks associated with the decline of their political patrons.

Because of factional struggles, cooperative arrangements such as joint ventures, collective technology development, market exploration, protection against market fluctuations, and collective bargaining with the state and other business associations are difficult if not impossible. Individual business clients reason that they could acquire all of these benefits from their official patrons and at the same time prevent their competitors from enjoying them. Individuals' rents are maximized, but the collective profits for business as a whole are reduced.

Clientelism exists in most developing countries and has a pernicious impact on economic development. Yet certain scholars have argued that its existence in some countries seems to combine economic advantages of integration and centralization. Analogous to economic oligopoly, it may combine the benefits of competition and pluralism. Japan's zaibatsu, Thai's landed oligarchs, Korea's chaebols, and their governments' clientelistic policies have not prevented these economies from producing impressive results (Oshima 1987, 214–15; Jones and Sakong 1980, 64–65). Furthermore, a deepening of clientelism or a transformation from other types of institutions to clientelism may stimulate growth at the initial stage, because the ostensible expansion of government involvement in a depressed market can boost business confidence. Italy's "economic miracle" in the early 1960s, Indonesia's New Order in the late 1960s, and the Philippines's "new society" in the early 1970s are exemplary of this confidence-boosting phenomenon.

This evidence of an alleged benign clientelism is dubious, however.[11] Scholars have pointed to the existence of strong business associations as an important cause of rapid growth in both Japan and South Korea. State corporatism helps to check oligopolistic inefficiency, while clientelism exacerbates it. Even if clientelism had contributed to economic growth, as in the cases of Italy, Indonesia, the Philippines, and South Korea, an exceptionally strong and energetic leadership would have been required to reduce rent-seeking behavior in the bureaucracy and business.[12] Furthermore, these growth records were always short-lived. Once short-term, conducive factors waned or leadership was replaced, clientelism in these countries produced a more serious fiscal and economic crisis than ever before.

State Corporatism

State corporatism as an institution lies between the free market and hierarchy (the developmental state or socialist state) as the third alternative for organizing an economy.[13] It resembles "administrative contracts"[14] in that it combines both the flexibility of the free market and the stability of hierarchy (Stinchcombe 1990). The major feature of state corporatism is that the business community is well organized by singular, hierarchical, powerful, state-sponsored, and functionally differentiated business associations.[15]

Within the business community, these associations resolve collective action problems such as coordination of production and sales, provision of club goods (e.g., sharing of technology and market information), negotiation between upstream and downstream producers, and networking with foreign buyers and sellers. In terms of state-business relations, these associations, as the sole representatives of their respective business sectors, provide a forum for their members to articulate their interests. Then the association can conduct research, engage in internal negotiation, filter out unrealistic and inconsistent demands, and finally, formulate concrete policy recommendations. The association also routinely participates in the decision making and implementation of national economic policies, monitors against detrimental policies and distorted implementation, and offers policy feedback to decision makers.

Equipped with collective legitimacy and powerful instruments, the association can punish free riders in the business community by cutting off club goods and initiating punitive actions jointly adopted by the association and the state. Clientelist activities may be reduced by means of the association's collective monitoring system, since business competitors have more incentive than state agencies to stop unfair competition immediately.

In terms of competition, corporatist business associations make a fine distinction between vicious competition and competitiveness. Because they are compulsory and functionally differentiated, corporatist associations do not restrict admission of new businesses, as many pluralist associations do. On the contrary, for the benefit of the entire business, corporatist associations tend to encourage the creation of "competitive advantages" (Porter 1990) through competition. But vicious competition within the business community or unfair competition from foreign countries is regulated by business associations.

The state assumes a cooperative role with the business association, a role similar to what Laumann and Knoke called an "organizational state" (1987). The most cooperative state simply formalizes business recommendations by turning them into laws.[16] But cooperation does not mean harmony. Although "structurally dependent" on business (Poulantzas 1973; Przeworski 1985), the state has political, bureaucratic, and developmental interests that may conflict with the interests of business. When such conflicts arise, the state and business associations mediate them through collective consultation and bargaining.

Because of the difference between the relative power and capacity of the state and those of business associations, state corporatism can be seen as a continuum, operating differently in different countries and time periods. Given the dominant role played by the state, for example, Singapore and South Korea are located at one extreme of state-business cooperation[17] while Taiwan, with more consultation and business initiatives, is located at the other extreme. Although the existing literature on Hong Kong's corporatism is limited, it seems to situate Hong Kong close to Taiwan.[18] Japan seems to be in the middle of the continuum and is properly called a "network state" (Okimoto 1989, 226).[19] In recent years, due to democratization and internationalization of capital, all of these countries have tended to move toward more consultation and business initiatives.

Why does the state want to cooperate with business associations? As organization theorists have argued, "organizations that incorporate societally legitimated rationalized elements in their formal structures maximize their legitimacy and increase their resources and survival capabilities" (Meyer and Rowan 1977, 352). As an organization itself, the state has more to gain from working with business associations. First, the state reduces the costs of collecting information. Business associations can provide timely and well-formulated policy proposals. The state gains legitimacy when it implements proposals initiated and supported by the business community. The state can reduce its political burden and risks by allowing the business community to hammer out their own differences and conflicts of interest. And finally, by delegating parts of policy implementation to business associations, the effectiveness of public policies can be improved and the administrative costs of the state reduced.[20]

Cooperation between the state and business as well as among business people themselves thus reduces collective action and policy problems. Slack in the economy is put to better use, and the economy as a whole grows more rapidly and more consistently than under the laissez-faire institution.[21]

State corporatism is particularly beneficial to developing countries. Most firms in developing countries are small or medium-sized. They lack the capital, management training, research capability, and marketing networks to compete with multinational corporations. To find a market niche, they have to gain access to these competitive advantages through collective arrangements. The state is certainly one such possibility. But as already seen, the state in developing countries cannot be expected to follow market signals closely. Private, bilateral networks among firms may also help create competitiveness. The bilateral efforts may not be sufficient, however, either in terms of quantity or quality. Only through business-wide cooperation can Third World firms significantly improve their competitiveness and bargaining situation in the international market. Furthermore, through collective pressure and information sharing, business associations can expand contributions of the state and of private networks to a firm's competitiveness.

State corporatism is, thus, different from the developmental state theory with regard to the theoretical relationship among state strength, state autonomy, and economic development. The developmental state theory suggests that a strong and autonomous state may contribute to economic development. Under state corporatism the state need not be strong or autonomous to help the economy.[22] On the contrary, by incorporating the business association into the decision-making and implementation process, state policies will be more effective and efficient, since business associations have a stronger incentive than the state to reduce the red tape, waste, and distortion associated with *their* policies. A nonautonomous state makes the state itself stronger and, hence, more helpful to the economy.

The distinction between state corporatism de jure and de facto is important to this study. Although the literature on state corporatism originated in the Latin American context, most Latin American countries seem to fit only the legal definition of state corporatism. Clientelism is, in fact, a more common reality in Latin American, as Kaufman (1977), Malloy (1977, 7), and Chalmers (1977, 35) have shown. As Stepan explains (1978, 47), the major reason Latin American states created these singular, hierarchical business associations was to provide an elite response to political crisis, to prevent political enemies from spreading their influence in the business community. As a result of the clientelism existing within these business associations, they lost their capacity to resolve policy and collective action problems.

In East and Southeast Asia, similar formal legal corporatism existed in Indonesia and the Philippines during Marcos's rule (Milne 1983). In other Asian countries, however, even though the creation of corporatist associations also had a strong political dimension (for historical and strategic reasons), the economic functions of these business associations soon replaced political functions among the organization's major goals.[23] State corporatism de jure was thus transformed into state corporatism de facto.

Table 2–1 summarizes the preceding discussion of the laissez-faire institution, state corporatism, and clientelism.

Institutions as Filters of International Impacts

Embedded in an increasingly interdependent world, economic development in most developing countries cannot but be affected by

Table 2-1

Typology of Institutions

	Laissez-faire	State Corporatism	Clientelism
Major actors	Atomized firms State bureaucracies	Business associations State bureaucracies	Individual business people as clients, state officials as patrons
Organization of business	Disorganized	Well-organized, powerful business associations	Disorganized or multiple factional associations
State cooperation	Not cooperative except in rule making, arbitration, and prevention of market imperfections	Very cooperative with some bargaining	Responsive to clients but not to entire business
Strength	Market efficiency	Policy quality and implementation Low market uncertainty and risks	Integration (?) Concentration (?) Mobilization of slack resources (?)
Weakness	High failure rate of efficient firms Uncertain investment climate Opportunism	Degeneration into pluralist politics or clientelism	High transaction costs Inconsistent policies Erosion of state capacity Fiscal crisis in state Waste in resource allocation
Growth patterns	Rapid growth Large fluctuations Continuous decline after external shock	Rapid and sustained growth Ratchet effect	Stagnation, low growth Occasional high growth accompanied by drastic decline
Empirical cases at national level	Hong Kong (?)	Japan, South Korea, Taiwan, Thailand (after 1970s)	Philippines, Indonesia, Colombia

Note: Question marks indicate that there are debates about the argument or case.

domestic and international factors simultaneously. Nevertheless, the impact of international factors on the economy—for example, foreign investments, foreign loans, and market fluctuations—often interacts with domestic factors (Aggarwal 1985; Grieco 1984; Ikenberry 1986; Katzenstein 1985; Milner 1988; Zysman 1983). Scholars of international political economy commonly assume that the international system presents essentially the same opportunities and obstacles to each nation. The causes of national variation in economic performance must then lie at the national level;[24] that is, certain types of institutions are more prepared than others to exploit opportunities and to overcome obstacles in the world economy. The next section will demonstrate how international opportunities (foreign direct investments and foreign loans) and constraints (market fluctuations), when filtered through different institutions, may have varying degrees of impact on the economy.

FOREIGN DIRECT INVESTMENTS

Many scholars have found that the impact of foreign direct investments on the host economy varies across industries and countries. In some cases, FDIs create forward and backward linkages with local producers; in others, they create enclave economies. The difference lie in natural endowments, economic structure, incentive policies, and sectoral attributes. In addition to these factors, however, each type of institution has an independent effect on whether FDIs create linkages or enclave syndromes.

Under the laissez-faire institution, FDIs are not obliged to establish linkages with the local economy. Local producers are either driven out of the market or merged by foreign companies. When local or international market conditions change, FDIs may quickly move their production elsewhere, leaving behind empty factories and unemployed workers. As a result, FDIs tend to increase instability and transitional costs in the local economy.

Clientelism tends to either deter FDIs or to reduce the beneficial externalities of FDIs. Clientelism deters FDIs because foreigners may find it too costly and risky to depend on local political patrons. Those who are able to break into the system are transformed from profit makers into rent seekers, engaging in oligopolistic behavior or speculative activities.

State corporatism, in contrast, facilitates linkages between FDIs and local producers. Close cooperation among producers and between the state and local producers gives the host country a better bargaining position vis-à-vis FDIs with regard to technology transfer and linkage effects. Through the introduction and coordination of business associations, FDIs can benefit from cheap and timely local supplies by providing local producers with necessary management and technology know-how. After establishing extensive linkages with local producers, FDIs establish vested interests in the local economy and hence are more willing to reinvest their profits locally.

FOREIGN LOANS

As Balassa (1984, 119) concludes, there is no significant statistical relationship between external financing and national economic performance. Why, then, do foreign loans accelerate growth in some countries while exacerbating underdevelopment in others? If it is assumed that developing countries have approximately the same access to foreign loans under similar terms, the difference may lie in how these loans are used.

The laissez-faire institution encourages the efficient use of these loans through competition. More efficient firms or national governments have better access to foreign loans. But information problems exist on both sides of the lending relationship. Firms may not know that such loans are available to them. Creditors may not know how efficient these firms are. Furthermore, since the allocation of foreign loans is often mediated through government agencies, implementation distortion may occur, resulting in the inefficient use of loans.

Clientelism greatly undermines the efficient use of foreign loans. Foreign loans are often used to finance white elephant projects or are siphoned off, ending up in private pockets as political rewards. Recipients of loans need not worry about payment because their political patrons can have their debts refinanced by the national treasury or can arrange for additional borrowing.

In contrast, state corporatism can maximize the efficient use of foreign loans. The state can formulate realistic loan policies by consulting with local producers. Because of the supervision and coordination mechanisms built into the corporatist institution, the possibility that loans will be unused or misused is reduced.

MARKET FLUCTUATIONS

Just as FDIs and foreign loans present similar opportunities to developing countries, international market fluctuations (including protectionism) constitute equivalent obstacles to all. Given a country's difference in export dependency and bilateral relationships, its institutions have varying capabilities for limiting the impact of market fluctuations on economic growth.

Under the laissez-faire institution, the performance of a national economy fluctuates with the same rhythm as the international market. Because of their sensitivity and vulnerability (Keohane and Nye, 19), most of the developing economies may incur irreparable damage from market fluctuations. Large-scale market turbulence may wipe out national industries and deter further investments.

The clientelist institution is no more capable than the laissez-faire institution of coping with fluctuations in the global market. Although business clients may receive exclusive state assistance to cope with market uncertainty and risks, this cooperation tends to be short-lived. Furthermore, there is no guarantee that state assistance achieves desirable policy goals. Import and export quotas, for example, may be resold for instant profit by those traders or manufacturers with strong political connections to other producers.

By comparison, state corporatism helps producers reduce the uncertainty and risks inherent in the international market. Through collective efforts, producers can devise risk-sharing or cost-sharing mechanisms to cushion the effect of market fluctuations, such as a rescue fund, export-encouragement fund, production order arrangement, or export diversification schemes. Furthermore, business associations may exercise collective pressure on FDIs and organize lobby groups to combat protectionism by the trading partner.[25]

The Dynamics of Institutions

Why have so few developing countries opted for the laissez-faire institution or for state corporatism? How do countries transform themselves from an inferior institution to a superior one if they are aware of the economic consequences of different institutions? Why does state corporatism sometimes degenerate into clientelism? Although history, international shocks, emulation, and other exogenous factors often provide good answers to these questions, understanding individual actors' strategic behavior within institutional constraints has more general theoretical importance. This section, then, attempts to provide a microfoundation for the institutional theory of economic development.

How do individual business people and state officials behave under different institutions? The game models in figure 2–1 offer an integrative scheme to study such strategic behavior. Figure 2–1 consists of two game models, the Prisoner's Dilemma in the lower part and the Stag Hunt in the upper part.[26]

First, the laissez-faire institution and clientelism are placed in the Prisoner's Dilemma model (PD). While the laissez-faire institution is the Pareto-optimal outcome, clientelism turns out to be the individual optimal outcome and the equilibrium of the PD model. The logic is as follows.

Assume that the cooperation strategy of each business person is to relinquish political connections and that the defection strategy is to build them. The best outcome (b) for a business person is to have a political patron when other business people do not. The second-best outcome (s) is the laissez-faire institution in which everyone has a fair chance to compete without the interference of political favoritism. The third-best outcome (t) is the clientelist institution in which everyone finds a political patron. Since risks and uncertainty increase under this institution, everyone is worse off than under the laissez-faire institution. But the outcome of clientelism is still better than the sucker's outcome (w) in which one business person relinquishes clientelist ties while all other business people retain theirs. Since defection is the dominant strategy for all business people, clientelism becomes the equilibrium outcome.

Figure 2-1 ■ Game-Structural Relationships Among Institutions

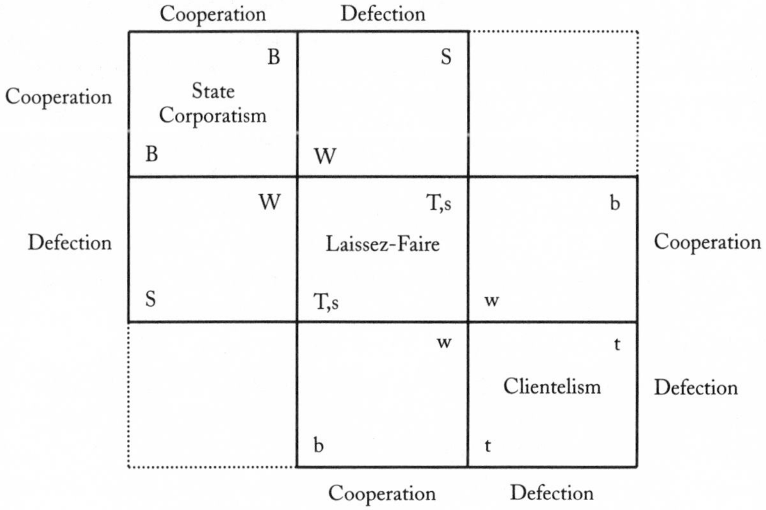

	Cooperation	Defection	
Cooperation	B State Corporatism B	S W	
Defection	W Laissez-Faire S	T,s T,s	b w	Cooperation
		w Clientelism b	t t	Defection
	Cooperation	Defection	

Key:

B(b) = Best outcome
S(s)   = Second-best outcome
T(t)   = Third-best outcome
W(w) = Worst outcome

The upper 2 x 2 table is a Stag Hunt game; the bottom table is a Prisoner's Dilemma (PD).

The upper-right payoff in each cell is the column player's; the other is the row player's.

The same reasoning applies to the relationships between state officials who have the choice of accepting a business client or not. A state official's preference orders are: to accept a business client when other officials do not, which increases the official's income and political influence; to refuse business clients when other officials do the same, which avoids breaking the law; to find a business client when other officials do the same, which destabilizes all officials' income while greatly reducing their political influence; and to refuse business clients when all other officials take clients.

State corporatism is located in a different model—the Stag Hunt model (see the upper half of figure 2–1). The cooperation strategy for each business person is to establish a strong, effective business association. The defection strategy is to take care of one's own business. State corporatism is both the collectively and individually optimal outcome (B). The second-best outcome (S) is to free ride and enjoy some of the association's club goods paid for by other business people. The third-best (T) is the laissez-faire institution, which in turn is better than the sucker's outcome (W). The sucker devotes his time and resources to building a business association that no one else cares about. Since no dominant strategy exists in the Stag Hunt model, state corporatism is a less stable outcome than clientelism but more stable than laissez-faire. The collective action problem is how to coordinate business people to reach the collectively and individually optimal outcome.

The Stag Hunt model also applies to the relationship among state officials. All state officials can benefit from a reduction of political and administrative burdens if they can help create powerful business associations. The second-best outcome for each official is neither to contribute to nor benefit from business associations, while other officials waste their time establishing business associations not fully recognized by the state as a whole. The third-best outcome is not to have business associations at all (the laissez-faire institution). The worst outcome for an official is to contribute to a business association that other officials do not recognize.

The results documented in figure 2–1 have three interesting implications. They explain why there have been so few empirical cases of state corporatism and even fewer of the laissez-faire institution. In the PD model the laissez-faire institution is hard to reach in the presence of clientelism because the latter is the equilibrium outcome. Although in the Stag Hunt the laissez-faire institution is also an equilibrium outcome, state corporatism is the preferred equilibrium for all members. Therefore, the institution of laissez-faire either degenerates into clientelism or is elevated to state corporatism. Since degeneration is in general easier than elevation, more countries end up with clientelism than with state corporatism. This may be the reason why, for example, most Latin American countries have degenerated into clientelism despite their corporatist formal legal structure.

The results shown in figure 2–1 also suggest the complexity of institutional transformation from the Pareto-inferior outcome of clientelism to the final Pareto-optimal outcome of state corporatism. In order to move from clientelism to the laissez-faire institution, effective mechanisms to prevent cheating in the PD model must first exist. Once this has been brought about, additional coordination will transform the laissez-faire institution into state corporatism. It takes two cooperative mechanisms to reach state corporatism.

Even when state corporatism is reached, the possibility of degeneration exists if a new payoff structure, consisting of state corporatism and clientelism, becomes a PD model. To show how this can happen, I have transformed figure 2–1 into a 3 X 3 table by including one additional cell at the upper right-hand corner and another at the lower left-hand corner. The payoff for the row player's choice of contributing to business associations is the worst of all if the column player decides to seek patrons. In this situation, the column player's payoff is either (a) the best of all or (b) the second-best. If (a), then the whole 3 X 3 game is a PD; if (b), then it is a Stag Hunt. Whether it is (a) or (b) depends on the marginal benefits of corporatism and clientelism. The institutional implication of this theoretical discussion is that state corporatism has to continually improve its function as provider of club goods while deterring free riders and cheating.

Summary and Hypotheses

Economic development involves the resolution or reduction of policy and collective action problems. The first section of this chapter revealed the insufficiency of current theories of economic development in addressing these problems. The second section studied the relative capabilities of three institutions (laissez-faire, clientelism, and state corporatism) in resolving policy and collective action problems and concluded that state corporatism tends to promote economic development, clientelism tends to produce stagnation, and the laissez-faire institution has a varying impact on the economy. Using game models, the third section provided a microfoundation to explain how individual actors (state officials and business people) behave under different institutional constraints and what the theoretical implications for institutional transformation are.

The following chapters apply the above theoretical hypotheses to the comparison of Taiwan and the Philippines. To refute the empirical validity of the developmental state theory, I will demonstrate that effective "developmental" policies are not initiated by the state but by corporatist business associations, that state autonomy often retards economic growth instead of assisting it, that a "committed leadership" either does not exist or is irrelevant to economic performance, and that state capacity increases as a result of the suggestions and pressure from business associations.

3

NATIONAL COMPARISON OF TAIWAN AND THE PHILIPPINES

In this chapter the national comparison of Taiwan's and the Philippines's political economy will demonstrate that Taiwan's economic success was not due to the existence of a developmental state, but rather to the transition from clientelism to state corporatism. In contrast, the failure of the Philippines's economic development during Marcos's rule is attributable to the emergence of an authoritarian clientelist state that happened to share the characteristics of a developmental state. The first section presents data to compare the economic performance of the two countries. The second section tests the applicability of the developmental state theory in the Taiwanese and Philippine cases. The third section elaborates the institutional causes of Taiwan's economic success and the Philippines's failure. The last section summarizes the findings of this chapter.

Comparing Economic Performance

The success of Taiwan's economic development and the failure of the Philippines's is now well known. A number of economic indicators, illustrated below, will suffice to support this general impression. What makes the comparison of Taiwan and the Philippines interesting and important, however, is not only the great difference in development outcomes but also the similarity in initial conditions.

Economic Indicators

The findings documented in table 3–1 show the difference in economic performance between Taiwan and the Philippines in terms of the growth rates of GNP, GNP per capita, and exports. To properly interpret these statistics, we need to keep in mind Taiwan's and the Philippines's developmental stages. For Taiwan, the 1950s has usually been called the import-substitution industrialization (ISI) stage. In the 1960s and 1970s the country experimented with export-led industrialization (ELI). In the late 1970s Taiwan began to have a mature industrial economy that replaced labor-intensive exports with more technology- and capital-intensive products. Hence, the high growth rates of per capita GNP, industrial production, and exports in the 1960s and 1970s represent the unleashing of Taiwan's economic potential, which was constrained during the ISI stage of the 1950s. The relative decline in these statistics during the 1980s should not be regarded as a deterioration of the economy, but rather as a sign of economic maturity.

The maturity of Taiwan's economy is further supported by the speed with which it recovered from the shocks of the two oil crises. The oil crisis of 1973 caught Taiwan and other countries off guard. Its growth rate of per capita GNP dropped from 10.7 percent in 1973 to −0.7 percent in 1974. The vibrant Taiwanese economy, however, managed to bounce back with two-digit growth rates in 1976 and 1978. The second oil crisis, in 1979, did not cause irrevocable damage to the economy either. Three years after the worldwide recession, Taiwan's economy resumed its momentum.

The Philippines's economic development went through two pe-

Table 3–1

Economic Indicators of Taiwan and the Philippines

	GNP Growth Rate		GNP/Capita Growth Rate		Export Growth Rate	
Year	Taiwan	Philippines	Taiwan	Philippines	Taiwan	Philippines
1950		8.7		5.5		
1951		8.6		5.3		
1952		8.1		4.9		
1953	9.3	8.4	5.8	5.2	35.1	
1954	9.6	8.4	5.8	5.3	−26.9	
1955	8.1	7.0	4.1	3.8	32.2	
1956	5.5	7.2	1.8	4.0	52.9	
1957	7.3	5.8	4.0	2.7	25.4	
1958	6.6	3.8	3.2	0.7	5.1	
1959	7.7	6.9	4.3	3.7	47.8	
1960	6.5	1.3	3.1	1.5	4.5	17.7
1961	6.8	6.5	3.5	3.1	30.9	7.4
1962	7.8	6.1	4.7	2.7	11.8	−24.3
1963	9.4	7.4	6.2	3.9	52.1	28.8
1964	12.3	2.5	9.1	1.0	30.7	2.0
1965	11.0	5.5	7.9	2.0	3.6	4.8
1966	9.0	6.0	6.1	2.4	19.3	18.3
1967	10.6	6.1	7.9	2.4	19.5	−0.7
1968	9.1	6.2	6.5	3.1	23.2	4.6
1969	9.0	6.2	6.6	2.7	33.0	−0.5
1970	11.3		9.0		41.2	21.9
1971	12.9	5.8	10.6	2.8	39.1	5.5
1972	13.3	4.9	11.2	2.2	45.0	0.2
1973	12.8	9.6	10.7	6.7	42.8	71.4
1974	1.1	6.3	0.7	3.5	25.2	44.6
1975	4.3	5.9	2.4	2.9	−5.7	−15.8
1976	13.5	6.1	11.2	3.3	53.8	11.4
1977	10.1	7.0	7.9	4.5	14.6	22.4
1978	13.9	6.8	11.8	3.4	31.9	8.8
1979	8.5	6.8	6.4	4.0	23.6	34.3
1980	7.1	4.4	5.1	1.8	22.9	25.7
1981	5.7	3.7	3.8	1.2	16.5	−1.5
1982	3.3	2.9	1.5	−0.0	4.2	−12.1
1983	7.9	0.0	6.1	−0.0	16.3	−1.6
1984	10.5	−0.1	8.9	−0.1	19.8	7.9
1985	5.1	−0.0	3.6	−0.1	1.5	−12.6
1986	10.8	0.0	9.5	−0.0	23.0	3.5

Sources: Data for Taiwan are from CEPD (1987, 2, 41, 208); data for the Philippines are calculated from Castro (1971, table 1), IMF (1987, 118–19), Rodriguez (1986, 6), and NEDA (1983, 190–95; 1988, 166–77).

Note: Data for the Philippines from 1947 to 1969 are based on 1955 constant prices. Data after 1969 are based on 1972 constant prices. The growth rate of the Philippine GNP in the late 1970s and early 1980s may have been exaggerated for political reasons.

riods, with Marcos's declaration of martial law in 1972 serving as the dividing line. Import-substitution industrialization characterized the first period and export-led industrialization the second. The growth rates of the economy were low and showed continual decline over the years. Especially during the martial law period (1972–1986), the economy was stagnant. The initial growth of the economy during this period was financed by a large number of foreign loans and was followed by the collapse of the economy.

The fragility of the Philippine economy is also reflected in its response to the two oil crises. The economy capitalized on the sharp rise of commodity prices after the first oil crisis and registered modest growth. But when the second oil crisis occurred in 1979 without a significant rise in commodity prices, the economy went bankrupt.

The figures in table 3–2 provide additional data on Taiwan and the Philippines by comparing them to other countries. In both dollar value and average growth rate of per capita GNP, Taiwan scores higher than other LDCs, while its inflation rate is lower than the averages of middle- and upper middle-income economies. Taiwan's industrial growth rate is also almost double the average growth rate of other LDCs. Especially interesting are the comparisons between Taiwan and two of the most advanced NICs in Latin America (Brazil and Mexico) and between Taiwan and three of the less energetic OECD countries (Greece, Portugal, and Spain). Taiwan's economy still fares better. In contrast, the Philippine economy does not consistently perform better than other developing countries. As compared to lower middle-income economies, the Philippines has a smaller per capita GNP, slower per capita growth rate, and slower industrial growth.

Initial Conditions

The success of Taiwan's economic development would not have been considered so remarkable if it initially had overwhelming economic advantages over other LDCs. In that case, there would have been no miracle to speak of and little to learn from Taiwan's experience.

Some scholars argue that Taiwan's economic miracle is attribut-

Table 3-2

Comparison of Economic Performance Among Taiwan, the Philippines, and Other Countries[b]

Country	GNP/Capita (In Dollars) 1986	GNP/Capita Average 1965- 1986	Inflation Rate (%) 1965- 1980	Inflation Rate (%) 1980- 1986	Industry 1965- 1980	Industry 1980- 1986
Taiwan	3,996[a]	7.5	8.3	5.7	15.6	7.2
Philippines	560	1.9	11.7	18.2	8.0	−3.5
Low-income economies	270	3.1	4.6	8.1	7.5	10.6
Lower middle-income economies	750	2.5	22.3	22.9	8.4	1.2
Upper middle-income economies	1,890	2.8	20.5	70.2	6.5	2.5
Latin American NICs						
Brazil	1,810	4.3	31.3	157.1	9.9	1.6
Mexico	1,860	2.6	13.1	63.7	7.6	−0.1
OECD Countries						
Spain	4,860	2.9	11.8	11.3	5.8	0.8
Greece	3,680	3.3	10.5	20.3	7.1	0.4
Portugal	2,250	3.2	11.5	22.0		1.4

Source: CEPD (1987, 2) and World Bank (1988, 222–25).
[a] This is calculated at the exchange rate of U.S. $1 = N.T. $35.45.
[b] Except for the first column of numbers, all numbers are growth rates.

able to its Japanese colonial heritage. In his classic work on Taiwan's economic development, Ho (1978) points out that Japan had developed Taiwan's agricultural sector into the major source of savings for rapid industrialization. The development of the agricultural processing industry during Japanese rule gave Taiwan a head start compared to former colonies of other imperialist powers. Crane (1982), Cumings (1984), and Gold (1981) also trace Taiwan's economic development to the infrastructural constructions completed during Japanese rule. The most distinguished example of these infrastructural projects was the construction of the Sun-Moon-Lake Dam, which the

Japanese designed to be the largest electric power plant in Asia (Zhang 1980, 75, 112). Furthermore, most of Taiwan's public enterprises were formerly established by the Japanese government, which allegedly contributed to Taiwan's capital formation (*FEER* 4/19/56).

These physical or agricultural legacies should not, however, be overemphasized, for several reasons. First, the high level of productivity of the agricultural sector is a common attribute of many LDCs. What distinguishes Taiwan from other LDCs is its transformation from a predominantly agricultural economy to an industrial economy. Second, Taiwan's alleged advantage in infrastructural constructions was shattered by the U.S. bombardment at the end of War World II. Half the railroads were paralyzed and only four-tenths of the roads were usable. Most harbors and surrounding facilities were completely ruined (Ye 1970, 2). Over two hundred factories were bombed, most of them housing Taiwan's vital industries. American bombing also burned down three of Taiwan's four electrical power plants. Consequently, Japan's industrialization efforts in Taiwan came to a virtual standstill by the end of World War II (Zhang 1980, 145).

Worse still, the Taiwanese economy encountered severe problems in the 1950s, which made its prospects dim. The *Far East Economic Review* reported then that the "general impression of [the] Taiwan[ese] economy seems that it has reached a 'bottled up' stage" (*FEER* 11/29/56). The import controls, tariffs, and multiple exchange rates of the 1950s resulted in inefficiency, deteriorating balance-of-payments problems, and discrimination against exporters (Ho 1978, 194–95). A high-level economic bureaucrat recalled that among the major problems in the 1950s were the scramble for profits derived from exchange rate differentials, excessive reliance on protection, speculation, and oligopolies (Yin 1959a). The government generously subsidized public enterprises with low-interest loans, which led to high interest rates on the black market where private entrepreneurs financed their capital needs (Yu 1975, 51–61). Militarily, Taiwan's safety during the 1950s was in limbo. Its "springboard of recovering the mainland," the island of Quemoy, was fiercely attacked by China in 1954 and again in 1958. Taiwan's president, Jiang Jeishi, had planned to use the second Quemoy war as a pretext for attacking the mainland. Deterred by this military uncertainty, no significant foreign investments came to Taiwan until the mid-1960s.

The transitional labor pain from ISI to ELI made the future of Taiwan's economy dim. In the late 1950s, "there practically had been no new development projects of any large scale, partly because of a shortage of investment capital as a result of ineffective control over consumption and partly because of the lack of investment opportunities" (Li 1959, 3). Then in 1958 a wave of business failures swept the country, caused by the overexpansion of industries, a saturated domestic market, and fraudulent bankruptcy claims (Li 1959, 10). In addition, the export sector did not perform well in the first few years of the liberalization program, which began in 1959. Between 1958 and 1961, Taiwan's trade deficit increased because the growth of exports could not catch up with imports (*FEER* 10/11/62). Exports did not expand rapidly, due to high production costs, the low quality of goods, high interest rates, a myriad of taxes and export fees, and poor marketing networks (Xu 1969, 199–200). Most Taiwanese producers were reluctant to export their products because they were afraid to compete with Japanese goods. The export drive also met with rising protectionism in the United States. Taiwanese exports became more precarious when Japan moved its export products from the protected U.S. market and dumped them on the Southeast Asian countries that had been Taiwan's major export markets before the late 1960s.

This evidence suggests that the importance of Japanese rule in Taiwan's economic development might have been overstated. Even if the allegations regarding the contribution of the "Japanese legacy" to Taiwan's industrialization are true, the transformation of Taiwan's economy from a precarious condition in the 1950s to the rapid growth period of the 1960s and 1970s requires another explanation.

By comparison, the Philippines had equal, if not better, initial conditions for promising economic development. During the 1950s and early 1960s, the Philippines had numerous political and economic achievements to be proud of. Politically, it was one of the few Asian countries where regular popular elections were held; civilian supremacy over the military was well established; and the communist insurgency was effectively suppressed in the mid-1950s (Corpuz 1965, 15).

This admirable political democracy was accompanied by an even more impressive economic achievement. During the half-century of American rule (1898–1946), extensive programs of infrastructure building, road construction, and human development had already fulfilled "the prerequisites or pre-conditions for economic development" (Castro 1971, 3–4). The postwar economy recovered rapidly. In addition to the period of hypergrowth between 1947 and 1949, the average growth rates of GNP and per capita GNP during the 1950s were 7.3 percent and 4.1 percent respectively—not much different from Taiwan's 7.7 percent and 4.1 percent for the period of 1953–1959 (see table 3–1). The manufacturing sector in the Philippines grew significantly in the 1950s and early 1960s, contributing more to the economy than its Taiwanese counterpart. In 1950 the Philippine manufacturing sector accounted for 12.5 percent of the gross domestic product; in 1955, 15.1 percent; and in 1960, 17.5 percent. The corresponding figures for the Taiwanese manufacturing sector were 10 percent, 13.8 percent, and 16.8 percent (Alburo and Shepherd 1985, 15; see also table 3–1). Production of food crops surpassed consumption requirements in 1954. Although the shift to cash crops in the late 1950s created stagnation in the agricultural sector, the problem was solved in the mid-1960s (Castro 1971, 15–16). The living standard was so high that one business leader nostalgically told me about the good old days when he traveled to Taiwan to buy "cheap-labor" goods.

The business sector was composed of well-educated entrepreneurs. The Filipinos, like the Chinese, Koreans, and Japanese, were very concerned about education. During American rule, one-fifth to one-fourth of the government's expenditure was on education. During the 1960s the average share of the government budget spent on education was 34.3 percent (Castro 1971, 3, 28). In 1960 more than 70 percent of the Philippine adult population was literate. In his study of Filipino entrepreneurs, John Carroll (1965, 106–10) found that 72 percent of his respondents had a college education and all had some schooling. By comparison, foreign entrepreneurs (Chinese and

Americans) in the Philippines had much less education than their Filipino counterparts.

The expansion of the economy and the emergence of entrepreneurs in the 1950s were results attributable to the government's import-substitution strategy, which was adopted as well by the governments of Taiwan, South Korea, and most of the developing countries. The Import Control Law was approved by the Congress in June 1948 and strengthened by Republic Act 650 in 1951. The Philippine government imposed exchange controls in December 1949 to cope with the shortage of foreign exchange. It was discovered then that exchange control could also be used as an industrial policy to protect domestic industries (Alburo and Shepherd 1985, 46). Direct controls of imports were lifted in 1953 but were immediately replaced by high tariffs. In 1957 tariffs were raised again to protect domestic industries.

In addition to these control policies, the government formulated various investment incentive acts to encourage industrial expansion. For example, Republic Act 35 of 1946 allowed tax exemptions for "new and necessary" industries. In 1951 Republic Act 901 further waived all taxes for new and necessary industries.[1] Under an investment incentive law passed in June 1961, "basic industries" enjoyed six-year exemptions of special import tax, compensation tax, foreign exchange margin fees, and tariff duties. The National Cottage Industries Law of 1962 established the National Cottage Industry Development Authority to solve problems of small and medium-sized enterprises. The government provided practical assistance to entrepreneurs to help them set up factories. Of the samples Carroll selected, 96 percent of respondents said they had received such assistance (1965, 179).

A number of U.S.-Philippine agreements further boosted the Philippine economy. The Philippine Rehabilitation Act passed by the U.S. Congress in 1946 helped the Philippine economy recover from war damages. According to the recommendation of the U.S. Economic Survey Mission (the Bell Mission) in 1950, the two governments signed the Quirino-Foster Agreement on Economic and Technical Cooperation, which began American developmental aid. In 1952 the Philippines approved the U.S. Investment Insurance

Program to encourage American investments. The Philippines was the first country in Asia to sign such an agreement with the United States (Shalom 1981, 132). To facilitate trade with the United States and to protect Philippine industries, the Laurel-Langley Agreement was enacted in 1954. The agreement gave preferential tariff treatments to Philippine exports for twenty years.[2] Agricultural aid, based on American Public Law 480, was accepted by the Philippine government in 1954 and arrived in 1957.

It is important to note that during the 1950s the U.S. government supported the import-substitution industrialization (ISI) strategy in the Philippines, as it did in Taiwan, South Korea, and other developing countries.[3] The International Monetary Fund (IMF) and the Bell Mission prescribed the ISI strategy for the Philippines (Cuaderno 1961, 26). The strategy was generally regarded as an effective way to cope with the foreign exchange shortage and to protect American interests in the host country. Although the Philippines imposed exchange and import controls, "new and necessary" industries could still import materials and machinery from the United States with dollar allocations and tax exemptions.

As in neighboring countries, ISI strategy in the Philippines encountered severe setbacks in the late 1950s. The domestic market became saturated due to successful import substitution (World Bank 1980, 2). Various investment incentive acts encouraged the development of capital-intensive instead of labor-using industries. As a consequence, unemployment problems increased. Foreign exchange crises recurred due to the overvalued currency and strong demands for imports. Black markets for dollar allocation and tax-free imports expanded.

With prior approval of the United States and the IMF, the government then experimented with a series of liberalization measures to cope with these ISI problems (Cuaderno 1961, 83; Macapagal 1968, 60–63). In April 1960 a multiple exchange rate system was adopted as a prelude to lifting exchange controls in January 1962. Import controls were further liberalized in 1962. In 1965 President Macapagal again devalued the Philippine peso and lifted the 20 percent retention rate of foreign exchange to reflect the market value of the peso.[4] Marcos reintroduced foreign exchange controls in 1968, yet the peso was allowed to float in accordance with market rates. In 1969 Marcos rejected the implementation of a congressional act that espoused the return of the ISI strategy. He approved the construction of the Bataan Export Processing Zone (EPZ) modeled exactly on Taiwan's Gaoxiong EPZ. The Export Incentives Act of 1970 further encouraged export industries.

From this evidence we can conclude that the initial conditions for rapid economic development in the Philippines during the 1950s and 1960s were as good as, if not better than, those in Taiwan and South Korea. Why, then, did Taiwan develop a vibrant economy while the Philippines under Marcos's rule, after emulating Taiwan's development programs, failed miserably? The developmental statists might suggest that this is because Taiwan had a developmental state while Marcos failed to establish one. The next section argues that the difference in economic development in the two countries had little to do with the existence of a developmental state. In fact, the state in Taiwan was not as developmental as the statists have argued; the Philippine state under Marcos rule seemed to fit more closely the theory's model.

Developmental States in Taiwan and the Philippines?

As explained in chapter 1, a developmental state has three characteristics: state autonomy, state capacity, and a developmental leadership. According to these criteria, Taiwan did not have a developmental state. First, the state was not autonomous from influential business people or from business associations. Second, it was not strong in terms of its planning agency, centralization, and bureaucracy. And finally, its leaders' commitment to economic development was shadowed by military and political concerns.

First, although the state was politically autonomous from the workers, landlords, and politicians, it was not economically autonomous from the capitalists. The statists correctly point out that Taiwanese workers were never able to exert significant influence on the state because of martial law (1949–1987). Taiwanese landlords, with the notable exception of the Gu family, were deprived of their influence after the land reforms of the late 1940s and early 1950s.

Politicians in Taiwan, surviving in powerless national legislatures, were at the mercy of the authoritarian party, the Guomingdang. But both the mainlander and Taiwanese capitalists were able to influence national economic policies through personal connections, party organizations, and the channel of corporatist organizations such as the National Industries Association, the National Chamber of Commerce, and especially their subsidiary professional associations.[5] Some capitalists were appointed or elected to core positions of the party and the state (for example, Lin Tingshen and Gu Zhenfu were members of the party's central standing committee; Lin was also a member of the powerful Economic Stabilization Board during the 1950s). Others assumed positions in city councils, provincial assemblies, and the national assembly (Numazaki 1986, 517). National economic policies were usually made after consultation with these corporatist organizations or with influential business leaders.[6]

Second, the Taiwanese state was not as strong (in terms of planning agency, centralization, and well-educated bureaucrats) as the statists have described. First, Taiwan's economic development plans during the 1950s and 1960s served few practical purposes. According to one planning official of the time, the development plans of the 1950s were formulated so that the country could apply for U.S. aid; they were not intended to be implemented (Li and Chen 1987, 276; Wanan Ye 1970, 1). In the mid-1960s a central planning agency, the Council on International Economic Cooperation and Development (CIECD), was established. CIECD officials, however, did not devote much energy to the plans because, as department heads, they were occupied with administrative chores (Wanan Ye 1970, 34). As a result, the plans underestimated, sometimes by as much as 70 percent, Taiwan's economic potential during the most crucial years of its economic development (Zhongbo Ye 1970).

Further, although the statists claim that the Taiwanese state was centralized, its centralization was the major obstacle to economic development during the 1950s. The state intervened in all important economic activities through control (foreign exchange), licensing (import and export), state ownership, and regulations (restricting entry to industries). In late 1959 the U.S. ICA China Mission in Taiwan had to threaten to terminate aid to achieve a drastic reduction in the Taiwanese state's intervention in the economy (Li 1985c). Following the eight-point proposal of the China Mission and recommendations from Taiwan's business associations, the state hastily formulated the now-famous nineteen-point economic development program and began to withdraw its power from the market, thus unleashing the potential of the private sector. Besides, the centralized state did not really penetrate Taiwan's local politics and economy at the county and city levels, where local factions had solid control (Chen 1991).

Finally, in 1949 the Guomingdang brought to Taiwan a group of well-educated bureaucrats (the statists, in fact, have not provided much statistical evidence to support this claim). These technocrats, however, were mainly technicians and not administrative experts. Several high-ranking technocrats had been associated with the most corrupt officials of the Chinese government before 1949. For instance, officials in charge of Taiwan's financial and monetary agencies, such as Yu Guohua, Xu Boyuan, and Yu Hongjun, were members of the notorious Kong-Song factions. Most ministers of economic affairs had served in public enterprises that were known for their inefficiency (Kuang 1987, 113–34; Li and Chen 1987, 260–62). Thus, the bureaucrats' high level of education did not directly contribute to Taiwan's economic success. An internal document of the U.S. AID/Taibei Mission dated 26 March 1962 severely criticized the Taiwan government's inefficiency and overstaffing:

Many Chinese officials . . . are well aware of this fact, but they have so far been unable to make strengthening government administration a high priority national goal. . . . The major missing ingredient is a strong nation-wide determination to improve administration. (Li 1985a)

The third component of a developmental state, a committed leadership, is also a debatable issue in Taiwan's economic history. After fleeing to Taiwan in 1949, President Jiang Jeishi restructured Taiwan's economy for the sole purpose of recovering the mainland through military means (*FEER* 6/21/56, 10/5/61). He did not give up this "sacred mission" until 1967, when he reluctantly adopted the slogan of "recovering the mainland through 30% military and 70%

political means." His son, Jiang Jingguo, had a more realistic assess-ment than his father about recovering the mainland. But in the 1960s and 1970s he was too occupied with political struggles over succes-sion. He fought battles simultaneously against the old cadres (e.g., Cheng Cheng) who had seniority over him, Madame Jiang's faction, which controlled Taiwan's economic authorities, the liberal intellec-tuals who opposed hereditary presidency, and local factions that re-sisted the party's intervention in local politics and economies.

To undermine Madame Jiang's influence, Jiang Jingguo went so far as to suddenly abolish the Foreign Exchange and Trade Control Commission (FETCC). In the 1960s the FETCC, though tempo-rary, was the most powerful agency in the economic bureaucracy (Cole 1967, 653). In March 1968, acknowledging FETCC's contri-bution and importance, the legislature passed a law making it a permanent bureaucracy. Nine months later, however, the FETCC was abolished by the soon-to-be vice premier Jiang Jingguo. Accord-ing to my interview with a former high official of the FETCC, the reason was that the bureaucracy had long been led by a follower of Madame Jiang's. Even the power of the government's planning agency was greatly curtailed for nine years, until Jiang Jingguo con-solidated his power in 1977—one year after his father died and Ma-dame Jiang left Taiwan for the United States, for "medical reasons." Therefore, Taiwan's transition from import-substitution to export-led industrialization in the late 1950s and its economic boom in the 1960s and early 1970s did not have much to do with the "committed" leadership of the two presidents Jiang.

This analysis, therefore, suggests that the Taiwanese state did not fit well the model of a developmental state and that the state did not contribute to Taiwan's economic miracle in the way the statists have described. This conclusion runs contrary to the recent research of a distinguished statist. In his research on Taiwan's political econ-omy, Robert Wade builds his "governed market theory" on the de-velopmental state theory to highlight the state's leadership role in the development of Taiwan's economy in industry generally and high-tech industries in particular (Wade 1990b). The contradiction be-tween my analysis and Wade's stems from different theoretical foci and the data used. The theoretical differences have been explained in previous sections. In terms of the data, while Wade and most statists have done extensive analyses of official sources (documents and interviews), I have also examined these official stories in the light of additional sources: industry association proceedings, a systematic set of newspaper clippings, and recently declassified documents. I have also supplemented this information with interviews with key business leaders. This difference in data results in a dramatically different interpretation of major events of state-business relationships in Taiwan's economic development.[7]

For instance, Wade describes the government's assistance to the textile industry between 1951 and 1953, when the industry was growing quickly. But this growth reflected only the performance of an emerging industry. He does not mention what happened after 1954, especially in 1959, when the entire industry almost collapsed due to the government's ever-changing control policies. Afterwards, it took the painstaking efforts of private cooperations which, for example, collectively reduced production and established an export-promotion scheme, for the industry to recover and prosper.

Wade also credits the state for promoting the electronics industry. But the industry had taken off around 1970, well before meaningful state promotion policies were implemented in the late 1970s. It was the industry association, the Taiwan Electric Appliance Manufacturers' Association, that initiated projects in the mid-1960s to both encourage cooperation and to benefit from foreign electronics assemblers. In the late 1960s and 1970s the association also implemented measures to promote production networks and technological development within the industry. Further, Wade misinterprets the development of the home appliances subsector, which had received the largest amount of state assistance but performed the poorest of all subsectors in the electronics industry.[8]

Finally, the story of the plastics industry has at least two sides. Wade briefly describes a farsighted state handing over a polyvinyl chloride (PVC) plant to a handpicked entrepreneur, Y. C. Wang, who later built up the multinational Formosa Plastics Group. The other side of the story, as told by an insider, is as follows: The PVC plant sold to Y. C. Wang was one of the government's reckless experiments aimed at spending as much U.S. aid money as possible to avoid a reduction in the next year's aid. The project was first proposed by the Yongfong Plastics Company, whose owner had prior political connections in China. He later backed out because he, as well as other big business leaders, did not foresee a bright future for the project. A timber processor at the time who had a problem even spelling polyvinyl chloride, Y. C. Wang approached the government on this project but was rejected due to his lack of experience in the plastics industry. He asked a mainlander friend to do the lobbying and got approval. Without strong support from other business leaders, he ended up throwing most of his own money into the project. Once PVC particles began rolling out of the machine, they soon accumulated in the factory stockroom and even in employees' homes because few, if any, PVC users existed at the time. Wang had to convince his relatives and employees to put up their property as collateral in order to build a small plastics molding factory. He then showed other businessmen how to use the new material to make plastic tubes, fabrics, toys, etc. After all this, the new experiment finally survived and prospered. "Without this plastics molding factory," a senior cadre of the conglomerate recollected, "the Taiwan Plastics Group would not have existed today" (*Koshu Lishi* 1989a, 209). Thus there is a good reason why Wang was popularly dubbed "the god of management."

Having examined the Taiwan case, we can now turn to the Philippine case, which presents a further challenge to the developmental state theory. The Philippine state under Marcos's rule was notoriously patrimonial and clientelistic. As a result, after Marcos's twenty-year rule the economy returned to the scale of the 1960s. But the Marcos state happened to share the characteristics of a developmental state; this casts further doubt on the relationship between a developmental state and economic development.

Although patrimonial and clientelistic, the Philippine state during Marcos's rule fit well the description of a developmental state. First, it was autonomous from major social groups, including landlords, traditional capitalists, workers, politicians, the military, and even the church. Second, the Marcos state had a relatively strong bureaucracy in terms of its planning agency, centralization, and technocracy. And finally, in his writings and public speeches, Marcos expressed his commitment to economic development.

First, the Marcos state was autonomous from social groups. After martial law was declared, traditional capitalists such as Jose B. Laurel (speaker of the House), Fernando Lopez (vice president), Alfredo Montelibano, Carlos Palanca, Antonio Madrigal, and the Osmena families lost their prominence and were replaced by loyal friends and relatives of Marcos and his wife. The political influence of landlords had declined in the 1960s due to the emergence of professional politicians and import-substitution industrialists (Alburo and Shepherd 1985, 72; Hawes 1987, 35, 43). After Marcos suspended the Congress in 1972, the landlords lost their major channel of influence. Coconut and sugar production, the livelihood of the Philippine landed class, was monopolized by quasi state institutions. The workers were suppressed by the martial law regime for the purpose of controlling prices, especially export prices. After 1972 politicians were arrested or simply had no forum to exert their influence. A powerless interim congress dominated by Marcos's followers was not established until 1978.[9] Moreover, the Marcos government effectively controlled the judiciary, co-opted the military, and silenced the most influential social organization in the country—the church.[10]

Second, Marcos established a planning agency and a centralized bureaucracy staffed by well-educated technocrats (De Guzman and Reforma 1988, 195–201).[11] The planning agency, the National Economic Development Authority, functioned as the statists have described. It formulated economic development plans, supervised their execution, and coordinated departments. The bureaucracy was centralized, and the state was able to penetrate into local institutions through periodic mass movements and plebiscites (Stauffer 1977, 402–03; Machado 1975, 546; Nowak and Snyder 1974, 1147–70). Barangay (town) assemblies were set up in December 1972 to assure "the national government direct control down to lowest local government level" and

the barangay record to date seems to indicate clearly that the New Society has been able to produce a centralized structure to mobilize mass action under firm administrative control in support of the regime's political goals . . . and carry out a variety of administrative tasks that involve mobilizing large numbers of persons. (Stauffer 1977, 402–03)

The efficiency (and corruption) of the bureaucracy was evidenced by such "white elephant" projects as a heart center, a culture center, government buildings, an electrical train system, and a Westinghouse nuclear power plant. Marcos recruited a group of highly educated technocrats, such as Roberto Ongpin, Gerardo P. Sicat, and Cesar E. A. Virata, whose expertise in economic theories had no equal in Taiwan's economic bureaucracy (Salgado 1985, 83). Marcos even joked once that he often mistook his cabinet meetings for faculty meetings at the University of the Philippines.

Finally, in terms of the leadership's commitment to economic development, official documents cannot differentiate the patrimonial Marcos state from the developmental state. Marcos repeatedly emphasized the priority of economic development in his presidential campaigns and in his declaration of martial law. He also published a number of books to demonstrate his commitment to economic development, though they turned out to be commissioned works written by the University of the Philippines faculty (Marcos 1970, 1973, 1983).

This comparison of Taiwan and the Philippines weakens the developmental state argument that the existence of a developmental state is a necessary condition for rapid economic growth. The evidence seems to indicate the contrary: Taiwan's economic success was associated with the existence of a nondevelopmental state, while the Philippine failure occurred in the presence of a patrimonial but developmental state. The South Korean case also presents a challenge to the developmental state thesis. Amsden attributes the success of Korean development to the developmental state's "market-augmenting" policies and the close relationships between the state and a few privileged big businesses (1989, 16, 150). But the same policies and relationships are discredited as sources of the Philippine developmental failure.

The statists might counter that the Philippine state under Marcos's rule was never a developmental state. It was infested and distorted by Marcos's cronies—a fact agreed upon by scholars from both the liberal economic and Marxist traditions. But the very existence of clientelism within a state that was strong and autonomous from the overwhelming majority of society may complicate the application of the developmental state concept.[12] Should the state's "relative autonomy" be defined not in terms of degree (how much autonomy) but in terms of kind (from whom), or both? Are the statists holding to a double standard when they ignore the omnipresent patron-client relationships within the Asian developmental states while exposing similar relationships in other cases of unsuccessful economic development? Are we compelled to resort to, in an ad hoc manner, concepts such as "developmental leadership" and "developmental ideology" to explain developmental consequences?

These problems with the developmental state theory prompt us to find an alternative explanation to the difference in development in Taiwan and the Philippines. The next section will suggest that Taiwan's economic success was due to its successful transition from clientelism to state corporatism, while the Philippines's failure was due to Marcos's adoption of authoritarian clientelism.

Institutions That Make a Difference

From Clientelism to State Corporatism in Taiwan

When the Nationalist government retreated from the mainland to Taiwan in 1949, it brought with it the practice of clientelism. Meanwhile, for the purpose of military mobilization and political control, the government imposed formal state corporatism on business by ordering the establishment of singular, hierarchical associations in all professions. During the 1960s, when the Taiwanese government replaced military recovery of the mainland with economic development as the country's first priority, a more cooperative and consultative form of state corporatism arose.

The dominant institutional arrangement between the state and business during Nationalist rule in China was state corporatism de jure but clientelism de facto.[13] The Nationalist government tried to incorporate the business sector into the decision-making process. It passed the Trade Association Law in 1929, which ordered the establishment of singular and hierarchical trade associations under the government's tight control. Only one such trade association was allowed in each administrative area. All other business associations had to join these state-sponsored trade associations.[14] Lower-level trade associations had to be members of higher-level ones. Their charter and association personnel had to acquire the prior approval of government agencies at the appropriate level. Trade associations could submit proposals concerning industry and commerce to local and central governments; in return, they had the responsibility of implementing government policies, especially to prevent market panic, which happened quite often during the anti-Japanese war. Later, the government further extended its control over business by passing the Industry Association Law, Commerce Association Law, Exporters Association Law, and the omnibus Regulations on the Agriculture, Mining, Industry, and Commerce During Emergency Periods.[15]

Fewsmith (1980) argues that such Schmitterian state corporatism existed in Shanghai (the economic center of China) during the 1920s and 1930s. It is not clear, however, whether such a corporatist arrangement was widespread in China and whether in reality the nominal corporatist policies served clientelist interests. As Fewsmith (1980, 273) notes, there were severe conflicts between the business associations created by the GMD and private business leaders affiliated with Jiang Jeishi. Jiang's rule resolved the conflicts in favor of the private leaders. This disparity between corporatist policies and clientelist practices is especially important when we analyze institutional transformation in Taiwan from the 1950s to the 1960s.

The Nationalist government brought these clientelist practices and corporatist laws to Taiwan in 1949. At the national level, patronage was distributed through various public enterprises and monopolies, which were the major economic actors during the 1950s; production of public enterprises constituted more than 50 percent of industrial production before 1959 (CEPD 1987, 89), while monopoly revenues amounted to about 17 percent of government revenue between 1954 and 1963 (CEPD 1987, 170).

During the 1950s the government and the GMD "recommended" that large-scale private enterprises hire retired government officials, cadres, and military personnel in exchange for preferential treatment in loan applications and other administrative conveniences. The largest steel company, Tang Rong Co., went bankrupt in the late 1950s, partly because it was staffed by too many unproductive retired officials (Kuang 1987, 37).

At the local level, the Nationalist government offered local monopoly rights to local elites in exchange for their political support. These rights included monopolies over logging, transportation, banking, agricultural cooperatives, and schools. Party cadres, especially retired military personnel, also engaged in rent-seeking behavior in transportation, construction, and gas retailing. Most of the firms whose company title began with the character "Xing" (in English, "prosper" or "happy") were controlled by veterans who could live on monopoly rents prosperously or happily ever after.

Clientelism in the 1950s was associated with modest economic growth. The growth in the 1950s should be interpreted as a recovery from war devastation. Clientelism and U.S. aid stimulated the economy through active government intervention and various patronage systems, as it also did in South Korea and the Philippines. The initial momentum of growth, however, faded away rapidly, only to be replaced in the mid-1950s by devastating problems of inefficiency, price wars, and oligopolies. When the economy stagnated in the late 1950s, both the state and business found it necessary to cooperate more closely through existing channels of business associations.

After the Nationalists emigrated to Taiwan, singular and hierarchical business associations were created that followed the corporatist laws passed in mainland China. These associations were characterized by their inclusive, participatory, and political nature: In terms of inclusiveness, all producers had to join at least one business association immediately after they began production. Otherwise, these associations could ask the government to cancel the producer's production license. All associations, regardless of their level, belonged to and paid a membership fee to one of the two national business associations, the National Industries Association or the National Commerce Association.

In terms of participation, all members of a business association had the right to participate in association affairs. Their voting rights, however, might vary depending on the size of their company. Each member had at least one vote. The maximum number of votes one member might have was seven (Legislative Yuan 1958, 383–444; Wen 1966, 5–17).

The political nature of these business associations is evidenced in the existence of party organizations parallel to each level of business association. There were at least three types of party personnel in a relatively well-established business association.[16] First, the divisional party chairman, usually one of the largest producers, reported directly to the enterprise department of the party central. The chairman of the enterprise department was concurrently minister of economic affairs of the Executive Yuan. Routine party activities such as the recruitment of party members, security checks, and political indoctrination were performed by professional party cadres within the industry division. Finally, and usually most important, the general secretary (Zongganshi) of each business association was "recommended" by the social works department of the party central and rubber-stamped by the Ministry of Internal Affairs. Most of the communication between the association and the party went through the general secretary whose tenure was not subject to any legal restriction, unlike that of association presidents, supervisors, and directors. All general secretaries reported regularly to the fifth division of the social works department of the GMD.

The original purpose for establishing business associations and parallel party organizations was both military and political. Militarily, President Jiang Jeishi needed to know the mobilization capacity of each business when the opportunity came for recovering mainland China. The General Mobilization Fee listed in all associations' balance sheet reflects this legacy. For the convenience of transmitting commands, several presidents of important business associations were recruited into the Economic Stabilization Board of the Executive Yuan in the early 1950s. Politically, the GMD needed to make sure that the business associations did not fall into the wrong hands. The triple-check system instituted by the party eliminated any possibility that the association could be penetrated by internal or external enemies. On national holidays and special events (e.g., the death of President Jiang Jeishi) and for other patriotic movements (e.g., the construction of Jiang's memorial hall and the manufacture of fighter planes and tanks), business associations were mobilized to make donations. Usually the party central, not the government, collected these donations.

When the hysteria of war preparation faded away in the late 1950s and economic development became the national goal, both the state and business found it necessary to strengthen the role of business associations in the decision-making process. The goals of cooperation were, first, to withdraw state power from the economy, and second, to redirect state power toward export promotion.

The state decided to withdraw unnecessary intervention from the economy but did not know where to start. In the nineteen-point program the United States suggested only basic principles of a free market but fell short on details. Lower-level bureaucrats would not tell what these unnecessary interventions were. If they did, they would be losing control, power, or even their jobs. Furthermore, state officials did not have the personnel or the resources to analyze the problems of each industry; only business people knew best. Through regular association meetings, business representatives summarized their problems and made policy suggestions to the state. The state then negotiated certain items or specific wording with association representatives. Most of the time, however, the state simply legalized these policy proposals, thereby reducing red tape and promulgating several realistic industrial policies. Unintentionally, state capacity was strengthened as a result of continuous policy input from the organized business community.

At the same time, business people found it necessary to cooperate among themselves to protect profits.[17] On the one hand, the business community had suffered from price wars during the second half of the 1950s because, as one official recalled, the business community was as disorganized as "a plate of sand." Major producers eventually called for a truce in price wars. On the other hand, the business community needed to resolve the fundamental problem of a saturated domestic market by exploring international markets. There was, however, too much risk and too little information about international markets, a problem the Taiwanese state did little to solve.[18] Exporters had to pool their resources to gather information, share market risks, avoid price wars among themselves, and lobby for state assistance. The singular, hierarchical, inclusive, and relatively democratic business associations were convenient tools for achieving these goals. Through business associations, large-scale trading companies such as the China Textile Trading Company, the China Paper Trading Company, and the Association for Exporters were organized by the business community with the blessing of the state.

The nature of the development crisis in the late 1950s might also explain why Taiwan did not choose the strategy of deepening import substitution, as most Latin American countries did.[19] First of all, the crisis was a result of domestic market saturation, not a drastic reduction in the export market. Deepening import substitution would have soon produced similar problems, or even made things worse. Second, during the crisis, local capitalists did not face strong competition from abroad due to the country's strong trade controls. Installing additional trade controls would not have had much effect on domestic production. Finally, before the mid-1960s there were no entrenched foreign companies in Taiwan eager to protect their market shares against other foreign competitors. Therefore, Taiwanese businesses organized themselves not to pursue protectionist measures but to explore the international market.

Business people also took advantage of the party organizations within business associations. In their regular meetings with party superiors, divisional chairpersons and general secretaries of business associations discussed problems of the industry. These meetings served both as an alternative channel of policy consultation and as a social occasion for business leaders.

Taiwan's business community was thus integrated through these business associations and their party organizations. Numerous professional, economic, social, and even political ties among business people merged and were consolidated (Numazaki 1986, 517). Because of the cohesion and power of the business community, one prominent business leader later allegedly contemplated modeling the Chinese National Association for Industry and Commerce (Gongshang Xiejinhui) after its powerful Japanese counterpart, *Keidanren*, to become the shadow Ministry of Economic Affairs (Kuang 1987, 41).

During the 1970s, Taiwan encountered drastic setbacks in international relations. In 1971 Nixon visited China as a prelude to establishing full diplomatic relations between China and the United

States. Taiwan was expelled by the United Nations in the same year. Then the majority of the nations, including the United States, withdrew their diplomatic recognition of the Taiwanese government. Without diplomatic relations, trade negotiations between Taiwan and foreign countries were often conducted through private organizations. Business associations were forced to step up to the bargaining tables and assume more responsibility and authority in coordinating the behavior of their members.

Within the business community, business associations prevented severe conflicts between large and small producers. Since all producers were required to join business associations and all producers had voting rights (albeit unequal) with regard to association affairs, large producers had to heed the needs of smaller ones who could outvote them. Business associations also provided information about members' production capacities and credentials. Hence, subcontracting systems between large and small producers were easily formed.

The state began to cooperate with the business community. In addition to various regularized meetings with association representatives, state officials often consulted with business leaders on industrial policies or macroeconomic policies.[20] State assistance was increasingly directed toward entire business sectors instead of individual firms. For instance, one American adviser described the FETCC (the decision-making center of economic policies in the 1960s) as having followed the principle of "justice to all, favoritism to none" (Xu 1969, iv). The state-business relationship could be characterized as "more cooperative, consultative, and less authoritarian" than Latin American bureaucratic-authoritarian institutions (Oshima 1987, 172). After the younger Jiang became premier in 1972, he convened numerous meetings with industry representatives to gather information for his administrative reform program and red tape reduction measures.

The delegation of decision-making power to business associations increased over time. This delegation started with minor proposals regarding tariff rates and tax revisions for each profession. Later, the government asked business associations to formulate industry-specific assistance acts. In the 1970s and 1980s, business associations, especially the National Industries Association and the National Commerce Association, participated actively in formulating macro policies such as economic development plans, the Fundamental Law on Labor, and the Industrial and Commerce Associations Law. The two national associations also formulated and implemented the Regulations on Association Administrators of 1972. Delegation of decision-making power to business associations was formally espoused by Premier Sun in the early 1980s. Business participation in decision making culminated in the formation of the temporary Economic Renovation Committee of the Executive Yuan in 1986. The committee, composed of business leaders, drafted the blueprint of Taiwan's economic development for the next decade.

In sum, Taiwan's rapid and consistent economic growth after the 1950s coincided with the institutional transformation from clientelism to state corporatism. The private sector and the state cooperated to resolve business's collective action problems and the state's policy-making and implementation problems, thus reducing waste, distortions, and obstacles in economic development.

From Clientelism to Authoritarian Clientelism in the Philippines

On 22 September 1972 Marcos declared martial law in order to establish a "New Society" free of antidevelopment forces such as landlords, cronies, corrupt politicians, the Congress, incompetent bureaucrats, rioting students, striking workers, and communist insurgents.[21] The means of achieving such a goal was glorified as "democratic revolution," "constitutional authoritarianism," "smiling martial law," and "revolution from the center." In the statists' words, Marcos intended to establish a developmental state that was strong and autonomous. Did Marcos actually establish such an autonomous state? The second section of this chapter has demonstrated that he did, but the new state did not work. The reason the "developmental state" did not work was that traditional clientelism was not constrained but was in fact strengthened during Marcos's rule.

Clientelism in the Philippines has a long history.[22] Onfre Corpuz (1965, 79–83) traces the importance of the family system back to the Spanish rule of the late nineteenth century. The colonial government was corrupt and weak. Many central and local government offices were auctioned off, both legally and illegally. The government itself failed to provide basic welfare services such as a public school system. People had to turn to their families to satisfy basic needs. As a consequence, "the intense family loyalties of Filipinos result[ed] in minimum identification of individual welfare with institutions outside the family" (Golay 1965, 290). When people contacted the government, they did so through their relatives in the government. Later, the auctioning off of government offices was discontinued only to be replaced by nepotism. Government offices were regarded as personal property through which the incumbents distributed favors to their clients (Talingdan 1966, 77).

American governance did not change the nature of the patrimonial bureaucracy. With the introduction of popular elections, elected officials had even stronger incentives to use government offices to reward their local supporters. The short, three-year rule by the Japanese (1941–1944) brought a deterioration of clientelism. Stealing government property and delaying the implementation of policies were regarded as patriotic behavior that could undermine colonial rule.[23] Some scholars (e.g., Veneracion 1988) blame the Japanese for the deterioration. No similar behavior, however, was found in the fifty-year Japanese rule of Taiwan.

The first case of massive government corruption, which resulted in neither legal prosecution nor popular opposition, occurred after Japan's defeat in 1944. In the so-called "surplus scandals," government officials openly appropriated military stocks left by the Japanese and redistributed them to their supporters. The same clientelist principle was later extended to reconstruction projects financed by American aid (Corpuz 1965, 85). The postwar Philippine bureaucracy became the distribution center of patronage (Fegan 1981, 11–12; Macapagal 1968, 129). It expanded continuously to accommodate new political clients. The recruitment of civil servants was therefore based more on the spoils system than on merit, as a research report conducted by the National Economic Council concluded in 1962 (quoted in Talingdan 1966, 77).

Political leaders were aware of the degenerating impact of clientelism on government morale and efficiency. In all presidential campaigns after the country's independence, opposition candidates routinely attacked the corruption and nepotism of the current administration. After the opposition won the race, predictable purges of government officials and a moral rearmament of the civil service followed. For instance, the Philippine government in the 1950s and 1960s had ten different anticorruption agencies in five administrations. None of them, however, was strongly supported by the Congress or by the presidents (Carino 1986, 129). The frequent change of anticorruption agencies not only made these agencies ineffective but also made them the ultimate source of corruption. Therefore, the same problems would reemerge soon after the installation of a new administration (Veneracion 1988, viii).

Clientelism also took its toll on the Philippine party system, on two fronts. First, local support became more important for winning elections than national party support.[24] Under American rule, family influence in politics was consolidated through the introduction of popular elections. A municipal election was held in 1899, then an election of provincial governors in 1900, and then a national election in 1907. The sequence of these elections was critical. Local leaders first mobilized their relatives and tenants (through economic as well as godparent-godchildren relationships) to compete in the local election. Family leaders acted as patrons, while their relatives and tenants acted as clients. After consolidating their strongholds, more influential leaders competed in provincial elections, using their broader clientelist ties. The subsequent success of national parties depended on the support of local leaders, not on the mobilization capability of the parties (Corpuz 1965, 96–97; Doronila 1985, 101; Nowak and Snyder 1974, 1153). Provincial politicians served as brokers between national and municipal levels (Wolters 1984, 145). Hence, the United States had tried to build the Philippine democracy in its own image through the introduction of local and national elections (Gregor 1984, 3), yet the democratic system was soon philippinized.

The second consequence of this clientelist party politics was the high mobility of politicians between parties. The two dominant parties after independence, the Nationalist party and the Liberal party, were virtually twins in terms of their ideology, policies, and social composition (Shalom 1981, 27; Tancangco 1988, 88–89; Wolters

1984, 140). They did not collect membership fees or keep membership lists because neither party had many core followers. Most of their funding came from donations or levies on illegal Chinese business people (Corpuz 1965, 100–17).

In addition to the tradition of appropriating government resources, these two attributes—the unimportance of party platforms in election campaigns and loose party organization—were caused by the importance of patron-client relationships and in turn reinforced these relationships. Instead of the party organization, political patrons mobilized their own clients to win elections. Their clients, dissatisfied with party platforms and the party system, looked for concrete rewards from their patrons. One survey conducted in the late 1960s found that both voters and candidates clearly understood the importance of pork barrels and the unimportance of the candidate's policy and party in winning an election (Averch, Denton, and Koehler 1970). Therefore, neither the patron nor the client had any incentive to stay in the party once the party was not in power. Massive exodus from one party to the other after each election thus became routine in Philippine postwar political history.

Interestingly enough, switching party membership was often an asset rather than a liability for politicians. One study shows that in the 1949, 1953, and 1957 congressional elections, candidates who had switched to the stronger party before the election were more likely to be reelected than those who had not (Lande 1965, 49). Switching parties was not the prerogative of local politicians. The first national turncoat (in Philippine terms, "Tangotician") was commonwealth president Quezon, famous for his motto, "My loyalty to my party ends where my loyalty to my country begins." President Magsaysay was a Liberal turned Nationalist. Vice President Emmanuel Pelaez turned Nationalist after he split with President Macapagal. Fernando Lopez, a former vice president of the Liberal party, turned Nationalist. And Ferdinand Marcos ran as a Nationalist against his former Liberal party patron, President Macapagal, in 1965.[25]

After each election, the patronage pie became relatively smaller as more turncoats tried to divide it. Dissatisfaction began to build until the beginning of the next election. Those who did not belong to the patronage center defected again to find a new patron or to establish their own networks, as Magsaysay and Marcos did.

Clientelism had a significant impact on political as well as business activities. First, it increased business costs in dealing with the government. In a survey of Philippine entrepreneurs, respondents replied that formal communication channels with the government were "an extremely time-consuming and unreliable process, or perhaps an impossible undertaking, unless one also made use of 'connections'" (Carroll 1965, 180). Business people had to pay "grease money" to facilitate their requests, but there were apparent political and legal risks for doing so.

The business sector was organized loosely before martial law. There were numerous business organizations, yet they were essentially organized along clientelist ties. Within each sector and industry, singular and hierarchical associations were rarely seen; there were usually more than two competing associations serving social functions. Felipe Miranda, a political scientist at the University of the Philippines, concluded his observation of Philippine interest groups to me by saying that "they do not exert coherent pressure on the government as their counterparts do in industrial democracies."[26] Business people could acquire more favors faster from their political patrons than they could from their interest groups, which went through ineffective formal channels. Not surprisingly, when asked in a survey about how to improve state-business relationships, most business people said that strengthening business associations was the last thing to recommend (Ramiro 1965, 32).

Scholars have noted the influence of the "sugar bloc" in Philippine politics. This influence, however, seems to have been employed for personal gains rather than for the benefit of all sugar producers.[27] The distinction between personal gains and association gains is illustrated in President Macagapal's handling of the sugar bloc. After he became president in 1962, Macapagal decontrolled foreign exchange and encouraged exports. Both policies strongly favored the sugar bloc. But prominent leaders of the sugar bloc fiercely attacked the administration through the mass media and through their political patrons during Macapagal's term and in his 1965 reelection campaign. "Why did they oppose a president who adopted policies in favor of the industry?" I asked President Macapagal during an interview. "The reason is very simple," he responded, smiling as if that question was a puzzle only to foreigners, "because I prosecuted some of their leaders for their corruption." He prosecuted the brother of his vice president, Lopez, House Speaker Jose Julo (who was also the leader of the Liberal party—Macapagal's own party), the powerful Yulo family, and other sugar producers involved in banking violations (Macapagal interview, 12/16/88). These influential sugar producers could have gained more from a president who was indifferent to the industry but sensitive to their personal needs than from a president who took care of the industry but tried to destroy their patronage powers. Personal considerations apparently outweighed association concerns in the sugar bloc case.

In addition to its erosive impact on political and business activities, Philippine clientelism also constrained the beneficial effects of foreign loans and aid on the economy.[28] As discussed in chapter 2, a clientelist state is also a very expensive state. The state needs to finance an ever-increasing bureaucracy and frivolous patronage projects. Since there are domestic constraints on monetary and fiscal policies, political leaders resort to foreign sources to strengthen their clientelist ties. In 1946 the newly created Liberal party gained power with help from the United States. The Liberal party granted privileges to American interests in the Philippines in exchange for postwar reconstruction aid, which was then used to reward political followers (Tancangco 1988, 91). The Philippine government submitted the first four-year economic development plan (1949–1953) to the International Bank of Reconstruction and Development and began the inflow of developmental loans to avoid "excessive drawing upon the currency reserve" (Cuaderno 1961, 19). Foreign loans were so available that Philippine president Quirino (1948–1953) thought "all that was needed to continue developing the economy was financial assistance from the United States Government" (Cuaderno 1961, 23). Since then, foreign loans have been regarded by political leaders as easy money for rewarding their clients.

Did Marcos's authoritarianism save the Philippine economy from the encroachment of clientelism? No. On the contrary, his authoritarian rule intensified the increasingly negative impact of clientelism.

In the 1950s clientelism in the Philippines was associated with modest growth, as it was in Taiwan and South Korea. The domestic market and foreign loans provided ample room for factional conflicts and patronage behavior. By the mid-1960s, however, both sources of capital were severely constrained. The old oligarchs were engaged in an increasingly bitter competition for political spoils (Shalom 1981, 161). The election of Marcos to the presidency in 1965 represented a temporary truce among oligarchs because Marcos had no independent oligarchical base from which to threaten their established interests (Miranda 1986, 10). Marcos then resorted to massive vote buying to get reelected in 1969, resulting in both fiscal and foreign exchange crises in the early 1970s.

The stage was then set for authoritarian clientelism: the old oligarchs were locked in a stalemate, different business interests could not agree on appropriate development strategies, the patronage sources that Marcos could control were severely limited, and most of all, Marcos was prohibited by the 1971 Constitutional Convention from running for a third term. Taking advantage of the outbreak of student movements and the bombing of Plaza Miranda, which raised a fracas only in the Manila area, he declared martial law on the whole country.

Marcos's authoritarianism did not and could not change the nature of clientelism in the Philippines. On the contrary, it magnified the impact of clientelism on the government, party system, business activities, and international capital, creating a "booty capitalism" that was filled with rent-seeking behavior (Hutchcroft 1992).

After the declaration of martial law, the first presidential decree (PD) Marcos issued was to reorganize the government. An anticorruption campaign followed to thoroughly purge the political clients of Marcos's opponents. Removed from duties by PD no. 6 in 1972 were seven thousand government employees. PD no. 46 in 1972 and PD nos. 677, 749, and 807 (the Civil Service Law) in 1975 continued the political purge. The reorganization plan was then tailored to consolidate Marcos's influence in the bureaucracy (Shalom 1981, 174; Veneracion 1988, 157–58). The result of the reorganization and purge was not the shrinking of the bureaucracy but the expansion of the bureaucracy to accommodate new clients, most of whom got jobs without taking competitive exams (Oshima 1987, 227; Rodriguez 1986, 131–36).

Technocrats, handpicked by Marcos, could not improve the efficiency of the government. In the first place, they had no independent political support to do so. Marcos's executive secretary Melchor was able to purge the political clients of Marcos's opponents at the outset. But in 1975, when he attempted to purge Marcos's own clients in the bureaucracy, he was fired (Canoy 1981, 133). Development agencies set up by the martial law government were soon infected by clientelist considerations (Oshima 1987, 228).

Nor were the technocrats able to resist clientelist considerations in formulating development projects. For instance, the overpriced Bataan nuclear power plant turned out to be a collusion between Westinghouse and Marcos crony Herminio Disini (Canoy 1981, 134). Marcos's family and their associates had substantial interest in the eleven major capital-intensive projects of the 1970s (especially mining and construction), to which the influential Chinese business community had voiced its opposition.[29]

The clientelist nature of the Philippine party system was intensified during authoritarian rule. For example, party activities were prohibited during the early years of martial law. In 1978 Marcos allowed political parties to reenter the scene of national politics by holding an election of legislative representatives. But the competition was limited. Marcos's newly established party, Kilusang Bagong Lipunan (KBL), was composed of leaders and members of the old Nationalist party, the Liberal party, and of his own political clients. The Liberal party suffered from an exodus of members because it boycotted all elections, which meant no patronage power for its members. Opposition groups did not constitute a significant threat to the one-party system because of official harassment and an internal split.

The KBL had a more elaborate organization than the Nationalist party and the Liberal party, and it recruited members down to the town level. It was not, however, a party based on a distinctive ideology or policy platform (Machado 1975, 525). The old elitist, patron-client relationships remained the backbone of the party. The sole criterion for selecting party candidates in local and national elections was their personal loyalty to Marcos (Tancangco 1988, 94–100). Hence, the interdependence between national and local leaders was even stronger than before. National leaders controlled a larger share of the political pie and were able to exert influence down to the local level. At the same time, they needed stronger support at the local level to confer legitimacy on their authoritarian rule. Numerous plebiscites and popular referenda on national policies were held during martial law to reinforce this interdependent relationship.

The most devastating and notorious impact of authoritarian clientelism on the Philippines surfaced in the area of business activities. One of the purposes of the martial law regime was supposedly to eliminate old oligarchs who had undue influence on national economic policies. An autonomous state, the argument went, would enable the Philippine economy to unleash its potential. Marcos was in an advantageous position to achieve such a goal. When elected in 1965, he had no strong oligarchical base; this, ironically, had helped him gain power because the oligarchs did not regard him as a threat to their established interests. After the declaration of martial law, Marcos launched a successful attack on the old oligarchs through imprisonment, land reforms, and various "rationalization" programs. Old oligarchs such as Jose B. Laurel (speaker of the House), Fernando Lopez (vice president), Alfredo Montelibano, Carlos Palanca, Antonio Madrigal, and the Osmena family lost their dominant influence or simply disappeared from the political scene. To penetrate the financial world of the old oligarchs, Marcos further ordered that the top one thousand corporations sell at least 10 percent of their stock to the public (Wurfel 1979, 150).

Did ordinary Philippine business people live happily ever after? By no means. The old oligarchs were soon replaced by new oligarchs who were clients of the Marcos family. The nouveaux riches included Roberto S. Benedicto, Rodolfo Cuenca, Herminio Disini, Herdis Group, Antonio O. Floirendo, Ricardo C. Silverio, and family members of both Marcos and his wife (the Romualdez family). The defense minister of the martial law regime, Juan P. Enrile, also belonged to this group of "smarter" people.[30] Old oligarchs such as the Ayalas and Cojuangcos, who survived the purge, became highly dependent on the good graces of the president.[31]

These new oligarchs derived their wealth mainly through various "rationalization" programs. The technocrats suggested that Philippine products would be more competitive if the production process were rationalized to achieve scale economy. Several industries, such as coconut, sugar, petroleum, logging, and wood processing, were thus rationalized.[32] Even the financial market was similarly rationalized in 1980 (IBON 1983, 97–100). Although theoretically sound, these rationalization programs were formulated and implemented through clientelist ties such that Marcos's cronies had tight control over the production, sales, and hence, profits of these products. Monopolies and oligopolies arose. Those business people, usually the more efficient producers, who could not or would not establish connections to these cronies, were deprived of government assistance, foreign exchange, tax and tariff exemptions, and import licenses (Alburo and Shepherd 1981, 18, 35; De Dios 1984, 59; Doherty 1982, 29–31).

In addition, Marcos cronies had easy access to the government purse in both good times and bad. During the 1977–1980 period, about 34 percent of government capital outlay went to corporate equity investment. During the 1981–1983 period, after the Philippine economy was devastated by the second oil crisis, the figure rose to about 46 percent (De Dios 1984, 10). Cronies such as Disini, Cuenca, and Silverio could not have survived these crises without government bailouts (Doherty 1982, 2). A common channel used by cronies to get public funds was public and quasi-public enterprises such as the sugar and coconut centrals. During Marcos's rule, these institutions expanded rapidly. Among ninety-three such enterprises existing in the 1970s and early 1980s, two-thirds were created by Marcos (Miranda 1986, 15–16).

How did the Marcos government finance these clientelist activities? It could not raise monopoly taxes because cronies would be the first to suffer. It could not impose taxes on small and medium-sized enterprises because they were already struggling in a failing economy. And there were large, poverty-stricken masses that had little income to survive on. The only way out was to borrow from abroad. The foreign liability of Philippine monetary authorities was only about $240 million in 1972, the year martial law was declared. That liability jumped to $1 billion in 1976, to $2.54 billion in 1980, and to $4.67 billion in 1984 (IMF 1987, 559). To make sure that these loans went to the "right" persons, the government established the Ministry of Human Settlements, headed by Imelda Marcos, to distribute the money (Sussman, O'Connor, and Lindsey 1984, 5).

The issue of foreign loans leads to the question of how authoritarian clientelism affected the relationship between international lending agencies and the national economy. The World Bank was aware of the corruption in the Philippine government. In fact, the bank had tried its best to increase the accountability of the use of foreign loans by stationing consulting groups in Manila. It had tremendous influence on the recruitment of Philippine technocrats, and it proposed or scrutinized major economic policies (e.g., the 1979 Structural Adjustment Loan). The influence of the World Bank was so omnipresent that nationalist economists and neo-Marxists have always blamed the failure of the Philippine economy on it (e.g., Bello, Kinley, and Elinson 1982; Broad 1988; Ofreneo and Habana 1987).

Nevertheless, tight supervision of foreign lending agencies over the use of funds was common in other developing countries as well. For instance, the United States had a stationary supervisory body in Taiwan—the International Cooperation Agency-China Mission. The Council on U.S. Aid (CUSA) was established outside Taiwan's regular administrative system to distribute aid. CUSA conducted meetings in English so that American advisers could understand. The exemplary case of American influence on Taiwan's economic policies was the Nineteen-Point Development Program of 1959, the watershed of Taiwan's transition to ELI. The program was simply an expanded version of the Eight-Point Outline formulated by Wesley C. Haraldson, director of the ICA China Mission.

Given the similar influence of international agencies, therefore, the cause of the Philippine "development debacle" should be traced to the way foreign loans and aid were distributed. Since foreign lending agencies could not replace the administrative system of the host country, economic institutions determined where the money went and whether the money was used efficiently. In the Philippines, Imelda Marcos spent the money on the splendid Cultural Center, elaborate government buildings, the elitist Heart Center, and her now-infamous shoe collection. The construction projects were undertaken by the Marcos family or their cronies. When these companies ran into trouble, the government easily bailed them out. As the World Bank observed, "a large part of the [government] deficit was due to foreign obligations of unprofitable private sector projects that the Government had to assume" (World Bank 1987a, ix).

Finally, under Marcos's authoritarian clientelism, the relationship between interest groups and government policies was further distorted. Marcos followed the authoritarian development models of South Korea and Taiwan to rationalize interest groups. Representative groups that previously competed in each sector were ordered to merge into one single national group sponsored by the government. In 1974 the capitalists were organized into the Employers Confederation of the Philippines. In 1975 the labor unions were organized into the Trade Union Congress of the Philippines. Other interest groups that were rationalized included the mass media, printing, petroleum, shipping, construction, logging, metal casting, and garment production (Doherty 1982, 29; Stauffer 1977, 398–99). The original purpose of this rationalization program was to facilitate communication between the state and respective sectors. A rudimentary form of state corporatism therefore existed in the early years of authoritarian rule.

But this state corporatism existed only on paper. In reality, these national associations became either empty shells or rent-seeking tools. In lucrative industries such as coconut and sugar, national associations dominated by cronies exercised tight controls over average producers to extract rents from below. These associations had rarely been responsive to the demands of producers (Hawes 1987, 97; Manuel Lim 1985, 162–66; Rodriguez 1986, 174). In other, less lucrative industries, these national associations served only nominal functions. Neither the state nor the producers took them seriously. After all, interest groups before martial law had not been an important source of policy input. Producers relied on their clientelist ties to get government assistance. They found it more necessary to do so under the authoritarian government. "If conflicts occur," as Robert B. Stauffer aptly observes, "the ideology and principles of . . . the New Society, including any corporatist components, are likely to take second place to the requirements of neo-patrimonialism" (1977, 176). Hence, under authoritarian rule, state corporatism existed de jure but clientelism was the reality.

Conclusion

What makes the comparison between Taiwan and the Philippines important is not only their great difference in development outcomes but also their similarity in initial conditions. The two countries were similar before the 1960s in terms of colonial history, infrastructure building, development strategies, and position in international politics and economy. But Taiwan later developed into a newly industrializing country while the Philippine economy, after Marcos's experiment with the authoritarian development model, ended in disaster. What went wrong? The developmental state theory would suggest that the Taiwan state was a developmental state and the Philippine state under Marcos's rule was not. The second section of this chapter, however, demonstrated that the Taiwanese state did not fit well the developmental state's criteria of state autonomy, strong capacity, and committed leadership. In contrast, Marcos established a state that resembled the developmental state model. An alternative explanation for the two countries' development difference was warranted.

The third section provided an institutional explanation. Because of its successful transition from clientelism to state corporatism, Taiwan broke away from the economic stagnation of the 1950s and entered the dynamic growth of the 1960s and 1970s. Business associations were transformed from formal corporatist organizations into effective coordination centers of business activities. The state also became responsive to the demands of these business associations. By comparison, the Philippines continued its traditional clientelism in the 1960s. When Marcos declared martial law in 1972, traditional clientelism was replaced by authoritarian clientelism, which stimulated pseudogrowth in the mid-1970s, only to be followed by a continuous decline and the final collapse of the economy. Although formal corporatism was introduced by Marcos, it was soon turned into an instrument of clientelist behavior and exacerbated business's collective action problems as well as the state's policy-making and implementation problems.

4

THE TEXTILE INDUSTRY

Taiwan's economic miracle began with the rapid expansion of the textile industry,[1] which is consistent with the liberal economics argument that developing countries should use their comparative advantage in abundant labor supply. But why did the Philippines's textile industry, which had a head start over Taiwan's, never develop into a self-sustained industry? Furthermore, within each country's textile industry, variations exist across time periods and between subsectors. Taiwan's textile industry almost collapsed at the end of the 1950s. It survived the crisis and developed into the main industry of the island in the 1960s and 1970s. After the oil crisis of 1979, however, the industry began its course of decline. In the Philippines, while the upstream textile industry (spinning and weaving) had been stagnant, the downstream garment industry grew remarkably in the 1970s and 1980s. This chapter provides an institutional explanation for these differences between countries and within a single industry.

The first section provides qualitative and quantitative evidence to describe the performance variations between countries and within the industry. The second section argues that the evolution of institutions in Taiwan's textile industry from clientelism to state corporatism, and eventually, to laissez-faire was in tandem with the industry's rise, prosperity, and decline. The third section explains the stagnation of the Philippine textile industry in terms of its clientelism and the growth of the garment industry in terms of its corporatist arrangements. The last section summarizes these empirical findings.

The Difference in Industrial Performance

The performance difference between the Taiwanese and the Philippine textile industries is demonstrated in tables 4–1 and 4–2. In terms of the growth of textile machinery, Philippine textile firms essentially discontinued their two-digit growth of spindles and looms after 1963, while Taiwanese firms maintained hyperexpansion throughout the decades.

The production of cotton fabrics, the major textile product before synthetic fiber became popular in the late 1970s, also indicates the difference in industrial growth between the two countries. Philippine cotton fabrics production reveals a pattern of slow and inconsistent growth. In contrast, Taiwan has a higher and more consistent growth record. Even South Korea, a latecomer in the development of the industry, came out stronger than the Philippines.

The failure of the Philippine textile industry is particularly puzzling in view of the fact that it had a head start over Taiwan and South Korea before the 1960s. A private Philippine Cotton Mills was established in 1930 with 7,400 spindles and 120 looms—a capacity close to the optimal production scale at the time. In 1939 President Quezon ordered the National Development Corporation to construct a large-scale mill with 10,000 spindles and 104 looms. Both mills were much larger and more modern than the mills in Taiwan during the same period. By 1941 the Philippine textile industry had a total of 27,688 spindles and 624 looms. World War II destroyed only a fraction of the equipment. In 1950 there were 20,288 spindles and 524 looms (*Industrial Philippines* 8/66; PDCP 1974, 107). These fig-

Table 4-1
Growth Rate in Scale of Textile Industry in the Philippines and Taiwan

Year	Philippines		Taiwan	
	Spindles (%) N	Looms (%) N	Spindles (%) N	Looms (%) N
1956	(68,368)[a]	(2,131)[a]	(207,140)[a]	(2,557)[a]
1957	63	50	19[b]	0
1958	55	31	0	10[b]
1959	56	53	0	10[b]
1960	46	53	67	66
1961	37	48	19	22
1962	10	−4	7[b]	16[b]
1963	4	17	7[b]	16[b]
1964	8	1	0	−4
1965	0	0	25	12
1966	3	2	9	15
1967	3	1	9	6
1968	7	7	2	3
1969	16	0	17	16
1970	−6	0	30	9
1971	5	−3	16	18
1972	−3	4	18	32
1973	9	4	3	3
1974	3	4	32	13
1975	3	4	17	11
1976	3	3	8	2
1977	−4	3	1	−29
1978	8	−5	12	50

Source: Data for the Philippines are calculated from DBP (1983, 6). Data for Taiwan are from TCSA (1972, 7; 1976, 3; 1987, 83).
[a]Numbers in parentheses are raw data.
[b]These are average growth rates.

ures were similar to those of Taiwan after the war—20,000 old spindles and 500 outdated looms.

In the early 1950s, new firms mushroomed in the Philippines. In 1952 the Yujuico family established the first private spinning mill, General Textile. Eleven additional private firms were operating by 1955. Together these private mills would be able to satisfy domestic demand by 1960 (*Manila Daily Bulletin* 9/29/55). Based on the per-

Table 4–2

Growth Rate in Cotton Fabrics Production of Various Countries

Year	Korea (%) N	Philippines (%) N	Taiwan (%) N	World (%) N
1958	(125)[a]	(155)[a]	(147)[a]	(46,699)[a]
1959	6.4	−23.9	6.1	6.8
1960	−5.3	50.0	12.8	−2.0
1961[b]	−11.9	−13.6	13.6	4.5
1962	13.5	9.2	5.0	−1.7
1963	16.7	−11.4	5.2	−2.2
1964	17.0	27.7	9.0	8.6
1965[b]	43.0	−5.8	11.2	3.5
1966	−4.5	−6.7	13.1	−2.9
1967	2.6	16.9	12.5	−18.8
1968	−49.8	19.6	11.4	25.5
1969	66.9	3.4	16.1	0.3
1970	−4.5	−2.9	30.3	−2.4
1971	21.2	−6.0	33.6	−0.1
1972	−14.1	2.7	35.4	0.6
1973	31.3	18.2	15.1	9.5
1974	−1.1	−17.3	0.3	0.2
1975	−2.3	4.5	0.0	−2.2
1976	15.3	6.1	4.8	3.5
1977	−2.0	−0.8	4.9	−3.4
1978	−5.2	−9.9	−1.5	−29.9
1979	16.1	−2.3	−1.5	2.5
1980	15.5	−6.6	4.8	6.9
1981	−3.3	22.6	0.6	−0.2
1982	26.3	−22.1	−4.7	2.3
1983	−1.1	13.7	−2.9	2.3
1984	−10.6		0.1	−1.6
1985	19.0		0.4	3.8

Source: Calculated from UNSO (1970, 73) and UNSO (1979, 186–87; 1988, 240, 243). Original data were in millions of square meters. Taiwan's growth rates after 1968 are caculated from DBAS (1968–1987).
[a] Numbers in parentheses are raw data, in millions of square meters.
[b] Taiwan's production volume surpassed the Philippines's in 1961, South Korea's surpassed it in 1965.

formance and potential of these firms, the Philippine Business Writers' Association cited the textile industry as the "Industry of the Year 1957." In 1959 Finance Secretary Jaime Hernandez proposed an integration program in view of the "far advanced stage" of the local textile industry. Japanese technicians visiting the Philippines found the quality of local products comparable to that of Japanese goods (*Manila Daily Bulletin* 9/11/59; 12/16/59). By the mid-1960s the president of the Textile Manufacturers' Association of the Philippines (TMAP) claimed that the industry was "in a position to export its surplus production" (*Industrial Philippines* 4/64; *Manila Daily Bulletin* 2/1/65). Landgrebe reached a similar conclusion in 1966 about the industry's export potential (1966, 147–48).

Several international factors contributed to the growth of the Philippine textile industry in the 1950s and remained present in later periods. The International Cooperation Agency (ICA) of the United States and the Industrial Development Center (IDC) of the Philippines, funded by U.S. aid, were actively involved in distributing dollar loans to new textile mills, hiring textile consultants, and formulating tariff policies against imports (*Manila Daily Bulletin* 9/29/55; 4/17/58; 7/17/58). The World Bank resident mission also prioritized the development of the textile industry in the early 1960s (Landgrebe 1966, 147). The industry benefited further from U.S. Public Law 81–85 (Commodity Credit Corporation Financing), Public Law 480, and Section 402 of the Mutual Security Act between the United States and the Philippines, which generously provided American cotton at relatively low prices, as had also been the case in Taiwan and Korea.

In addition to the Laurel-Langley Agreement, which gave preferential tariff treatment to Philippine exports to America, the United States had bilateral textile agreements with the Philippines in 1964, 1968, 1974, 1975, and 1978, similar to those it had with Taiwan and Korea during the same period. U.S.-Philippines agreements reached in the 1970s were even more generous than earlier ones. They were also more generous than those between the United States and other Asian nations,[2] despite the fact that the Philippine utilization rates of export quotas had been very low. For instance, in 1972 the Philippines could not fill one-half of the quotas under the New Bilateral Cotton Textile Agreement (BOI 1972); its utilization rate in 1974 was only 7.5 percent (*NEDA Development Digest* 4/15/74). In the history of the Philippine textile industry, protectionism or export quotas have never been a serious concern (World Bank 1987a, 60; USITC 1982, A270). On the contrary, these abundant quotas could have served as market guarantees for Philippine textile exports, thereby encouraging the expansion of the industry.

In contrast to the Philippines's head start, Taiwan's textile industry did not have a good beginning. At the time of Taiwan's retrocession from Japanese rule in 1945, Taiwan's textile industry consisted of two cotton spinners, dozens of weavers, one wool spinner, and one jute spinner (Lin 1978, 5). These factories were equipped with machines retired from Japan—they might even have been second-hand machines the Japanese had bought earlier from England's Lancashire mills (World Bank 1987b, 56). The scale of the entire textile industry was very small, having a total of only 8,268 spindles and 428 looms (CCIS 1983, 12).[3] Taiwan's textile industry, therefore, was not a legacy of Japanese rule; it was a new *foreign direct investment* brought in by the mainlanders.

But with the exception of the state-owned China Textile Company, none of the large-scale textile mills in China moved to Taiwan. They either stayed in China or migrated to Hong Kong. According to one respondent, those who did move to Taiwan were basically "small potatoes," having few connections to China's political and economic inner circle. The new ruler also granted a few prominent Taiwanese the privilege of establishing textile factories as rewards for their allegiance.

The government began to develop the textile industry in the early 1950s for two related reasons: to satisfy domestic demand and thereby to save foreign exchange. Facing more than 1 million emigrants from China, the government found Taiwan's textile industry too meager to meet even the demands of the native population. The government thus had to import textiles to clothe the people, and more important, the military. In 1951 the cost of imported cotton textiles reached U.S. $11 million; in 1952 it was U.S. $18 million (Lin 1969, 78). In the government's trade plans of 1953 and 1954, textiles remained an important import item (Qu 1964, 72). The cost of textile imports, therefore, constituted a heavy drain on the dwindling foreign exchange reserves. The government decided to develop the textile industry to cope with this crisis, not because it foresaw that the industry would become the locomotive of future industrialization.

Riding on the wind of the Cold War, American surplus cotton arrived in time. Since the supply of cotton was restricted by the U.S. aid program, the Taiwanese government could distribute cotton only to a limited number of producers. At the beginning, the government adopted the so-called "entrusted spinning and weaving" scheme (Daifang Daizhi) to control production and sales.[4] The government allocated cotton to spinners who in return sold yarn back to the government at a small profit margin. The government then exchanged yarn with weavers for fabrics. The original scheme lasted for only two years, from 1951 to May 1952, when its side effects (corruption and a black market) had come to outweigh its benefits. The government experimented with variations of the scheme without success until 1957, when it finally decided to deregulate the industry (Lin 1969, 103–04).

Because of the guaranteed profit under such schemes and the trade protection erected in the early 1950s, the industry expanded steadily during the 1950s. Some textile products were even exported to other Southeast Asian countries (Wang 1987, 83; Li 1957, 12; *FEER* 7/2/59). But the textile industry's initial boom came to a halt by the late 1950s. Like other import-substitution industries, local textile products soon saturated the small domestic market. A government report revealed that Taiwan's textiles were self-sufficient in 1956, and by 1957 the market was saturated (*Xinshen News* 12/2/57). To keep their market shares, producers engaged in price wars instead of technological improvement or export expansion (Li 1985b). In 1961 vicious competition, coupled with a sudden credit control, resulted in the bankruptcy of Daqin Textile, the largest textile company at the time. The other two large companies, Taiyuan and Yuandong, barely escaped the same predicament through a government bailout. One veteran producer equated the seriousness of the crisis with the 1929 crisis in China caused by world recession (Jiang 1988, 20).

The curse on the industry did not dissipate at the end of the import-substitution period. First, Taiwan's export-oriented industrialization experiment encountered the cold shoulder of American protectionism in the early 1960s. In early 1961 Taiwanese textile exports to the United States declined sharply and were nearly discontinued (*United Daily News* 5/19/61). In October of that year, the United States suddenly imposed quotas on Taiwan's textile exports. Six months later, the United States requested that Taiwan exercise voluntary restraint on its cotton textile exports; Taiwan complied. But a few months later, the United States restricted another thirteen major categories of Taiwan's textile exports. This series of protectionist measures, as one official complained to the U.S. Agency of International Development, "[has] dealt a serious blow to our young textile industry now struggling for its very survival" (Li 1985b; 1985c).

The prospect of Taiwanese textile exports looked dim for two additional reasons. First, due to American protectionism, Japan dumped its textile exports that were originally destined for the United States on Southeast Asian countries where Taiwan had some market shares. Japanese products were more competitive than Taiwanese in both quality and price. Second, because of technical innovation in the 1960s, "many textile industrialists predicted a sharp reversal of comparative advantage in favor of the advanced industrialized countries" (World Bank 1987b, 48). Although the prediction was never realized, it was a strong deterrent for Taiwanese textile exporters. Therefore, given the Philippine textile industry's head start and the Taiwanese textile industry's rugged beginning, the difference in development outcomes between the two countries' textile industries is particularly perplexing.

In addition, within each country the performance variation across time periods and subsectors requires attention. As indicated in tables 4–1 and 4–2, the performance of Taiwan's textile industry can be divided into four periods. The first period lasted from 1949 to the late 1960s, during which the industry grew at an inconsistent pace; it ended with an industry-wide crisis. The second period lasted until the oil crisis of 1973 and was characterized by sustained and rapid growth. Between the two oil crises was the third period, representing the industry's unsuccessful effort to adjust to market pressure. The final period began after 1979 and lasted until the middle of the 1980s, during which time the industry stagnated.

In the Philippines, variations also existed within the industry, between upstream textile production, which was stagnant over the decades, and downstream garment production, whose products became one of the Philippines's top two export items. Although the Philippine garment industry began during American colonial rule (*Industrial Philippines* 10/66), its expansion was halted because of persistent harassment by the government and textile producers. But beginning in the early 1970s, the garment industry revealed tremendous growth potential. Despite the termination of the Laurel-Langley Agreement in 1974, which gave preferential tariff treatment to Philippine exports entering the American market, Philippine garment exports registered consistent growth records. The proportion of garment exports rose continuously, from 3.2 percent of total exports in 1970 to 10.9 percent in 1983 (Manuel Lim 1985, 215; *Central Bank Review* 2/85, 15). In 1977 garments became the largest export item among all Philippine export products (*Export Bulletin* 3/77). In 1983 they remained the Philippines's second largest export item, after electronic products. In terms of export value, the average growth rate of garment exports between 1970 and 1982 was 25.2 percent (Lim 1985, 214). Not only did garment exports increase in the 1970s, but the portion of consigned garment exports declined and was replaced by regular exports. In 1975 consigned garment exports constituted 74 percent of total garment exports. The ratio declined steadily to 42 percent in 1983 (*Central Bank Review* 2/85, 14).

What caused these variations in industrial performance between countries, across time periods, and within the industry? The following sections will provide an institutional explanation for these questions.

Clientelism, State Corporatism, and Laissez-Faire in Taiwan

Organization of the Cotton Textile Industry

The cohesion of Taiwan's cotton textile industry fluctuated in tandem with the growth and decline of the industry as a whole: weak cohesion during the import-substitution period, strong cooperation during the export boom, declining cooperation after the first oil crisis, and further decline after the second oil crisis. In the 1950s the industry was organized under a clientelist institution in which all producers used their strong political connections to maximize short-term interests (see table 4–3). Mainlanders owned ten of the fifteen cotton textile companies existing in 1955. The remaining five were owned by prominent Taiwanese leaders. Wu Sanlian (Tainan) and Li Qingyun (Taizhong) were factional leaders in southern and central Taiwan. Wu helped another Taiwanese business person acquire "special permission" to establish the Zhonghe Textile Company in northern Taiwan after the government banned entry to the industry in the early 1950s (Wang 1987, 91). The New Taiwan Textile Company was owned by a provincial representative who had been the director general of the local textile association before 1949.[5] The last Taiwanese company, Taiwan Gongkuang, was owned by a factional

Table 4–3

Taiwan's Textile Producers in the 1950s

Company	Scale[a]	Ethnicity	Established
Huanan	Small	Mainlander	1951
Zhanghua	Medium	Mainlander	1951
Liuhe	Medium	Mainlander	1948
Shenyi	Medium	Mainlander	1950
Yuandong	Medium	Mainlander	1953
Taibei[b]	Medium	Mainlander	1951
China Textile[b]	Medium	Mainlander	1951
Yongxing[b]	Large	Mainlander	1949
Daqin	Large	Mainlander	1949
Taiyuan	Large	Mainlander	1951
Tainan	Small	Taiwanese	1955
Taizhong	Medium	Taiwanese	1952
New Taiwan	Medium	Taiwanese	1952
Zhonghe	Large	Taiwanese	1955
Taiwan Gong- kuang	Large	Taiwanese	1946

Source: TCSA (1955[?]).
[a]Small: fewer than 10,000 spindles. Medium: between 10,000 and 20,000 spindles. Large: more than 20,000 spindles.
[b]Publicly owned.

leader but managed by mainlanders. Together these producers carved up the lucrative domestic market, which was tightly controlled by the government through entry restriction and allocation of U.S.-aid cotton.

Despite, or perhaps because of, the government's favoritism, most mainlander firms went bankrupt in the 1960s and 1970s. Taiyuan and Yuandong would not have survived the 1960 crisis of the industry if they had not been bailed out personally by Chairman Yin Zhongrong of the Foreign Exchange and Trade Control Commission (*FEER* 12/22/60; Shen 1972, 27–32). The poor performance of mainlander firms cannot be explained by protectionist policies or price wars alone because all other Taiwanese firms survived with little government help. One explanation for their poor performance might be related to the fact that many mainlander companies hired retired officials and their relatives in exchange for government favoritism. These firms, especially the three public enterprises,[6] were therefore filled with employees who had few technical or management skills (Hu 1969, 36; *United Daily News* 10/3/62). In contrast, Taiwanese firms were able to avoid the problem of redundant employees because cultural and language differences discouraged many mainlanders from working for Taiwanese-managed firms.

Except for one instance in which a mainlander lent cotton to a Taiwanese producer so that he could start production, there was no significant cooperative effort among producers during the 1950s (Wang 1987, 71). Such an effort was unnecessary, since the government distributed cotton and capital to individual firms, the amount determined by each producer's personal network. Because the domestic market was lucrative and safe due to trade protection, all producers aimed for a larger share of it. When the market became saturated in the second half of the 1950s, producers began to engage in price wars.

Due to unnecessary reorganizations, political control, and its small size, the industry's association was not active during the 1950s. The first textile association, Taiwan Textile Industry Association, was established in May 1946. In July 1948 the government ordered its reorganization into the Taiwan Machinery Cotton Textile Industry Association, which consisted of 205 Taiwanese producers who made various textile products. In February 1950 the association was expanded to include a few newly arrived mainlander producers. In 1951 the association was again reorganized and renamed the Taiwan Cotton Spinners and Weavers Association. Mainlanders became dominant in the association in June 1955 when the association was reorganized yet again into the current Taiwan Cotton Spinners Association (TCSA). A mainlander who was the president of a public enterprise replaced a Taiwanese as the association's director general. Total control of the association by the government and mainlanders was then complete.

In the 1950s TCSA could not actively serve the industry because of its small budget and political interference from outside. Its revenue was N.T. $134,200 around 1955, compared to almost ten times that, N.T. $1,112,782, in 1966. Given its small budget, the association could provide few technical services and lobbying efforts for its members. The only major cooperative effort among textile producers during this period was the establishment of the Zhonghua Textile Trading Company (ZTTC) in May 1958, and even it was not sponsored by the association. Another competing textile trading company was established a few months later because a business client of FETCC chairman Yin Zhongrong was not supported by the major producers in ZTTC. According to one respondent, Yin immediately ordered the establishment of another trading company and slated his client as its president. The effect of the cooperative effort, therefore, was partly offset by the official's patronage considerations. Some officials and producers later complained about the unnecessary competition between the two trading companies (*United Daily News* 5/27/61; 5/30/61).

In the early 1960s two factors forced textile producers to cooperate. First, the price war of the late 1950s resulted in financial crises for all producers. The deregulation of the industry in 1957 further exacerbated the financial crises. The fact that the largest textile producer at that time, Daqin Textile, went bankrupt in 1961 sent a clear signal to all producers that if they did not cooperate, they would go down together. Their first priority, therefore, was to collectively reduce production to keep prices above costs.

Reducing production was merely a temporary measure, however.

It could not solve the fundamental problem of the industry—a small domestic market.[7] The international market was the only alternative. Yet to most producers it was filled with uncertainty and risk, since few had experience in exporting. International protectionism was on the rise. International prices were lower than either domestic prices or production costs.[8] At the same time, Japanese textile products were very competitive in both price and quality. Too much risk and uncertainty needed to be overcome, and it could only be done collectively.

All of these problems were addressed in the Contract of Cooperation reached by producers in July 1961. This contract was adapted from the Japanese model of the 1950s when the United States imposed quotas on Japanese textile exports (*Central Daily News* 7/15/61). Taiwanese producers agreed to reduce their total production by one-fourth. They collectively purchased cotton and set prices. Each firm could sell only 40 percent of its products on the domestic market; the other 60 percent had to be exported. This was called the Responsibility Export Scheme, under which all producers shared equally the risk and uncertainty of the world market.

To further encourage exports and reduce competition in the domestic market, an Export Encouragement Fund was established by exacting a levy on cotton purchase, called the Export Cooperation Contribution. If a producer exported more than its allocated quota, it received from the fund not only the original contribution but also a cash reward equivalent to 5 percent of its export sales. Those who failed to fill their quotas lost their contribution.

An arbitration committee, the Coordination Committee on the Improvement and Cooperation of Sales and Production, was established by TCSA to enforce these agreements. The government also assisted in the enforcement (*Gonglun News* 8/26/61). The association could ask the government to cut off loans and electricity to violators. TCSA also requested the government to compel nonmember producers to join the association and to forbid importation of cotton yarn and fabrics that could be made locally.[9]

By increasing the benefits of cooperation and the costs of defection, the Cooperation Contract encouraged producers to cooperate. At the same time, its effective enforcement by the association and the government discouraged free riders. These cooperative measures continued throughout the 1960s and early 1970s. The Contract of Cooperation, for example, was renewed periodically throughout the 1960s. Similar contracts on new products were added to strengthen the order of production and sales.[10]

Several other associational features favored the cohesion of the industry. First, TCSA's voting rule tended to encourage cooperation between large and small members. In 1967 the largest firms had at most five votes, while the smallest firms had at least two. Because of their relative importance in decision making, smaller producers did not feel alienated. Second, TCSA had several standing committees to coordinate sales and production. In addition to the arbitration committee, there were committees on the supply of yarn, price of cotton, taxes, exports, and technology, among others. The association also began to collect statistics on the textile industry for the purpose of quota negotiations (*Central Daily News* 8/8/71). Third, the association either assisted or joined the government in negotiating textile agreements with foreign countries. For instance, TCSA pressed the government to negotiate with the United States on import taxes, quota transfer, and quota expansion (*United Daily News* 1/11/62; 8/10/65; *Economic Daily News* 5/9/69; 11/20/70). Producers also participated in the government's negotiations with foreign countries (*Xinshen News* 7/27/62; TCSA 1972, 4). If the government was not active enough, the association would send its lobbying groups to foreign countries. A number of such groups were organized by producers after the government showed signs of passivity or weakness (*United Daily News* 10/22/62; 10/27/62; 5/4/69; *Economic Daily News* 11/2/67).

The fourth associational factor promoting the industry's cohesion were the negotiations TCSA held with other industry associations when conflicts or common interests arose. For instance, TCSA negotiated with the weavers' association to resolve the conflict over yarn imports. The weaving industry supported the liberalization of yarn imports, while the spinning industry resisted it. With the help of state mediation, a compromise was worked out. TCSA agreed to lower the price and stabilize the supply of yarn in exchange for abandoning the liberalization proposal (TCSA 1972, 5–6). To facilitate communication among different textile products associations, textile producers proposed a national textile industry association modeled after the Japanese and Korean associations (*China Times* 2/19/71). The government approved. The plan materialized in 1975 with the establishment of the Taiwan Textile Federation. In 1971 TCSA also headed a project to establish the Textile Building to house all textile associations (TCSA 1972, 23). Better communication among producers and between associations and the state resulted in high utilization of textile export quotas. In 1964 the utilization rate was 87.3 percent; in 1965 it increased to 93.5 percent; and in 1966 it registered 99.97 percent (*Xinshen News* 9/9/67).

Fifth, the association coordinated its members to establish a textile technology college in 1972 in order to stabilize the nation's supply of technicians. TCSA also contributed, in cooperation with other textile associations, to the establishment of the private China Textile Industry Research Center in 1971.

Sixth, all of the above-mentioned cooperative efforts were supported by the association's increasing revenues and power. TCSA's revenue was merely N.T. $134,200 in 1955 but increased to more than N.T. $1 million by 1966 and to almost N.T. $5 million by 1973 (TCSA 1974, 53). The association's power increased concomitantly. In addition to the power of enforcing collective agreements, it received government authorization in 1961 to issue the export licenses required by both the Taiwanese government and the importing countries (TCSA 1974, 27). Later, TCSA acquired the authority to allocate export quotas (*Economic Daily News* 7/23/73). Externally, the association represented the industry in negotiations with the government and sometimes with foreign governments.

Based on these organizational strengths, TCSA became active in coordinating and promoting its members' interests during the 1960s and early 1970s. It coordinated the supply of raw materials when there was a shortage (*United Daily News* 12/22/72) and initiated proposals to simplify tariff collection procedures, which were later expanded by the government to cover other industries (TCSA 1972, 13–15; 1974, 18). Other TCSA activities included collective pricing, marketing, bargaining with other associations, and constructing a cotton storage company (TCSA 1974). In September 1974 the association once again implemented a cooperative scheme to reduce production in order to cope with the impact of the first oil crisis (TCSA 1976, 32–33).

After the 1973 oil crisis, cooperation among producers remained strong. Together with other textile associations, TCSA asked the government to control imports; to reduce taxes, interest rates, and tariffs on machinery; to lower the *minimum* requirement on a firm's products sold in the domestic market; and to cooperate with producers on their labor-saving initiatives (TCSA 1978, 7–16; 1979, 14). TCSA formulated the Measures for Rescuing the Cotton Textile Industry in 1977 to seek adjustment assistance from the state (TCSA 1979, 29). Working with other textile associations, it formulated the Measures for the Self-help of the Textile Industry, aimed at inviting government intervention (TCSA 1980, 27).

Signs of division within the industry emerged during the 1970s, however. In the early 1970s, there were heated debates about quota allocation. Small producers complained publicly that 80 percent of the quotas were controlled by less than 10 percent of the producers (*Economic Daily News* 10/12/71). New producers opposed the concurrent allocation system because it tended to protect old, inefficient firms (*Minzhong Daily News* 10/19/71). The disputes were temporarily resolved by the adoption of an eclectic method of calculation. The debate, nevertheless, continued full steam during the 1970s and 1980s, causing bitter resentment among producers (TTF 1987; Huiqing Li 1985, 156).

Small producers felt increasingly alienated when the association widened the discrepancy in voting rights between large and small producers. In contrast to the five-to-two ratio in the 1960s, large producers in the 1970s and 1980s had seven times more votes than small ones but did not pay an equivalent proportion of membership fees (TCSA 1972, 3; 1985, 60–61).

Producers lost their credibility with the government when they refused to implement a merger proposal and a labor-saving initiative suggested by the association itself (TCSA 1978).[11] Instead, they opted for short-term profits during the mild economic recovery in the mid-1970s by overloading existing production facilities.

The association also fumbled its handling of the Export Cooperative Fund around 1970, resulting in the termination of the Cooperation Contract two years later. The mishandling came about because, by that time, most Taiwanese textile products were exported, not sold to the domestic market as they had been in the 1950s. The reward for export performance should have been adjusted accordingly. The association's director general, however, insisted on the old formula, and hence promoted an unfair practice; members who had applied earlier for the reward had drained the fund.

After the second oil crisis, TCSA failed to meet from 1982 to 1985, thereby constituting a violation of the Industry Association Law. When they did meet in 1985, the association's director general complained about the declining support of members, the impotence of the association, and the state's noncooperation (TCSA 1985, 1).

Association revenues declined during the 1980s. After 1981 most revenues came not from membership fees but from rent on association property—another legal violation. In November 1986 the government announced that imports of cotton no longer needed the approval of the association, thus further reducing TCSA's authority over its members (TCSA 1987, 7).

Today the coordination of the entire textile industry falls into the hands of the Taiwan Textile Federation (TTF). TTF is a relatively well-established organization, providing valuable technical and market information to its members. TTF's power over its members remains restricted, however, since all textile associations were working independently of one another long before the association's establishment and wish to preserve that autonomy. Furthermore, the government has shifted its attention and resources from the textile industry to the electronics industry. TTF is not as influential as it was in the 1970s. For these reasons, it remains to be seen how effectively TTF can serve the industry in the 1990s and beyond.

In sum, the growth and decline of the textile industry was associated with its degree of cohesion. Clientelism in the 1950s resulted in modest growth in the first half of the decade but crisis in the second. Strong cooperation among producers during the 1960s and early 1970s helped the industry overcome the crisis and turned it into Taiwan's major industry and foreign exchange earner. After the first oil crisis, cooperation among producers began to decline. Industrial adjustment efforts were postponed by producers themselves, resulting in slower growth of the industry. The second oil crisis further weakened the cohesion of producers. The rise of a laissez-faire institution in the industry corresponded to its further decline in the 1980s.

Similarly, a close relationship existed between the state's cooperation and the industry's performance.

Cooperation of the State with the Industry

In the 1950s the first economic priority of the Taiwanese state was to prevent foreign exchange reserves from being depleted. To do so, the state controlled textile imports while it promoted the domestic textile industry as a substitute for imports. In August 1949, to expand the domestic industry, the state promulgated an incentive law specifically for the industry. A textile committee was established under the Provincial Production Control Board. The Council on U.S. Aid (CUSA) also set up a textile committee to handle the allocation of U.S.-aid cotton. Another executive order was issued in 1951 to control the production of yarn and fabrics. The scheme of entrusted spinning and weaving took effect between 1951 and 1952. All of these measures were aimed at both developing and controlling the industry to meet domestic demand.

The state made these developmental and control policies heavy-handedly. It decided which policies it preferred regardless of the industry's interests, though not necessarily contrary to them. A few textile producers did sit on the government's Textile Committee, but they acted only as transmission belts for government policies. For example, the state imposed the entrusted scheme that had been tested without success in China before 1949; Taiwan's textile producers had no choice but to follow the scheme. The state thought textile prices were too high and put a ceiling on them in 1953; producers obeyed without public complaints. When this price control resulted in the expansion of a black market in 1955, the state authorized a government agency to allocate yarn. At the same time, the state froze entry into and expansion of the industry; producers also followed these orders. Prices of textile products nevertheless skyrocketed as a result of these restrictions. Ultimately, the "autonomous" state gave up all these ineffective, ad hoc controls, and in 1957 it decided to let the free market reign. Furthermore, in November 1958 the Ministry of Economic Affairs lifted the ban on entry into and expansion of textile firms (*Xinshen News* 11/22/58). Textile prices dropped immediately, but too far and too fast. The ensuing price war gave birth to the industry's first major crisis around 1960. To finance their price wars, producers acquired easy loans through their clientelistic connections with political and financial patrons.

The state tried unsuccessfully to encourage exports during the 1950s. Export rebates were introduced in July 1955. The Measure for Assisting the Processing of Imported Materials for Exports was proclaimed in August 1956. In 1957 the Bank of Taiwan began to provide export loans. Before these export incentive measures were adopted, the state had issued an executive order in 1954 to encourage textile exports (Zhang 1980). But neither state officials nor producers paid much attention to the formulation and implementation of these measures or any other export incentive measure of this period (Liu 1980, 72–73). These measures were used like chicken soup—they might not help, but they couldn't hurt.

Serious cooperation between the state and producers began in the late 1950s when both realized that free market competition and clientelist bailouts were incapable of saving the textile industry. In late 1957 a few textile producers formed a survey group to explore export markets in other Asian countries. They were particularly impressed by the experience of South Korea, where textile exporters received strong cooperation from the Lee government in terms of low-interest loans, loan applications, and procurement of raw materials and machinery. A number of suggestions recommended by the group were finally adopted by the Taiwanese government and translated into executive orders, but only after they went through enormous red tape (*Zhengxin News* 11/25/57; *Xinshen News* 12/18/57; *United Daily News* 12/21/57).

The major problem with state policies toward the industry during the 1950s was the proliferation of decision-making agencies, which resulted in policy inconsistencies, overcontrol, and favoritism.[12] Even when producers tried to make suggestions, as in the case of the survey group, they more often than not ended up appealing to the wrong agency. Beginning around 1959, the Ministry of Economic Affairs took the initiative to respond to the demands of the textile industry. The ministry held frequent meetings with producers and worked with other government authorities to satisfy the industry's needs.[13] For instance, in coordination with the Finance Ministry, it issued executive orders to facilitate the establishment of bonded factories and simplify tax rebate procedures (*Central Daily News* 2/1/59). After an export promotion meeting with producers in 1959, the ministry formulated guidelines to establish export syndicates and unify inspection criteria on textile exports (*Central Daily News* 5/5/59; *Xinshen News* 5/8/59). The responsibility of quality inspection was later delegated to a private organization established by producers (*United Daily News* 4/9/60). Several other important executive orders were likewise promulgated by the ministry after meeting with producers; for example, the Measures for the Supply of Imported Textile Materials (*United Daily News* 6/15/60; *Zhengxin News* 5/21/61), the Assistance Guidelines for Textile Factories (*Xinshen News* 10/5/60; *Zhengxin News* 1/31/61), the establishment of the Working Committee on Cotton Textile Exports under the Ministry (*Zhengxin News* 7/14/61),[14] and the Measures for Rescuing the Textile Industry and Export Promotion of 1962.

Another coordination center between state officials and producers was the omnipotent economic decision-making center—the Foreign Exchange and Trade Control Commission (FETCC). The FETCC helped draft and implement the reduction scheme for the cotton textile industry in 1961. FETCC chairman Yin Zhongrong urged cooperation among producers and provided enforcement assistance should the association request it (*United Daily News* 7/15/61; *Central Daily News* 7/22/61). Yin adopted the suggestion of a Taiwanese textile producer to subsidize exports with domestic sales (Wang 1987, 71). The FETCC also held monthly meetings with textile producers to discuss the development of the industry. Occasionally *all* textile producers were invited (*United Daily News* 6/29/62). When negotiating with the United States on Taiwan's textile quotas, the FETCC was very attentive to the suggestions of producers. Formal consultations with producers were reported frequently by local newspapers between 1962 and 1969, and embassy officials stationed in the United States were sometimes summoned back to consult with producers (*Economic Daily News* 1/11/67; 7/12/67).

After the dissolution of the FETCC in 1970,[15] the Bureau of Industry and the newly created Bureau of International Trade (BIT), both under the Ministry of Economic Affairs, took over the main responsibility for coordination between the government and producers. These two bureaus continued to consult with producers on matters concerning the development of the industry. With assistance from BIT, in 1973 producers organized a Textile Export Committee to promote exports. Subsequently, a committee on quota allocation was established by BIT after consulting with producers (*Economic Daily News* 3/1/73; 7/23/73). Frequent consultations were also reported in the early 1970s. Jiang Jinguo, then vice premier, even presided over a meeting with textile producers (*Xinshen News* 9/5/70).

Most of the proposals suggested by the textile producers during the 1960s and 1970s were aimed at reducing red tape. In other words, the industry asked the government to withdraw the arbitrary intervention introduced during the 1950s (or even before 1949 in China). These proposals included revisions of expansion and entry requirements, bonded factory systems, tax rebates, tariff reductions, loan applications, administrative fees, and export inspections. In particular, producers asked the government "to help the industry without favoritism" (*United Daily News* 7/25/62). These vital revisions all came under the administration's legal jurisdiction and did not impose extra administrative burdens on the state. Ironically, they helped the state reduce its routine work and concentrate its resources on other more important and productive issues.

Some association proposals requested active state intervention— for example, trade protection, restriction on foreign direct investments, low-interest loans, contract enforcement, quota negotiation, and the collection of foreign market information—but did not impose an unusual burden on the state. Moreover, TCSA shared some of the responsibility for negotiation and information collection. Only once did TCSA ask the state to punish two major textile producers for their violations of a collective pricing agreement (*Zhengxin News* 11/4/67). Witnessing in retrospect the fast growth of the industry during the 1960s and 1970s, we realize how little the state had to pay to reap the magnificent harvest.

Faced with various proposals by the industry association, the state did not take all of the industry's wishes as its commands. The state occasionally bargained with the industry based on macroeconomic or developmental interests. For instance, when producers asked for a relaxation of import controls on raw materials and machinery, the state struck a bargain by setting aside a certain percentage of the imported materials and machinery for use in exports. When producers asked for an easing of requirements on entry and expansion, the state insisted on a minimum economy scale and the purchase of the latest technology. At the same time, the state provided financial incentives for producers to do this. The massive retirement of old machines and the purchase of new technology in the second half of the 1960s were a result of this bargaining (*Economic Daily News* 5/18/ 67). Concerning quota allocation, the state provided more incentives to producers of high-tech products and to those who exported to nonquota countries.

On only one occasion did the state flex its muscles toward TCSA. In the mid-1960s the price of cotton yarn increased sharply due to greater demand in the international market. The association raised the price above the international market level, which hurt the competitiveness of downstream products. After being pressed by weavers and garment makers, the government asked TCSA to lower its price and threatened to import cotton yarn if TCSA did not comply. The TCSA director general rejected the state's proposal. The association thought the government was bluffing; it thought wrong. The government immediately purchased three thousand bales of cotton yarn and threatened to purchase more if the association did not comply. The association backed down and the state discontinued its yarn imports.

During the 1970s, cooperation between the state and the industry eroded. The first major confrontation emerged after the first oil crisis. Following the advice of economists, the state planned to let the Taiwanese dollar appreciate to control inflation. All textile associations opposed the move and urged the state to adopt the American lawmaking system of holding hearings before the decision was made

(TCSA 1974, 9–10). As a compromise, the state allowed the Taiwanese dollar to appreciate only 5 percent and then stabilized it for five years.

TCSA asked the government to forbid foreign investments in the textile industry within export processing zones (EPZ), but the request was denied. Two separate associations were later established to safeguard the interests of EPZ firms. TCSA pleaded for the resumption of production incentives; again the state refused. TCSA then asked for a freeze on entry; the state said no (TCSA 1976, 31). How about reducing the minimum ratio of products that a company was required to sell to the domestic market? No, the state replied (TCSA 1979, 7–8). The association's requests for reducing and removing the cotton tax were rejected, postponed, and compromised; they were finally accepted when the association petitioned Premier Jiang directly. This entire process lasted four years (TCSA 1974, 19–20; 1978, 12). Similarly, TCSA's request for reducing taxes on imported machinery was rejected when the industry launched a laborsaving initiative.

The state remained cooperative on other issues such as the extension of loan dues, tax reduction on yarn, and minor revisions of administrative procedures. The association was also cooperative with the state's effort to control inflation by supplying enough textile products to the domestic market, even though international prices were higher (TCSA 1974, 1). But the "team spirit" between the state and producers of the 1960s no longer existed. The state began to shift its attention to the rising star of the electronics industry.

Textile producers were partly to blame for the state's increasing apathy toward the industry. First, signs of division among producers emerged in the 1970s but went unheeded. Then, the heated debate concerning quota allocation intimidated mediating state officials who often ended up being accused of favoritism by all sides. In the recession year of 1975, TCSA asked the government to purchase surplus yarn and fabrics. The government cleared all the legal and political hurdles, assigned officials to the association's committee, and began the requested purchase. The result: only one producer applied; the same producer later bought back the goods from the government and sold them abroad once the international market recovered slightly.

The biggest blunder committed by the textile industry was the laborsaving initiative of 1977. TCSA initiated the plan and the government responded generously. TCSA members, however, backed out to take advantage of the temporary economic recovery in the late 1970s. State officials were frustrated and infuriated. The initiative was terminated by the Ministry of Economic Affairs in 1980 (TCSA 1980, 62).

The state's cooperation with the industry declined rapidly after the 1979 oil crisis. TCSA again sought investment incentives for their laborsaving efforts and formulated several concrete proposals. Yet the government either rejected, postponed, or at best, only partially accepted these requests (TCSA 1982, 15–41; 1985, 19; 1986, 5). Other demands for tariff protection, loan application, the revision of quota allocation, the reduction of harbor tax, and a freeze of currency appreciation faced similar outcomes. In 1982, in the original draft of an incentive bill concerning machinery imports by strategic industries, the textile industry was not even included (TCSA 1985, 25). On one occasion the state went so far as to reduce tariffs on cotton yarn by 50 percent to punish the association's alleged involvement in price manipulation (TCSA 1986, 13–14).

During the 1980s, the state essentially adopted a laissez-faire attitude toward the industry in the name of free market philosophy. By this time state officials were treating textiles as a sunset industry. But was it? One study conducted in the early 1980s argued it was not. Among the thirty major textile products studied, few exhibited the symptoms of the end of a product cycle (Cai 1983, 85–86). The state's prophecy, however, fulfilled itself when it prematurely withdrew its assistance from the industry. The state was then fully "autonomous."

Over the decades, the Taiwanese state took a number of arbitrary, "autonomous," and counterproductive actions against the interests of the textile industry, such as hiring retired military officials and requiring "voluntary" contributions to government and party activities. But the most expensive burden shared by association members was the political purchase of cotton from countries of diplomatic importance. These countries, knowing that the purchase was intended to promote diplomatic relations, often deliberately raised the price, mixed in low-quality cotton, and charged higher transportation fees. The United States was the major country from which the association purchased cotton above market price.[16] TCSA was also ordered to buy cotton from Latin American countries, the Ivory Coast, Greece, and even Hungary (whose cotton was donated by the Soviet Union). Association members had no choice but to obey. The state would occasionally subsidize the markup over market price. Textile producers, however, had to assume other costs and risks associated with the transaction. These costs often totalled millions of U.S. dollars (TCSA 1972, 9; 1974, 44; 1976, 29; 1978, 37; 1979, 55; 1980, 61; 1982, 54; 1985, 17–22). Thus, whenever the state became truly autonomous to meet its political goals, it caused trouble for the textile industry.

Weaving Clientelism in the Philippines

Organization of the Philippine Textile Industry

The Textile Mills Association of the Philippines (TMAP) has been a major association of the textile industry. It was established in January 1956 when modern, large-scale mills emerged. Compared to its competitors, the TMAP has also been the most active and influential association representing the industry. Through hiring retired public officials to handle government relations,[17] it helped pass a number of protectionist measures and acquired tax-exemption privileges to import machineries and raw materials (*DataFil* 7/1/74).

Despite its long history and activism, however, the TMAP was not able to resolve the industry's collective action problems and the state's industrial policy problems as effectively as the Taiwan Cotton Spinners' Association. The reasons for its ultimate failure were many.

First, it was not a very inclusive organization. The TMAP was composed only of large, integrated textile mills—about 10 percent of the total.[18] Its high membership fees deterred smaller producers, who either established rival associations or remained unaffiliated. In the late 1950s Filipino producers organized the Filipino Textile Mills Association in an effort to regain Filipino (versus Chinese) dominance in the industry. The association soon disappeared; its members either joined the more influential TMAP or gradually sold their factories to the Chinese (*Manila Daily Bulletin* 6/12/59; 9/22/59; 2/13/60). In the mid-1960s and early 1970s the Chamber of Textile Manufacturers, the Philippine Knitting and Weaving Association, and the Textile Producers' Association of the Philippines (TEXPAP) were organized (*Manila Daily Bulletin* 6/17/70; 2/3/72; PDCP 1974). TEXPAP had a larger membership but smaller political influence than TMAP. It was essentially a "social club [that] rarely interacted with the government or other relevant industry associations," one high official of TEXPAP told me. Later, the Texturizers Association of the Philippines joined the factional struggle in the industry.

The Marcos government finally ordered the merger of the twenty-seven-member TMAP with the twenty-five-member TEXPAP in 1982 to form the Federation of the Textile Association of the Philippines (DBP 1983, 8). Other textile associations were subsequently directed to join the federation (*Trade, Industry, and Investments Development Digest* 3/82). Yet the federation was essentially an organization only on paper. The exclusive TMAP remained independent, as did TEXPAP. The federation never worked as well or lasted as long as its Taiwanese counterpart (Taiwan Textile Federation).

Second, TMAP and Philippine textile millers in general were obsessed with protecting their share of the domestic market instead of expanding exports. TMAP successfully pushed for high tariffs and import bans on various textile products, such as the 1965 customs administrative order, which controlled textile imports, and the 1973 Amendment of the Tariff and Customs Code, which raised tariffs on used clothing and rags to 100 percent. When high tariffs stimulated rampant smuggling, TMAP invested its precious resources in fighting (technical) smuggling[19] through a propaganda campaign and by offering assistance at customs (*Industrial Philippines* 10/66; *Manila Daily Bulletin* 1/12/66; 3/19/69). TMAP rarely even espoused the idea of exporting its products; it was far from formulating an export incentive program like Taiwan's Export Cooperation Contract.[20] "The

Philippine textile industry," the president of the Confederation of Philippine Textile/Garments Exporters said, "strives to be a dollar-saving and not a dollar-earning industry" (*Economic Monitor* 10/30/78).

Third, TMAP and Philippine textile millers could not work closely with their downstream or upstream producers. What Philippine textile producers failed to do was to develop long-term relationships with downstream producers by lowering prices and improving quality. Instead, textile producers, especially TMAP members, did what most oligopolies do—they raised monopoly prices as high as possible without improving quality. Downstream producers (i.e., the garment industry) had no choice but to import or smuggle in their materials. Many garment producers even found it more profitable to sell their textiles to the local market rather than process them for export. Philippine textile producers thus fell into a vicious circle: the higher the prices they asked, the smaller the quantity garment producers would purchase from them. To compensate for the reduced sales, textile millers charged even higher prices, thus encouraging even more smuggling.[21]

Ironically, the same logic prevailed in the relationship between textile producers and their upstream producers. In the 1970s textiles with mixed fibers became fashionable. Philippine textile producers failed to reach an agreement with the local producers of synthetic fiber to cut down material costs. Synthetic fiber producers, in the name of infant industry protection, charged local textile mills two to three times the international price.

Why did textile producers fail to work collectively with downstream and upstream producers? In addition to the aforementioned rival industry associations, producers were divided over different private interests. Some producers played the role of the wolf who cried wolf; they accused garment producers of smuggling while they themselves were engaged in smuggling. They used government discount loans to buy tax-exempt machinery (usually secondhand), spare parts, and textile materials, and then sold them to the black market in Manila's Divisoria district rather than produce textiles with them (*Manila Daily Bulletin* 4/6/67). Others textile producers such as Universal Textile, General Textile, Continental Manufacturing, and

Eastern Textile Mills had presidents who were also major shareholders and officers of Filipino Synthetic Fiber (*Manila Daily Bulletin* 3/20/70; 2/17/72). These presidents could not have cared less about higher prices of synthetic fibers charged to other textile millers.

The case of Filipino Synthetic Fiber (Filsyn) deserves a closer look here because of its tremendous impact on the Philippine textile industry in the 1970s and 1980s. Established in July 1968, Filsyn was a joint venture of Japanese firms (Teijin and Toya Menka Kaisha) and of the local textile producers mentioned above (*Manila Daily Bulletin* 3/20/70; 3/10/73). The Japanese firms subsequently withdrew from the partnership because of Filsyn's poor sales record compared to its sales networks in the Philippines. As the dominant local supplier of synthetic fiber, Filsyn was politically powerful enough to protect its interests at the expense of those of the textile millers. For instance, Filsyn got government approval to restrict imports of synthetic fiber even before it began production in late 1971. This approval not only violated a legal requirement of the tariff law but also disregarded the strong opposition of most textile millers (*Manila Daily Bulletin* 9/16/71). Textile millers offered to buy all of Filsyn's products in exchange for its withdrawal from protected status. Filsyn bluntly rejected this proposal (*Manila Daily Bulletin* 1/13/72). All textile mills using synthetic fibers were required by the government to buy 70 to 100 percent of their materials from Filsyn (*Bulletin Today* 4/19/83). Some imports of synthetic fiber were allowed only when Filsyn's inventory level was low (*Bulletin Today* 6/21/83). With government approval, Filsyn's monopoly was further strengthened in 1980, when it took over the unprofitable Lakeview Industrial Corporation, which also produced a small amount of synthetic fiber (*Bulletin Today* 3/6/86). Despite its poor management, Filsyn was appointed by the government in 1981 to manage a large, integrated textile firm, Alfa Integrated Textile Mills. The latter, however, was never revitalized by the new management (*Bulletin Today* 10/3/81; 4/25/83).

Why was Filsyn so influential that it was able to override even the powerful TMAP? Two major shareholders of Filsyn were the key: Patricio L. Lim of Universal Textile and the Dee brothers (Dewey and Donald) of Continental Manufacturing. Lim was known in the textile industry as the "all-season" power broker. In the late 1950s, he single-handedly persuaded President Garcia to ban printed cloth imports after TMAP's similar formal request was not acted upon (*Manila Daily Bulletin* 2/26/57; 8/10/57).[22] Lim, not TMAP's president, was invited by the martial law government to attend the first official meeting on the textile industry (*Bulletin Today* 12/5/72). Lim was closely associated with Imelda Marcos through whom Filsyn was granted tariff protection and monopoly privileges.

Dewey Dee, a banker and industrialist, headed the eleven-subsidiary textile conglomerate—the Continental Manufacturing Company. He organized the Confederation of Textile Exporters, which represented the private sector in the U.S.-Philippines textile negotiation in 1976 (*Bulletin Today* 3/30/76). He was also the one who triggered the banking crisis in January 1981 when he defaulted on his debts and left the country. His brother, Donald Dee, subsequently bought back the seized Continental Manufacturing from the government at a discount price. My respondents charged that Continental Manufacturing had been engaged in "ghost exports."[23] The Dee brothers thus made a good fortune from the ownership transfer of the family business. Donald Dee has also been president of the Confederation of Garment Exporters and Producers (CONGEP), which represented large textile and garment exporters.

In sum, the division of the industry into rival groups, the obsession of textile millers with protectionism over export drive, and the failure of textile millers to cooperate with downstream producers resulted in the underdevelopment of the Philippine textile industry after the 1960s. During the authoritarian rule of the 1970s and 1980s, clientelist relationships between owners of Filsyn and government leaders further dwarfed the industry's development.

A Clientelist State

Those Philippine state agencies that could greatly influence the textile industry seemed to be more interested in clientelist behavior than in their organizational goals. Because of their different clients, these state agencies were divided over major policies concerning the industry. Corruption and favoritism were widespread within these agencies. As a result, few significant industrial policies existed. Even those few policies tended to be inconsistent over time, in conflict with one another, or simply not implemented.

A number of Philippine state agencies were involved in the development of the Philippine textile industry. The most influential agency was the Central Bank, which regulated imports and exports through foreign exchange controls. The Philippine Central Bank responded to the call of textile mills to restrict or ban textile imports (*Manila Daily Bulletin* 5/24/58; 1/26/61). Yet the implementation of these policies was filled with loopholes and tended to favor large mills (Buffington 1957, 7; *Industrial Philippines* 8/66; *Manila Daily Bulletin* 9/22/59; 8/22/61; 8/15/70; 4/7/72). In the late 1960s the Central Bank set as its priority the conservation of foreign exchange. As a result, imports of textile materials were severely restricted. Due to the protest of textile millers, the Central Bank later granted them an exemption from the 50 percent margin deposit on foreign exchange used to import machinery, equipment, and raw materials. This exemption, however, was granted only to TMAP members (*Manila Daily Bulletin* 8/27/67; 12/21/69; *DataFil* 7/1/74).

While small textile mills had difficulty acquiring foreign exchange, government agencies, veterans organizations, and consumers' cooperatives had easy access to foreign exchange allocation to import a large quantity of textiles (Buffington 1957, 5; *Manila Daily Bulletin* 12/18/62; 7/8/63; 9/23/69; 4/16/70). The Reparations Commission, for example, allowed imports of Japanese textiles in the late 1950s and throughout the 1960s in the name of reparation. In 1968 alone, the commission authorized $3 million in such imports (*Manila Daily Bulletin* 3/11/68). Another prime example was the National Development Corporation (NDC), which had its own finishing mill, the Illocos Textile Mill. In the 1950s the NDC suggested that President Magsaysay impose a ban on textile imports (*Manila Daily Bulletin* 3/8/55; 7/11/55; 8/13/55). But NDC employees were more interested in selling imported textiles on the black market than in processing them (*Manila Daily Bulletin* 12/11/56). The debt-ridden Illocos Textile Mill was finally forced to close down because no private investor was willing take it over (*Manila Daily Bulletin* 4/20/62).

The third state agency that had a significant impact on the development of the textile industry was the Philippine Customs Bureau, which, unfortunately, was perhaps the most corrupt agency in the Philippine government. In the 1950s Magsaysay once proposed to fire all customs officials and start a new bureau, but his proposal was rejected by the Congress because bureau jobs were protected by law. The Philippine economy thus was left with a doorkeeper who let all kinds of goods enter as long as their owners had the correct passport—bribes.

The Customs Bureau had a very good record for spotting and seizing illegal textile imports, especially when a new administration was inaugurated. In addition, TMAP, and later the Chamber of Industries, had representatives stationed at customs to check for textile smuggling (*Manila Daily Bulletin* 6/17/65). Yet customs officials could decide which textile goods should be categorized under which tariff rate and which imports should be declared illegal.[24] Those imports that were unfortunately declared illegal and seized could be released (and most of them were) for unstated reasons (*Manila Daily Bulletin* 7/31/63; 5/10/65; 1/31/66; 10/18/70). In one sense, the Customs Bureau was a very efficient government agency because it had full knowledge and control over imported goods. It could boast of its good performance in immediately seizing smuggled goods whenever its political leaders demanded. Yet it was even more efficient in allowing smuggled goods to fly through customs or be released later. Because of this "efficiency," garment producers had to bribe customs officials to facilitate their textile imports. Even TMAP was once allegedly paying fifty thousand pesos a month to former customs commissioner Juan Ponce Enrile *not* to release illegal textile imports (*Manila Daily Bulletin* 12/24/66; 8/14/69). In the end, both garment producers and textile producers suffered from the Customs Bureau's pendulous policies (*Manila Daily Bulletin* 4/23/67).

This pendulous attitude toward textile millers and other textile importers also existed in the Embroidery and Apparel Control Inspection Board (EACIB) throughout the 1960s and early 1970s (*Manila Daily Bulletin* 9/2/61; 1/9/62; 5/7/66; 5/3/67; 9/12/67). After all, the Customs Bureau alone could not monopolize the exercise of favoritism. The granting and release of illegal textile imports needed EACIB's approval (and that of the Manila Police). EACIB's ineffectiveness and corruption resulted in its being restructured in 1966 and in its demise in the mid-1970s (*Manila Daily Bulletin* 6/7/66; 5/11/68; 6/14/71).

During Marcos's authoritarian rule, these clientelist practices were intensified and dominated by a few textile millers who had connections to the Marcos family. One example mentioned earlier was the case of Filsyn, whose major owners were Marcos cronies. In the name of rationalization, the authoritarian state not only granted a long-term monopoly to Filsyn at the expense of textile millers but also increased the assets of the poorly managed Filsyn by appointing it the caretaker of other smaller synthetic fiber companies (the Lakeview, Philippine Polyamide Industrial, and Texfiber) and of the large Alfa Integrated Textile Mills (*Bulletin Today* 2/24/72; 10/3/81; 4/19/83; 6/21/83; 4/15/85). Before these takeovers, textile millers were allowed to buy products from other synthetic companies or to import needed materials only when Filsyn could not meet the demand (*Bulletin Today* 10/2/73).

Another example of the clientelist state is demonstrated by the privileges given to the Tanco family, which owned the Manila Bay Spinning Mills and the Southern Textile Mills. In the early 1980s Manila Bay Spinning Mills was one of the two largest exporters of textiles.[25] It was accused by other textile millers of engaging in ghost exports involving officials of the Customs Bureau and the Ministry of Trade and Industry.

The case of the Southern Textile Mills (STM) is even more intriguing. In 1983, after its export quotas were cancelled because of misrepresentation, STM was rewarded by the government with the ownership of Mindanao Textile (MinTex). MinTex was established by the National Development Corporation in 1981 as a textile mill that would contribute to Mindanao's economy. MinTex soon met the fate of its predecessor, the Illocos Textile of the 1950s: it was soon transformed by NDC into a garment manufacturer that owned a lucrative quota share but produced few garments. MinTex became such a national scandal that NDC had to give up ownership. Who was heir to this lucrative quota? The Southern Textile Mills' owner, Eusebio N. Tanco, who happened to be a godson of the most powerful Marcos crony, Eduardo (Danding) Cojuangco. STM later went bankrupt because of mismanagement. Danding Cojuangco bought it back from the government at a discount—a lucrative replica of the Dee brothers' Continental Manufacturing affair (*Bulletin Today* 10/16/83; *Manila Bulletin* 4/4/86; 4/13/86).

All of this important clientelist behavior of the Philippine state could have been overlooked if the analysis were limited to the policy level. If we judge by proclaimed policies, Philippine governments, both before and after the declaration of martial law, seemed responsive to the needs of the textile industry. These policies, however, were either not implemented or they favored certain groups of producers. In 1963, for instance, President Macapagal launched the "clothes for the masses" project to encourage the use of a new local fabric called "Pag-asa." But the project was assigned only to TMAP members for production and distributed exclusively by the publicly owned National Marketing Corporation (*Manila Daily Bulletin* 1/1/63). The fabric was of such poor quality and was so high in price that the whole project was discontinued at the end of the Macapagal administration in 1965.

The 1964 Textile Assistance Acts (RA 4006 and 4068) granted textile mills tax exemptions on raw materials, chemicals, and spare parts. Few textile millers took advantage of these laws because of their short period of validity (three years) and the tremendous red tape involved in tax rebate procedures. For example, producers did not receive the certificates of qualification for tax exemptions until two years after the laws were passed (*Industrial Philippines* 8/66; *Manila Daily Bulletin* 8/7/66).

To assist the research and development of the textile industry, the government established the Philippine Textile Research Institute in 1967. Since then, however, it has been poorly staffed and funded. It did not even have complete statistics on the Philippine textile industry (*DataFil* 7/1/74).

After its inauguration, the Marcos authoritarian government allocated $60 million to textile millers to purchase raw cotton for textile exports. The $60 million, nevertheless, went to only 3 mills out of a total of 129 (*DataFil* 7/1/74). In the second half of the 1970s, powerful industry-specific agencies such as the Garments and Textile Export Office, the Subcommittee on International Trade in Textiles, and the Garment and Textile Export Board were established to help textile exportation. But they were created only to help garment exports, not textiles (*COPE* 3/78; *Sunburst International Magazine* 11/78). In 1981 the Philippine government and the World Bank initiated a textile modernization program (part of the famous Structural Adjustment Program) with a budget of $550 million. The program qualifications were so restrictive, however, that few Philippine textile mills applied. In 1985 the government embarrassingly returned $100 million of the authorized $150 million to the World Bank (*Bulletin Today* 5/23/81; 11/2/84; 6/26/85; DBP 1983, 8–12; *Philippine HRD Yearbook* 1985).

The failure of the Philippines's textile industry is in sharp contrast to the success of its garment industry. Because of their different types of institutions, these two closely related industries had very different levels of performance.

The Corporatist Garment Industry

The Philippine garment industry had been a disorganized industry until the end of the 1960s. No influential industry association representing a significant portion of the garment industry existed. Perhaps there was no need for such an association, since most garment exports were produced on a consignment basis. The industry was ruled under a laissez-faire institution, although government policies and red tape tended to retard the industry's development.

In the second half of the 1960s, increasing government harassment of the garment industry to protect the aging textile industry forced garment producers to organize themselves defensively. There emerged the Philippine Association of Embroidery & Apparel Exporters (PAEAE), the Filipino Chamber of Embroidery & Apparel Products, the Export Processing Zone Chamber of Exporters and Manufacturers, and the Garment Business Association of the Philippines (GBAP). In 1969 Donald Dee established an umbrella association for these four major garment associations, the Confederation of Garment Exporters of the Philippines (CONGEP).

According to my interviews with Donald Dee and other garment producers, CONGEP served its members well throughout the 1970s and early 1980s. The government began to see the legitimate interests and foreign exchange earning potential of the garment industry as a whole, and import controls on textiles and garment materials were relaxed. In 1974, for example, CONGEP began to expand the links (i.e., subcontracts) between large and small producers as well as between FDIs and local producers. As a result, export quotas were better utilized and technology transfer was facilitated.

GBAP was the major contributor to CONGEP in terms of its policy initiatives and enrollment effort. Established in 1968, the GBAP aimed to represent the interests of small producers, though it also welcomed medium-sized and large producers. Membership dues were low but association services were abundant. The GBAP was a well-organized association, with eleven standing committees specializing in international relations, Garment and Textile Export Board (GTEB) affairs, export promotion, and productivity, among other concerns. It disseminated government regulations and trade opportunities to its members each week. It also published a quarterly magazine called *The Garment Journal*. At the time of its establishment, the GBAP had only 7 members. In 1982 it enrolled 230 members. By 1988 it had 383 members representing about one-third of the whole industry but more than 90 percent of the industry's production capacity (*Bulletin Today* 8/13/82; my interview with GBAP president Anastacio delos Reyes).

Serious friction between large and small producers began to develop in the early 1980s when quotas became more competitive among producers. In 1983, when the export quotas of 21 GBAP members were arbitrarily cancelled by the government for alleged "dollar salting,"[26] CONGEP sided with TMAP to support the cancellation. GBAP, which represented small and medium-sized producers, broke with CONGEP and asked the government to reinstate these quotas instead of redistributing them to large producers; the government refused (*Bulletin Today* 10/11/83; 10/27/83; 11/12/83; 1/13/84).

A daughter of Imelda Marcos, Imee Marcos Manotoc, became interested in selling quotas. So in 1984 the government forced the third-largest garment exporter, Glorious Sun, to transfer its quotas to two newly established companies, De Soleil Garments (owned by

Imee Manotoc) and American Inter Fashion (owned by former deputy prime minister Jose Rono). In two years, the two companies accumulated the largest and most profitable export quotas to the United States and Canada (*Bulletin Today* 11/10/83; *Manila Bulletin* 9/10/86; 11/19/86). These indeed were the "smarter" people to whom Imelda Marcos referred.

Before the 1970s, the Philippine state had not been very kind to the garment industry because of the influence of large textile millers. In the early 1950s and 1960s textile imports were tightly controlled. Garment producers had to rely on either smuggling or consignment to remain competitive in the international market. In June 1961, Republic Act 3137 (the Embroidery Law) created the Embroidery and Apparel Control and Inspection Board (EACIB) under the Finance Ministry for the purpose of constraining, rather than developing, the garment industry. EACIB issued import licenses to a limited number (less than fifty) of Embroidery Law firms, some of whom did not even engage in production. The Embroidery system was "an exclusive club for political spoils," one industry leader commented. EACIB scrutinized applications for textile imports, which always caused a delay in the release of textile materials and an increase in the costs of garment production (BOI 1972; *Industrial Philippines* 10/66).

In the late 1960s Marcos was particularly harsh with the garment industry. He put constant pressure on EACIB to tighten its import controls, purged those EACIB officials who were sympathetic to the garment industry, ordered the customs commissioner to stop issuing licenses to importers of embroidery materials, scaled down the quantity of textile imports, and finally, froze the entry of Embroidery Law firms in October 1970 (*Manila Daily Bulletin* 5/15/66; 6/7/66; 4/28/67; 10/27/68).

The Marcos government did not change its hostile attitude toward the garment industry until the late 1960s and early 1970s, when it badly needed foreign exchange to rescue itself from financial crises. The inward-oriented textile industry was unable to help. The garment industry, therefore, became the new star. The government first released the garment industry from the list of "overcrowded industries" in January 1972, which resulted in an increase in the number of Embroidery Law firms. A tripartite dialogue among the state, producers, and labor was subsequently established.[27] EACIB relaxed its control over the import of garment materials. Because of its declining importance, the regulation-oriented EACIB was finally merged into the export-oriented Garment and Textile Export Board (GTEB) in 1982.

The creation of GTEB in June 1977 represented, for the first time in Philippine history, close cooperation between producers and the state in developing the garment industry. It was a very powerful, interministerial agency composed of the minister and deputy ministers of the Ministry of Trade and Industry, finance deputy minister, and customs commissioner. GTEB gathered production statistics, handled foreign negotiations on quotas and tariffs, issued export licenses, allocated quotas, supervised bonded warehouses, and disciplined violators (*Sunburst International Magazine* 11/78; *Trade, Industry and Investments Development Digest* 9/82; 4/83). The two major producers' associations, CONGEP and GBAP, made regular presentations in GTEB meetings. It was, therefore, no coincidence that garments became the largest export item of the Philippines in 1977— the year GTEB was created.

But the performance of the garment industry had little to do with the autonomy of the state or authoritarianism. Marcos changed his mind about the garment industry when the government was still democratic. The trademark of the state's cooperation with the industry—the creation of GTEB—was not realized until five years after the declaration of martial law. By then the garment industry had been relatively well organized by GBAP and CONGEP. In effect, the creation of GTEB was more a response than a stimulus to the boom in the industry.

Ironically, industry leaders recalled that whenever the state or GTEB had its own opinion about the industry's development, harmful effects followed. They cited the examples of the arbitrary cancellation of smaller producers' export quotas, the transfer of the Glorious Sun's export quotas to Marcos cronies, and an inflexible attitude toward penalties for producers who failed to fill up their quotas during world recession (*Bulletin Today* 1/23/82; 6/7/82; 8/5/82; 10/11/83; 7/10/84).

In my interview with him, one industry leader commented on the adverse impact of the autonomous state on the industry:

If the government had been more responsive to the demands of the industry as a whole, garment exports could have broken the one-billion-dollar mark in the late 1970s instead of in this year [1988]. But it was the style of [MTI] Minister Ongpin and the style of the authoritarian government. Those technocrats thought they knew more than we industrialists did. Hence whatever came from the top had to be followed.

This claim is supported by the fact that no formal development program for the industry was established despite the industry's repeated requests for one. The only industry-specific policy was the Embroidery Law of 1961. Yet in the past, non-Embroidery Law mills contributed to the growth of the garment industry more than Embroidery Law mills did. In 1976, for instance, Embroidery Law mills increased their export value by 41 percent, while non-Embroidery Law mills increased by 144 percent, accounting for 43 percent (compared to 25 percent in 1974) of total garment exports. Embroidery Law firms enjoyed various tax incentives which, if applicable to all other smaller producers, could have doubled the growth of the industry (*Export Bulletin* 3/77; *Bulletin Today* 5/21/79).

Conclusion

The comparison of Taiwan's and the Philippines's textile industries has revealed several weaknesses in the developmental state theory. First, the "developmental" industrial policies were initiated either by corporatist associations alone or by close consultation between the state and business. These policies were not promulgated by "farsighted" developmental states alone. The industrial adjustment and expansion of Taiwan's textile industry in the 1960s and the Philippines's garment industry in the 1970s were such examples.

Second, corporatist associations often made proposals to improve the capacity of the state by cutting its red tape and excessive intervention in the market. Thus, state capacity should not be regarded as the ultimate cause of industrial growth but rather as a consequence of state-business cooperation.

Third, whenever the state became autonomous, the industry began to perform poorly. The state either ignored the developmental plans of industry associations or imposed antidevelopmental policies on the industry. This was the case for Taiwan's textile industry during the 1950s and 1980s, as well as the Philippines's garment industry before the 1970s.

Finally, the state's commitment to the industry's development might explain the fluctuations of industrial performance. For instance, the Taiwan state's attention to the textile industry in the 1960s and withdrawal of commitment in the 1980s were critical to the industry's performance. Yet the commitment was often a reaction to the industry's performance, not its precondition.

The previous sections have demonstrated that types of institutions had a significant impact on industrial performance. In Taiwan during the 1950s clientelism stimulated the industry's rapid growth at the outset. This growth soon decelerated and resulted in a major crisis in the late 1950s. During this period, the industry association was weak and was reorganized frequently for political reasons. Producers looked for political and financial patrons in the state to divide the small domestic market. The state did not have coherent policies toward the industry. Rather, it imposed arbitrary policies on the industry for its own political and fiscal purposes.

The financial crisis of the textile industry in the late 1950s and early 1960s brought together producers and the state. Producers began to cooperate among themselves in production, export promotion, and domestic sales. The association became a powerful coordinator, arbitrator, and club goods provider. The state was very responsive to the proposals formulated by the industry; it reduced red tape, favoritism, and arbitrary intervention in the industry. The state and the association cooperated in international negotiations and in upgrading production technology. The emergence of state corporatism generated the rapid and sustained growth of the industry in the 1960s and early 1970s.

A mild decline in state corporatism began just before the oil crisis of 1973. Problems of quota allocation, resistance to industrial adjustment, alienation of smaller producers, and the association's administrative errors weakened cooperation among producers. The state's cooperation declined due to splits within the textile industry and the growing importance of the electronics industry. Therefore, the growth of the textile was capped after the first oil crisis.

After the second oil crisis, in 1979, producers withdrew their support for the association. The association lost its credibility in the eyes of its members and of the state because of its reduced power and activities. At the same time, the state regarded textiles as a sunset industry and refused to provide assistance in industrial adjustment. The premature withdrawal of state assistance made the sunset industry argument a self-fulfilling prophecy. The laissez-faire institution replaced state corporatism in the 1980s and caused the stagnation of the industry.

Compared to Taiwan's textile industry, the Philippine textile industry before the 1960s had an equally, if not more, promising potential for rapid growth. It was modern, protected by a lucrative domestic market, and strongly supported by the United States through technical, financial, fiscal, and material assistance. The Philippine textile industry, however, failed to capitalize on its potential.

The existence of clientelism was the major cause of stagnation in the Philippine textile industry. The industry was not well organized and was deeply divided among factional industry associations. The most influential association, TMAP, was interested only in protecting existing market shares, not in expanding export markets. TMAP members and other textile millers also failed to establish constructive links with the emerging garment industry in the critical years of the 1960s. Within the group of large producers, an even smaller group of producers pursued individual maximization at the expense of the whole industry.

The state was basically a clientelist state. Because of their different clientelist and organizational interests, government agencies implemented conflicting policies with regard to the development of the textile industry. During authoritarian rule, clientelist practices by state officials were intensified toward a small group of cronies.

The Philippines's garment industry provides an interesting contrast to its textile industry. Despite the harassment by both the state and textile millers, the corporatist garment industry finally emerged in the 1970s as one of the top earners of foreign exchange. Evidence suggests that the organization of the industry by its associations, GBAP and CONGEP, contributed to its rapid growth. The state then became responsive to the demands of the industry, which further boosted the industry's development.

5

THE PLYWOOD INDUSTRY

In the previous two chapters, the comparisons between Taiwan and the Philippines began with the puzzle that the two countries had relatively equal initial conditions but ended with vastly different development outcomes. The history of the plywood industry in these two countries reproduces this development puzzle. In fact, instead of having equal initial conditions, the Philippine plywood industry had obvious advantages over Taiwan and other Asian competitors. But institutions made a difference. When it emerged and thrived, Taiwan's plywood industry benefited from the laissez-faire institution. It also faded away on the waves of international market fluctuations. In contrast, the Philippine plywood industry enjoyed the fruits of state corporatism before the 1960s only to be destroyed by the clientelism of the 1960s and authoritarian clientelism in the 1970s.

The first section provides evidence for the difference in growth patterns of the two countries' plywood industries. In particular, it will elaborate the initial advantages of the Philippine plywood indus-

128

try. The second section describes how the laissez-faire institution influenced the growth and decline of Taiwan's plywood industry. The third section explains how state corporatism contributed to the success of the Philippine plywood industry in the 1950s and how clientelism disarrayed the industry's potential. The last section summarizes this chapter.

Patterns of Industrial Growth

The growth patterns of Taiwan's and the Philippines's plywood industries are reported in tables 5–1 and 5–2. When these tables are read alongside table 5–3, in which Korea's, Indonesia's and the world's plywood productions are also included, the differences between Taiwan's and the Philippines's plywood industries become significant.

First, the average growth rate of the Philippine plywood industry in the 1960s and 1970s was lower than that of the Taiwanese and Korean plywood industries. The Philippines had a 7.7 percent average growth rate in production in the 1960s, while Taiwan registered 36.1 percent. Philippine plywood exports grew on average 14.1 percent in the 1960s, while Taiwanese products grew by 33.6 percent. The contrast between the Philippines on the one hand and South Korea and Taiwan on the other is even sharper.[1] The Philippine plywood industry had the worst average growth record among the three in the 1960s and 1970s.

Second, before the 1979 oil crisis, Philippine plywood production and exports had more negative growth rates than its Taiwanese and Korean counterparts. The condition of the international market, especially American housing construction, had a significant impact on the industry's performance in all three countries. Most of the time, however, Taiwan and South Korea were able to maintain positive growth rates; as a result, machinery and labor were not idle, as they often were in the Philippines.

Third, the Philippine plywood industry did not fare well either in net production volume or in exports. Its production volume was surpassed by Taiwan in 1963, by Korea in 1966, by Malaysia in 1975,[2] and finally by Indonesia in 1979. The Philippines's export

Table 5-1
Growth Rate of Taiwanese Plywood Industry

	TPMEA Membership (%) N	Total Production (%) N	Exports (%) N	Domestic Sales (%) N	Domestic Sales (Percentage of Total Sales)
1953		(26,443)[a]	(807)[a]	(25,596)[a]	97
1954		58	34	32	97
1955		7	54	-2	95
1956		-11	63	6	93
1957		17	166	14	85
1958		57	350	8	57
1959		52	72	5	45
1960	9	20	11		43
1961	80	163	8		24
1962	(15)[a]	35	40	11	20
1963	7	74	84	9	13
1964	0	49	56	7	9
1965	13	10	7	7	9
1966	6	18	18	7	8
1967	16	1	2	2	8
1968	5	45	40	141	13
1969	26	40	53	-36	6
1970	21	25	18	35	7
1971	9	16	14	38	8
1972	11	51	43	209	16
1973	52	1	0	-17	14
1974	17	-18	-28	25	22
1975	5	-5	-5	-15	20
1976	3	18	13	30	22
1977	-1	4	10	5	21
1978	-3	26	31	41	23
1979	3	-10	-13	-39	17
1980	-10	-10	-20	96	34
1981	1	5	10	-3	31
1982	-3	-9	-13	-2	33
1983	-3	1	5	4	33
1984	-1	-20	-30	2	42
1985	6	-15	-8	-9	42
1986	6	6	-9	8	46
1987	8 (82)[a]	7	8	6	46

Source: TPMEA (1988b, 5–6).

[a] Numbers in parentheses are raw data on production volume, measured in thousands of square feet, 1/8 inch thickness.

Table 5-2
Growth Rate of Philippine Plywood Industry

Sales	Production (%) N	Exports (%) N	Domestic Sales (%) N	Domestic Sales (Percentage of Total Sales)
1949	(3,980)[a]	(74)[a]	(3,906)[a]	98
1950	174.7	205.4	174.1	98
1951	103.9	105.8	103.9	98
1952	71.0	−48.0	73.9	99
1953	53.9	−24.4	54.4	99
1954	11.8	801.1	9.3	98
1955	23.7	144.6	20.6	95
1956	29.4	130.0	24.2	91
1957	28.4	167.9	4.9	82
1958	24.9	112.0	5.3	69
1959	76.6	246.3	−0.3	39
1960	8.6	−1.7	25.0	45
1961	19.7	−37.7	2.7	57
1962	21.7	29.6	15.7	54
1963	26.4	34.3	19.7	51
1964	17.5	106.6	−66.7	15
1965	27.1	−19.5	300.1	46
1966	−9.6	−36.2	21.9	62
1967	−3.4	42.1	−31.5	44
1968	33.2	46.7	15.8	38
1969	−24.6	−23.1	−27.1	37
1970	9.4	−26.9	71.4	58
1971	3.0	35.9	−21.1	44
1972	33.1	49.7	12.3	37
1973	58.0[b]	74.5	30.2	31
1974	−3.7	−49.0	787.1	50
1975	−61.1	−59.2	−63.0	48
1976	54.2	46.8	62.4	50
1977	17.5	−15.3	72.6	55
1978	0.2	6	−52.1	26
1979	2.6			
1980	9.9			
1981	−17.4			
1982	−28.0			
1983	36.8			
1984	−15.3			
1985	0.0			
1986	−15.4			
1987	20.8			

Source: *Philippine Forestry Statistics* (1970, 1978, 1988) and PWPA (1983–1987); data after 1982 are calculated from PWPA (1982–1987).

Note: For the period from 1949 to 1973, original numbers were reported in square feet or thousands of square feet; for 1974 to 1987, in cubic meters. After 1976, statistics are reported by calendar year rather than fiscal year. Export data after 1979 are not available.
[a]Numbers in parenthese are volumes measured in thousands of square feet.
[b]Philippine plywood production reached its peak volume in 1973.

Table 5–3
Growth Rate in Plywood Production of Various Countries

Year	Korea (%)	Philippines (%)	Taiwan (%)	Indonesia (%)	World (%)
1956	27.3	66.1			
1957	50.0	29.0			
1958	9.5	39.2	100.0		
1959	17.4	58.1	83.3		
1960	7.4	8.7	72.7		
1961	−17.2	−19.9	−21.1		
1962	87.5	21.7	6.7		
1963	120.0	−38.6	1087.5		
1964	49.5	17.4	64.7		
1965	45.3	27.2	12.1		
1966	64.2	−9.7	21.4		
1967	24.6	−3.4	7.0		
1968	59.8	33.5	21.3	33.3	
1969	16.8	−24.7	−2.4	75.0	4.4
1970	3.2	20.4	50.0	0.0	7.3
1971	20.9	3.7	44.7	−14.3	10.9
1972	6.7	20.3	12.9	33.3	7.8
1973	35.5	57.7	21.5	−35.7	4.4
1974	−17.8	−37.9	−31.9	166.7	−8.4
1975	18.0	−8.8	−0.6	345.8	−4.5
1976	16.4	−10.6	15.1	100.0	13.6
1977	37.0	17.8	2.4	30.4	7.1
1978	11.8	0.2		52.0	1.4
1979	−8.7	5.1		47.2	1.4
1980	−32.6	7.4	62.0		−7.6
1981	1.5	−16.3	53.5		2.1
1982	−11.0	−6.3	60.2		−3.2
1983	4.8	8.1	26.2		13.3
1984	−11.1	7.5	14.7		0.4
1985	−7.3	−29.22	8.2		2.4
1986	−9.6	24.6	24.6		8.4

Source: Figures for countries before 1977 are calculated from FAO data as reported in the *Philippine Lumberman* (November 1979, 6). These data are relatively consistent with those reported by each country. Data on world production are from UNSO (1963, 1969, 1970, 1977, 1986). Original data were in thousands of cubic meters.

market share in the United States met a similar fate. Taiwan's plywood exports exceeded those of the Philippines in 1963. Korea surpassed the Philippines's export record in 1965 and dominated the
American plywood import market until the early 1980s, when it was
replaced by Indonesia.

Finally, the number of Philippine plywood mills has not increased
substantially since the early 1960s. In 1987 the industry was about the
same size as it was in 1964. There were thirty-four plywood firms in
1964 (Landgrebe and Brussier 1964, 10); twenty-nine in 1976
(PLPMA 1976, Appendix); thirty-three in 1977 and 1980 (PDCP
1977, 12; *Philippine Lumberman* 7/80); and thirty-eight in 1987.

The Philippine plywood industry had many advantages over Taiwan's at the beginning. First, the Philippine plywood industry
emerged early and performed well. The first plywood company,
Cadwallader-Gibson Lumber, was founded in 1936 during American
rule. Several more plywood firms were set up in the 1940s and 1950s.
The growth rates of production and exports of Philippine plywood
were remarkable in the 1950s (see table 5–2). The average growth
rate of production from 1954 to 1959 was 32.5 percent, higher than
Taiwan's 30 percent for the same period. In 1956 the Philippines
ceased to import plywood (*Manila Daily Bulletin* 8/10/56). In 1958 the
Business Writers Association cited plywood as the Industry of the
Year for its contribution to the Philippine economy and export earnings (*Manila Daily Bulletin* 6/14/57). Plywood's export value was three
times that of textiles and thirty times that of footwear and garments
in 1962 (Sicat 1972, 76).

In contrast, there were virtually no plywood factories in Taiwan
during Japanese rule. Three so-called plywood companies existing
before 1945 produced goods other than plywood: one company produced veneer only[3] and the other two manufactured tea boxes (Ye
1968, 150). Fewer than ten plywood companies were established in
the late 1940s and early 1950s and most of these companies were
owned by the Taiwanese. In the early 1950s plywood was produced
mainly for domestic consumption. More than 90 percent of total
products were sold locally before 1956 (see table 5–1), and a small
quantity was exported to other Southeast Asian countries (*Taiwan
News* 2/28/72). Because of its great dependence on the domestic

market, plywood production slowed drastically in the mid-1950s when the market became saturated.

The second advantage of the Philippine plywood industry was that its exports faced little competition in the international market. By 1949, when the Nationalist party fled to Taiwan, the Philippines was already producing and exporting high-quality plywood products. In fact, the Philippines kept a comfortable edge over Taiwan in production until 1962 and in exports until 1961(TPMEA 1988b, 5–6; *Philippine Forestry Statistics 1970*). Plywood production in South Korea, Malaysia, and Indonesia was insignificant until the mid-1960s. The only competitor in Asia in the 1950s was Japan. But Philippine plywood exports were not under serious threat from Japanese plywood because, first, Japan soon reduced its exports to satisfy domestic demand, and second, Philippine plywood producers adopted American standards of quality control to compete with Japanese products.[4] Furthermore, the quality of products and the size of firms in the Philippines were comparable to those of the United States and Europe (*Philippine Industry* 1/14/56).

Third, Philippine plywood exports enjoyed the advantage of preferential treatment from the United States. According to the Laurel-Langley Agreement of 1954, Philippine exports to the United States paid only 40 percent of the lowest U.S. tariff duty on the same product. The agreement was in effect until the end of 1970. Philippine exporters paid 60 to 80 percent of basic U.S. duties between 1971 and 1973 and the full rate after 1974. This preferential tariff meant that Philippine products enjoyed a comfortable 26 percent margin over Taiwanese products, despite the fact that Philippine plywood exports met with higher labor and freight costs when they landed on American soil (*Manila Daily Bulletin* 2/24/70).

Finally, and most ironically, the Philippines had been *the* major log supplier to the plywood industries in Taiwan, South Korea, and Japan in the 1950s and 1960s. None of these competitors was using a significant portion of its forest reserves to produce plywood. Instead, each imported almost 100 percent of its supply from the Philippines, where Lauan trees, which provide the best plywood material, grew. Therefore, Philippine producers should have had a lower cost for log supplies than their competitors. Since log cost constituted

60 to 70 percent of the total cost of plywood, this lower cost was significant. Furthermore, it meant that all profits realized by these competitors would have belonged to the Philippines if the Philippines had only banned log exports. Why, then, was the Philippine plywood industry unable to grow and compete with its Asian neighbors?

Another puzzle to be explained is why Taiwan's competitive plywood industry failed to sustain its growth record after the 1960s. By several standards, Taiwan's plywood industry had a very distinguished performance in the 1960s: it had stronger forward and backward linkages to other economic activities and generated higher net foreign exchange earnings than the textile industry (Lin 1969, 121–22; Xu 1969, 203). Plywood was the number one industrial export produced by private firms in 1966 (*Economic Daily News* 2/23/68). Wood products (mainly plywood products) were ranked between the second- and the fourth-largest export products from 1964 through 1970 (TPMEA 1968; City Bank of Taibei 1973, 5). In 1964 Taiwan became the largest exporter of plywood to the United States, occupying 25 percent of the American plywood import market (*Central Daily News* 6/12/64). And finally, the number of plywood producers increased rapidly during the 1960s and reached its peak in 1973. After the 1960s, however, negative growth rates occurred frequently in membership, total production, and exports (see table 5–1). The entire industry shrank rapidly. What happened? The next two sections provide an institutional explanation for these questions.

Taiwan's Neglected Child

Organization of the Industry

Taiwan's plywood industry was not organized as well as its textile industry. Although the industry association provided certain coordination efforts and club goods over the years, cooperation among members was modest and irregular.

Before the establishment of the Taiwan Plywood Manufacturers & Exporters Association (TPMEA) in 1962, there were no reports available on the cooperation among plywood producers. Producers arranged for their own material supplies, production needs, and sales. American importers made individual sales contracts with Taiwanese producers, who competed with one another through pernicious price wars. Fortunately, the export market remained lucrative in terms of profit margin and volume.

In the early 1960s the Taiwan government's Council on U.S. Aid convened a meeting with plywood producers and asked them to organize an industry association to further expand exports. Most of Taiwan's industries organized their associations according to the Industry Association Law. But TPMEA was organized under a different law, the Exporters Association Law. The law allowed more autonomy for the association vis-à-vis the state while it gave less authority to the association over its members' production and sales. For instance, the Industry Association Law stipulated that industrial associations had responsibility for implementing government policies and participating in social movements as well as regulating members' equipment, materials, conflicts of interest, and labor-management problems. These responsibilities were not included in the Exporters Association Law, which listed only three functions, all concerned with export matters (Legislative Yuan 1958, 424–44). Plywood producers wanted to keep both the state and the association away from their business.

In 1963 the director general of the Japanese plywood association visited TPMEA to explain how cooperation among producers and with the government had contributed to the brisk growth of Japan's plywood industry. For instance, the Japanese association, with the participation of government officials, jointly decided on the price, quantity, and quality of plywood exports. Export inspection was conducted by the Japanese Plywood Inspection Corporation, a semiofficial organization belonging to the industry. When there was an export slump in 1955, Japanese producers implemented a reduction scheme (TPMEA 1963).[5] Most of these suggestions and examples, however, fell on deaf ears because Taiwanese producers had prospered under a relatively laissez-faire institution and did not want to change it.[6]

Cooperation among producers during the 1960s and early 1970s was modest or irregular. TPMEA paid membership fees to the U.S.

Importers of Hardwood Products Association (IHPA), which acted as a watchdog over the interests of foreign plywood exporters. The other major cooperative activity among producers was the construction in 1969 of a water reservoir to store imported logs. With the exception of these two cases, cooperation efforts failed.

An export committee was organized within TPMEA in 1964 to coordinate export prices. The committee met once every two weeks, but it was neither powerful nor effective. It collected information on export prices, which had reference value only and not regulatory power. Producers set their own prices to compete for foreign orders. Despite a reorganization of the committee in 1966 to reinforce communication among producers, price wars continued.

Shipping cost was a major concern for Taiwanese plywood producers. They cooperated once in negotiating with their shipping companies (TPMEA 1964), which led to a temporary reduction in transportation costs. Proposals to cooperate in chartering ships, however, were repeatedly rejected by most producers (TPMEA 1969; 1972, 22). Another proposal to establish a trading company for plywood products never materialized (*Central Daily News* 10/2/68).

One failed cooperation effort that had a great impact on the development of the industry concerned the problem of log supply. In the 1960s the Taiwanese government encouraged plywood producers to collectively explore the Indonesian forest so as to ensure a stable supply of logs. Some of the big producers, however, rejected the idea because the supply of Philippine logs was abundant at the time. Only one producer went ahead and acquired the license for forest development in Indonesia. In contrast, Korean producers and the government jointly established the Korean Development Company in 1967 to manage the log supply of the entire industry (Zhou 1973, 106) and prepared the ground for the later revitalization of Korean plywood companies in Indonesia. In 1978 Korea's largest overseas investment was in Southeast Asia's timber and totalled $20 million (Jo 1981, 60).

The poor organization of TPMEA was also a reason for the disunity of the Taiwanese plywood industry. First, the general secretaries of the association whom the GMD had recommended were incompetent. The first general secretary, who held the position during the 1960s, was fired because he forged accounting records for personal gain. The second general secretary resigned in 1977 because of his political ambition. Neither general secretary had paid much attention to the welfare of the industry. TPMEA directors general did not actively promote the interests of the industry either; most spent as little time as possible on association matters, and no one in the association's history served more than two terms (for a total of four years).

Second, the association had only a small budget compared to the Taiwan Cotton Spinners' Association (TCSA), for example. Both associations had a similar number of members throughout their history. In 1966 TCSA's revenue was N.T. $1,112,782; TPMEA had only about half that amount—N.T. $661,233. By 1972, while TCSA's revenue reached N.T. $3,885,956, TPMEA had only about one-fourth that amount. TPMEA's small budget constrained its activities, including its lobbying efforts in the United States (TPMEA 1968).

Third, the association did not provide its members with the extensive technical services or market information TCSA provided. TPMEA did not even have a library to store production and market information. It had few, if any, staff members to conduct market and product research. And there was little contact between the association and other research facilities in the government or in universities.

Finally, TPMEA did not actively enroll plywood producers. Many small plywood producers joined either the Taiwan Wood Products Association or the Taiwan Wood Exporters Association. Legally, TPMEA could force these small producers to become members, yet for some unknown reason it was not interested in doing so. No statistics on the number of nonmember producers before 1974 are available. In 1975 about 40 percent of Taiwan's plywood producers were *not* TPMEA members (TPMEA 1976, 19).

Hence, the fast growth of the Taiwanese plywood industry in the 1960s was nurtured by a relatively laissez-faire institution. The disorganized industry could not compete with its well-organized counterpart in Korea, however, which in 1968 replaced Taiwan as the largest plywood exporter to the United States.

During the 1970s and 1980s the disorganized industry could not cope with severe external shocks. Between 1969 and 1974, Taiwanese plywood producers attempted to strengthen their cooperation. The association doubled its membership fees to cope with inflation and to purchase a permanent office, which it did in 1973. TPMEA distributed more documents to its members and officials, though the number of its meetings with government and party officials decreased (see table 5–4). Within the association, four standing committees were established to deal with issues of production and sales, log supply, marine transportation, and taxes. TPMEA also organized a committee in preparation for the exploration of overseas forest reserves. In 1969 producers established a transportation and storage company to handle log imports. And finally, many nonmember producers were persuaded to join the association.

These attempts, nevertheless, were short-lived and did not have much impact on the organization of the industry. First, TPMEA's doubled revenue in the 1970s was offset by the 50 percent inflation rate. Net growth rates of revenues during this period were minimal or negative. Second, only twenty out of seventy-five association members participated in the Overseas Forest Reserve Exploration Company established by TPMEA in 1974. Third, the transportation and storage company was poorly managed by an ex-convict. According to one of my respondents, several producers later withdrew from the company in protest. Fourth, there were almost as many nonmember as member producers. And finally, vicious price wars among producers continued (*Economic Daily News* 6/8/71).

After the 1973 oil crisis, the association attempted to reduce its members' production to keep plywood prices above costs. Following the Japanese model of 1955, TPMEA formulated an export contract and in 1974 established an export cooperation committee. Neither the contract nor the committee, however, was effective because both lacked coercive power over participants, and not all association members participated in the reduction scheme; six members refused to sign the agreement, and about sixty to seventy nonmembers were not constrained by the scheme (TPMEA 1975, 26–27). The association established another committee in 1975 to coordinate production and sales. The effort was soon aborted due to lack of support from member producers (TPMEA 1976, 10).

Around this time, the association reduced its activities. The ex-

Table 5–4
Associational Strength of TPMEA

Year	Revenues in N.T. Dollars	Documents Sent N	Export Committees N	Official Meetings[a] N
1962	314,750			
1963	620,932	183		
1964		230	24	28
1965	683,728	227	24	46
1966	661,233	211	24	36
1967	747,398	220	24	40
1968	1,289,110	209	26	62
1969	1,854,430	206	26	62
1970	1,294,258	326	25	25
1971	1,327,643	341	26	
1972	1,065,586	398		31
1973	7,543,898	507		15
1974	3,215,151	403		31
1975	3,597,705		26	18
1976	2,566,240		23	23
1977	2,499,101		19	34
1978	2,806,494	372	18	36
1979	2,393,270	350	10	33
1980	2,122,409	275	6	34
1981	2,371,861	246		40
1982	2,382,273	198	15	22
1983	2,311,676	189	4	19
1984	2,106,822			28
1985	2,108,897	288		26
1986	4,467,597	241		28
1987	4,873,070	202		20

Source: TPMEA (1962–1988).
[a]After 1974, "official meetings" refer to those with government and party officials. Before 1974, these also include association activities.

port committee, which had been meeting once every two weeks, met much less frequently after 1975 (see table 5–4). The association also issued fewer documents to its members and to government agencies.

Two other developments in the 1970s further undermined the cohesion of the industry. In 1976 the government, disregarding the association's wishes, ordered that members' voting rights match their membership fee levels (TPMEA 1974, 17; 1977, 16). Before 1976 members were classified into four levels by their export sales, and membership fees were assessed accordingly. Each member had one and only one vote regardless of membership fee level. Smaller members had as much say in association matters as larger ones. After 1976 smaller members and nonmembers were further alienated from an association they had not been very attached to even at the beginning.

The second development was the expansion of second-stage processing of plywood. During the 1960s most Taiwanese plywood producers imported logs and then processed them into unfinished plywood for export. During the 1970s some producers foresaw a tightening of supply by log-exporting countries and began to expand their second-stage processing of pre-finished, overlaid, fancy, and printed plywood. Smaller and nonmember producers also found the second-stage processing more profitable because the production of processed plywood required less capital and generated higher value-added. Initially, due to a division of labor, the expansion of second-stage processing did not cause bitter conflicts with those who persisted in the first-stage production of unfinished plywood. But when some producers pushed the government to adopt the bonded factory system for second-stage processing, the interests of the first-stage plywood producers were threatened (TPMEA 1979, 20). Second-stage processors shifted to foreign suppliers for unfinished plywood. The conflict culminated in the resignation of the association's director general, who supported second-stage processing.

After the 1979 oil crisis, the Taiwanese plywood industry deteriorated rapidly in terms of total production and exports (see table 5–1). A one-time jump in domestic sales in 1980 flooded the domestic market and resulted in negative or minimal growth rates of domestic sales throughout the 1980s.

Concurrent with the industry's deterioration was the further decline of cooperation among producers. The export committee of the association rarely met; an ineffective export price agreement was abandoned in 1983 (TPMEA 1984, 19); the association distributed even fewer documents to its members and government agencies; the number of meetings with government or party officials decreased in the 1980s (see table 5–4); and the growth rates of association revenues were either minimal or negative during the 1980s. After 1984

TPMEA acquired additional revenues by issuing export licenses for certain plywood products. But the additional revenues came too late; few association activities that needed financing remained.

The association reported that some bonded factories sold the imported plywood to the domestic market instead of engaging in second-stage processing for export (TPMEA 1984, 45). According to one of my respondents, these bonded factories sold the imported plywood to smaller or nonmember processors not qualified for bonded factory status. First-stage and second-stage producers negotiated with each other several times to resolve this conflict, but no concrete results followed (TPMEA 1985, 19). At the same time, the Indonesian plywood industry, via Taiwanese second-state processors, drove out Taiwan's producers of unfinished plywood from both the international market and Taiwan's domestic market. Then it strangled Taiwan's second-stage processors by reducing its exports of unfinished plywood. The disorganized Taiwanese plywood industry in the end yielded to the whims of market forces.

State Cooperation with the Industry

"We couldn't pay much attention to the plywood industry," is how one economic official summarized the state's attitude toward the industry over the past four decades. During the 1950s the state was preoccupied with recovering the mainland. In the 1960s and 1970s its attention was focused on the textile industry. During the 1970s and 1980s the electronics industry became its favorite child. As a result, the plywood industry has been a neglected child, exposed to the whims of market forces with little state protection or assistance. The industry had an institution with a corporatist formal structure but laissez-faire was the reality.

During the 1950s, preventing foreign exchange reserves from depletion was the major economic concern of the government. Import controls were imposed on almost all industrial materials and products, including logs. The real opposition to log imports came from one of the most powerful state bureaucracies at that time—the Bureau of Forestry of the Provincial Government. The bureau monopolized the harvest of Taiwan's forest reserves. National and local representatives as well as the military competed for the limited allocation of logs during the construction boom in the early 1950s. The bureau would not allow imported logs to destroy its power base.[7]

After the purge of corrupt officials from the Forestry Bureau in the late 1950s, the chairman of the Foreign Exchange and Trade Control Commission overruled the bureau's opposition and decontrolled log imports in order to earn foreign exchange (Shen 1972, 28). Taiwanese plywood exports immediately jumped to an annual average of 154 percent growth rate between 1957 and 1961.[8] The unleashing of market forces contributed to the tremendous growth of the industry. No other government aid, such as export assistance, was provided during this period.

Government control over the plywood industry did not disappear immediately, however. First, the decontrol of log imports was replaced by a high tariff rate. Second, the government issued the Guidelines for Assisting Plywood Exporters in May 1962. As discussed in chapter 3, most of the industry assistance acts initiated by the Taiwanese government during the 1950s and early 1960s were passive regulatory orders aimed at restricting entry and expansion. The guidelines were of this genre. Third, the government ordered the establishment of the plywood industry association for the purposes of political control and war preparation.[9]

Once organized, Taiwanese plywood producers began to push the state out of the market with some cooperation from the state. The establishment of TPMEA in accordance with the Exporters Association Law instead of the more regulatory Industrial Association Law was the producers' first attempt to keep the state's visible hand out of the industry. The government wanted the inspection of plywood exports performed by a government agency. Producers requested that the inspection be conducted not by the government or by the association but by individual firms, a routine that had worked well in the 1950s. Moreover, they argued that differences in inspection criteria between the national and local governments would result in confusion and delay in exports. The government agreed and withdrew its plan (TPMEA 1963; *Central Daily News* 11/30/63). Envisaging the rapid growth of the industry in the early 1960s, the government revised the guidelines and decontrolled the industry in 1965. TPMEA was content with this decontrol.

Most of the demands of the plywood industry in the 1960s and 1970s focused on three issues: log tariffs, red tape, and ammonia supply. The fight for reducing log tariffs did not begin until the mid-1960s, when Korea threatened Taiwan's leading position in the American plywood import market. Korean and Japanese log imports were not subject to control or tariffs, whereas Taiwanese producers had to pay a 25 percent tariff (*Economic Daily News* 5/26/67). The government adopted the bonded factory system for the industry in 1970 to reduce the producers' burden. The measure was implemented without prior consultation with TPMEA, which had voiced its opposition in 1966 over the draft's troublesome red tape (Zhou 1973, 104). The government, however, did not take this opposition into consideration. The industry's reaction to the bonded factory system was understandably indifferent or negative. Due to the ineffectiveness of the system, the government finally agreed in 1971 to lower the tariffs on log imports from 25 to 6.5 percent.

Another motive behind the tariff reduction might have been pressure from the United States, which sought compensation for Taiwan's growing trade surplus. Taiwan also imported a small quantity of logs from the United States that were not grown in the tropical countries of Southeast Asia. To the surprise of the Taiwanese tariff authority, tariff revenues on logs increased dramatically after the tariff reduction. An additional reduction in 1973 and the removal of log tariffs in 1976 were also related to both TPMEA's request and American pressure.

The second major demand of the plywood industry was a reduction in red tape in both national and local governments. At the national level, red tape in tax rebate procedures slowed producers' capital turnover. Plywood producers were not very successful in persuading the Ministry of Finance to simplify its regulations. Ironically, several requests were delayed by red tape (TPMEA 1963, 1964, 1967; 1973, 18). In contrast, the Taiwan Cotton Spinners' Association was more successful in reducing bureaucratic routines within the national government, probably because TPMEA members were not as influential politically as those in the textile industry. The highest authority TPMEA representatives could meet with was the minister of economic affairs, not the premier or president, as in the cases of textile and electronics industries. Besides, high-level meetings concerning the plywood industry were rare and occurred only briefly in the early 1970s.

At the local level, TPMEA had some success in reducing red tape, though the process was slow and erratic. Most red tape concerned transportation. Taiwan's port authorities often arbitrarily raised the cost of harbor transportation and imposed stringent regulations on the storage and handling of wood products. New prices and regulations often caught TPMEA by surprise. Some TPMEA counterproposals were accepted, others were bluntly rejected, and still others were approved only after TPMEA appealed to a higher authority in the government. For instance, the city government of Gaoxiong, a harbor city, often raised storage fees and imposed unrealistic regulations on the transportation of logs through its port (TPMEA 1966; 1969). TPMEA's decade-long petition for allowing direct business transactions on the deck had to climb bureaucratic ladders and was finally approved by the Executive Yuan in 1971 (TPMEA 1972, 11).

The third major demand of the plywood industry was a reduction in the price of ammonia, which was a key ingredient in the production of plywood. The only legal supplier of ammonia in Taiwan was the government-owned Taiwan Fertilizer Company, which was known to sell overpriced fertilizers to peasants in order to squeeze capital out of the agricultural sector. Yet at the same time, the company overpriced industrial ammonia in the name of assisting agriculture. Prices of both agricultural and industrial ammonia were much higher than the international market prices.

Since the 1960s TPMEA had been requesting the reduction of ammonia prices (TPMEA 1964, 1968). The best TPMEA got was a slight reduction in price differentials between agricultural and industrial ammonia and between domestic and international ammonia. Plywood producers were still overcharged, especially compared to Korean and Japanese plywood producers. The issue of overpricing became most serious after the first oil crisis. Because of a shortage in ammonia supply, the government suddenly announced that plywood producers should manage their own ammonia imports (TPMEA 1974, 19) and the local supply would be terminated temporarily in early 1974 (*Economic Daily News* 12/18/73). Being extremely dependent upon the Taiwan Fertilizer Company and having no previous contact with foreign suppliers, Taiwanese plywood producers had no choice but to discontinue production. Later, a rationing system was worked out jointly by the association and the government to meet part of the ammonia demand.

After the first oil crisis, the autonomous state remained indifferent to the demands of the plywood industry. Although the state listed it as one of the three major export industries qualified for state assistance, no substantive assistance came. Nor did the industry benefit much from the Executive Yuan's Seven Measures for Assisting the Industry and Business to Solve Current Difficulties in 1975. TPMEA asked for authorization to issue permits for log imports and plywood exports to control production and price, but the government refused (TPMEA 1975, 42; 1976, 16). Several requests for industrial adjustment loans, entry freeze, and reduction of red tape in both national and local governments were similarly rejected by the government (TPMEA 1975, 23–26; 1977, 17, 24; 1978, 23; 1979, 20).

After the second oil crisis, the state's cooperation with the plywood industry remained insignificant and tended to be clientelistic. The state granted the continuation of the bonded factory system for which only a few producers qualified. After listing the plywood industry as a "hardship industry" in 1982, the state agreed to provide emergency loans, reduce the prices of ammonia and electricity, authorize TPMEA to issue export licenses for certain plywood products that only a few companies produced, and delegate to TPMEA the supervision of bonded factories (TPMEA 1982, 26; 1983, 25; 1986, 19–27).

TPMEA formulated a draft of the Plywood Industry Assistance Act in response to the second oil crisis. Most of the key proposals, however, were rejected by the Taiwanese state on the principle of noninterference in the market, while the state was in fact actively promoting the electronics industry (TPMEA 1983, 43–44). The act finally proclaimed by the Bureau of Industry in 1983 was useless to the industry (TPMEA 1984, 18).

The issue of ammonia supply continued to plague the industry after the second oil crisis. In 1982, it was only after TPMEA reported that price differences between agricultural and industrial ammonia had created a black market that the state agreed to bridge the price gap. Plywood producers were also allowed to import ammonia (TPMEA 1981, 15–16). When they did, however, the Bureau of Industry suddenly forbade ammonia imports in 1983 because the Taiwan Fertilizer Company expected a surplus in ammonia production. But Taiwan Fertilizer's projected surplus was miscalculated; ammonia imports were then resumed. The state's erratic policy toward ammonia imports discouraged most plywood producers from buying imports and forced them to continue to pay a higher price for local ammonia (TPMEA 1984, 25; 1987, 24). Thus, instead of serving the agricultural and industrial sectors, the state-owned Taiwan Fertilizer Company in effect enslaved both.

The state's refusal to protect the Taiwanese plywood industry against the Indonesian dumping of plywood led to the destruction of the industry in the 1980s. Contrary to the liberal economic view, Taiwan's plywood industry was most competitive when it was highly protected and became noncompetitive after the protection was removed. Before 1971 the tariff on plywood imports was around 90 percent of the import value; after 1971 the rate was reduced to 50 percent. In terms of effective protection, however, the rate remained around 105 percent. (Yen 1976, 110). In 1974 the nominal rate declined further to 35 percent and in the early 1980s stabilized at 30 percent. When the United States pressed for liberalization, the Ministry of Finance proposed a tariff rate of 15 percent. The association suggested either a 20 percent tariff rate on all plywood imports or a dual system strongly favoring American plywood imports, which were limited in quantity; yet all government agencies rejected TPMEA's proposal.

When the tariff bill was discussed in the Legislative Yuan in 1985, one congresswoman, whose brother was an importer of Indonesian plywood, sneaked in an amendment to reduce the tariff to 7.5 percent. The amendment was passed in the first reading but intercepted by the association in the second. TPMEA publicly denounced the congresswoman and asked the GMD not to nominate her in the next election (TPMEA 1986, Appendix). At the same time, the association filed several antidumping suits against Indonesia and a number of Taiwanese plywood importers. None of these actions worked, unfortunately. The congresswoman was reelected because of her strong cliental base in the local precinct. As a result of her reelection, tariff rates on plywood imports were further reduced. One committee of the Ministry of Finance found evidence of Indonesian dumping and decided to levy antidumping taxes (TPMEA 1987, 13); the decision was overruled by the Executive Yuan (TPMEA 1988, 14).

In retrospect, none of the plywood producers and TPMEA staff members I interviewed could think of any public official who had contributed to the industry. Most producers never took out or even knew about special industry loans. No specialized state agencies were responsible for the welfare of the industry. The Sixth Department of the Bureau of Industry had jurisdiction over the industry, but no special committee or official was in charge of the industry. Occasionally, producers mentioned the Forest Experiment Institute (FEI) whose major function, however, was the preservation of forest reserves, not the development of the plywood industry. Summarizing past state-industry relationships, one senior association official said during my interview, "No one in the economic bureaucracy knows anything about wood. . . . The general attitude of the government toward the industry has been laissez-faire."

Although the autonomous state was not helpful to the plywood industry, its political considerations did not unduly hurt the industry as they did the textile industry. TPMEA, like other associations, contributed to the memorial funds of FETCC chairman Yin Zhongrong and President Jiang Jeishi, to Madame Jiang's call for helping Vietnamese refugees in 1968, and to the Self-Sufficiency Patriotic Fund in 1979. The association was indeed very patriotic. It collected more contributions than its own annual revenues for the Self-Sufficiency Fund at a time when the industry was requesting assistance loans. In fact, TPMEA was the number one contributor to the fund (TPMEA 1979, 21). The association also routinely assisted the GMD in various election campaigns (TPMEA 1973, 18; 1974, 21; 1981, 19; 1984, 15). There was no political purchase of raw materials like that imposed on the Taiwan Cotton Spinners' Association by the government, because log-exporting countries such as the Philippines and Indonesia were not as diplomatically important as the United States.

The Taiwanese state was certainly autonomous, as judged by its ability to ignore the industry's demands. Yet the state's autonomy had little to do with the development of the plywood industry. It was autonomous when the industry began to prosper in the 1950s. It was autonomous when the industry registered a peak in exports in the 1960s and early 1970s. And it remained autonomous when the two oil crises and Indonesia's strategic dumping of plywood devastated Taiwan's plywood industry. In sum, the state did not actively promote or impede the development of the industry; it simply ignored it.

The Philippines's Disarrayed Potential

Organization of the Plywood Industry

In terms of the two development stages of the Philippine plywood industry (before and after 1960), state corporatism was associated with the hypergrowth of the industry in the 1950s, while clientelism existed in the second period, characterized by smaller and negative growth rates and large fluctuations in sales.

The Plywood Manufacturers' Association of the Philippines (PMAP) was organized in January 1952, ten years earlier than the Taiwan Plywood Manufacturers and Exporters Association. PMAP was the sole national industry association and all the major plywood and veneer producers joined it (*Industrial Philippines* 3/60). A Veneer Producers Association of the Philippines existed and had the potential to compete with PMAP for members (*Manila Daily Bulletin* 8/12/60), but it did not last long. None of the wood producers I interviewed even remembered such an association. The Veneer Association posed a threat to Philippine plywood exports because some American importers preferred to purchase the more versatile veneer products rather than the final plywood products.

PMAP was an active, cohesive organization in the 1950s. The founders of PMAP cooperated with one another to improve the competitiveness of the industry in the world market. PMAP conducted seminars on quality control (*Industrial Philippines* 3/60), sent producers abroad to survey modern technology and management (*Manila Daily Bulletin* 7/8/55), and maintained close contact with the Forest Products Research Institute, the International Development Corporation, and other government agencies on matters of industrial development and exports (*Manila Daily Bulletin* 12/10/57). American commercial standards of plywood were adopted by PMAP in 1957 to coordinate plywood exports. It engaged in extensive and successful lobbying efforts to prevent the United States from imposing trade barriers on Philippine plywood (*Manila Daily Bulletin* 2/21/58; 2/24/58; 3/4/58; 3/20/58; 3/24/58).

From mid-1960 to the end of 1961, a recession hit the American housing market. Plywood industries in the Philippines, Taiwan, and South Korea were similarly affected by this reduction of demand. In 1961 Philippine plywood production was reduced by about 20 percent, Taiwan by 17 percent, and Korea by 21 percent.

The divergence in development between Taiwan's and the Philippines's plywood industries began at this time. Taiwanese producers were organized by the state in 1962. TPMEA provided certain coordination and club goods to its members. A mild form of state corporatism emerged in Taiwan's plywood industry. Taiwanese producers were then able to tap the international market and harvest the profits from trade. The Philippine plywood industry, in contrast, moved toward clientelism. Producers withdrew from export markets and targeted the more comfortable domestic market.

Three factors might have caused the institutional transformation from state corporatism to clientelism in the Philippine plywood industry in the 1960s. First, by late 1960, the veneer industry association constituted an organized force that threatened the international competitiveness of Philippine plywood. Unable to incorporate all veneer producers in its organization, PMAP could not develop effective and coherent policies to expand plywood exports (*Commerce* 8/60). Plywood producers consequently lost their interest in PMAP and began to rely on the more familiar domestic market to protect their profits. PMAP tried to implement self-imposed quotas on local sales (*Manila Daily Bulletin* 6/24/60; *Commerce* 8/60), but judging from the growth record of domestic sales in the early 1960s, PMAP's proposal was apparently not followed by producers.

Second, PMAP did not actively enroll new plywood producers, especially those who specialized in plywood and veneer production (in contrast to those larger producers who also had interests in logging).[10] By 1970, PMAP had only twenty-four members, whereas eighteen other producers did not belong to the association (PMAP 1970). These nonmembers might have been nonconcession producers whose sole interest was to see the plywood industry grow rather than to sell logs to their Korean and Taiwanese competitors.

Third, those plywood producers who had forest concessions began to shift their interest to the logging business. The rapid development of the Taiwanese and Korean plywood industries provided both pushing and pulling forces in this transition. On the one hand, Philippine plywood exports encountered increased competition from these two countries. On the other hand, both countries imported logs mainly from the Philippines, thus driving up the total revenue of Philippine log exports. These producers (usually the larger ones) had a greater influence over association affairs than those who engaged solely in plywood production. Therefore, when major producers shifted their attention to the logging business, PMAP's focus changed accordingly. Without changing its name, PMAP was transformed from a plywood producers' association to a loggers' association.

Three anecdotes illuminate this transformation. First, PMAP had espoused a total ban of log exports before 1960 (*Manila Daily Bulletin* 3/7/58; 7/22/60). After 1960 PMAP opposed this ban by claiming that its members' plywood production needed to be financed by log exports (PMAP 1970, 8; *Republic Weekly* 2/12/71). Second, when the Export Tax Law (RA 6125) was discussed in 1970, PMAP did not oppose it because the law imposed export taxes on plywood and veneer but not on logs. In a country where "80 per cent of the log producers . . . are politicians, and of that 80 per cent, only 20 per cent are plywood or veneer producers," PMAP's reaction was hardly surprising (PMAP 1971, 8). And third, almost none of the seminars sponsored by PMAP during this period was directly related to plywood (PMAP 1970, 14).

By moving toward the logging business, the plywood industry introduced clientelism. Fegan (1981) has described how clientelism works in the logging business. The Philippine government issued a limited number of timber licenses to loggers, who then had exclusive rights to exploit forest resources in their concession areas. In return, concessionaires paid taxes to the government for the timber they harvested. The government, however, lacked the personnel to monitor how much timber concessionaires harvested and whether they cut trees outside their concession areas. The monitoring responsibilities were delegated to local authorities who could easily detect or tolerate any violation on the part of concessionaires, as they saw fit. This arrangement gave great leeway to local political leaders to reward their clients and punish their opponents.

These patron-client relationships tended to be self-serving. The instability of local political leadership and hence of the patron-client relationship encouraged the expansion of illegal logging and tax fraud by concessionaires as long as the relationship existed, which in turn made the relationship both more important and unstable. Political opponents and those producers who lost their concession rights tried hard to overthrow the incumbents to grab patronage power.

Under clientelism there was little incentive on the part of concessionaires to engage in more complicated plywood production. Instead, they harvested as many trees as possible and sold them immediately for instant cash. As the Presidential Committee on Wood Industries Development (PCWID) concluded in 1971, "the exploitation of these [forest] resources has largely been characterized by gross inefficiency . . . and the concentration of resources to a privileged few" (PCWID 1971, 2).

When PMAP members became involved in the logging business and clientelist activities, they had little interest and capital left to attend to plywood production. Nor did they devote much energy to association affairs, most of which were insignificant social activities (PMAP 1970, 3–6, 21). Exchange of market information was rare. After 1960 Philippine plywood production did continue to grow, though it did not receive the attention from major producers that its counterparts in Taiwan and Korea received. The growth momentum of Philippine plywood production, therefore, could not match that of the other two countries.

Despite the introduction of some formal corporatist arrangements during the 1970s and early 1980s, the clientelist trend continued in the industry. Since the organization goal of PMAP had gradually shifted to logging, the association shared more of its interests with other wood industry associations composed of loggers. In 1970 the Secretariat of PMAP was merged with that of the Philippine Lumber Producers Association (PLPA), though the associations remained independent of each other (PMAP 1971, 23). These two associations were finally merged into the Philippine Lumber and Plywood Manufacturers Association (PLPMA) in 1972.

During Marcos's rule, the central government encouraged mergers of associations within the same industry so that only one association represented the entire industry. One member of the politically powerful Puyat family, Jose Puyat, Jr., was then president of the Philippine Chamber of Wood Industries (PCWI) as well as director of PLPMA. He proposed a merger of the two associations in order to "rationalize" the associations (PLPMA 1976, 4). The merger was realized in 1979 and a new organization, Philippine Wood Products Association (PWPA), was born. PWPA was intended to be an inclusive, representative, peak association of the entire wood industry.[11] It even had regional chapters to deal with local problems and vice presidents in charge of timber, lumber, and plywood/veneer production (PWPA 1980, 1–3).

These formal corporatist features might have helped timber and lumber producers, but they did not help plywood producers. Neither PLPMA (the first merger of wood associations) nor PWPA (the second merger) was an institutionalized, productive, inclusive, and representative association.[12] Two years after the first merger, some powerful members of PLPMA started holding informal Saturday forums to discuss association affairs, instead of going through the channel of regular association meetings (PLPMA 1974, 9; 1975, 3). PLPMA had no authority to control members' production and prices (PLPMA 1979, 12–13). Except for lobbying for the lifting of log export bans, it did not do anything substantial to improve the welfare of its members. It spent most of its revenues on inconsequential international associations of wood producers. Both PLPMA and PWPA loved to join and sponsor such international events (PLPMA 1976). Finally, PLPMA's enrollment effort was not aggressive. In 1973 there were thirty-one plywood mills and eighteen veneer mills in the country, but PLPMA had only sixteen members that produced plywood and veneer. The enrollment ratio remained the same throughout the 1970s (PDCP 1977, 12; *Philippine Lumberman* 7/80).

Being *the* national association for wood products producers, PWPA generated initial enthusiasm. In 1973 PLPMA had only ninety-two members; two years after the merger in 1979, PWPA had three hundred and seventeen members. But membership dropped by half from 1983 to 1985. Only after the 1986 revolution did membership begin to rise again. In the first half of the 1980s, PWPA reported problems of cooperation among members: "We have experienced difficulty in obtaining information from you and getting your consensus when necessary," the president of PWPA told its members (PWPA 1983, 2). In another PWPA report, the president said that "we still face the continuing problem of keeping our members united and thoroughly satisfied about the role that your association plays in ensuring the survival of the industry" (PWPA 1984, 2).

What caused disunity in PWPA? Clientelism. "Political patronage and cronism," PWPA reported after the 1986 revolution, "wrought havoc on the ideals set by the founders of our predecessor Associations. Moreover, opportunists pervaded our ranks and burdened our drive for a cleaner image" (PWPA 1986, 2). This passage refers to, among others, Lawrence V. Lim of Taggat Industries, which later was sequestered by the Aquino government. Before the sequestering, Lim was PWPA's vice president of marketing.

This series of mergers further reduced the importance of plywood on the associations' agenda. PMAP had already been shifting its emphasis toward logging. When it merged with other loggers' associations (PLPA and PCWI), the relative importance of plywood producers declined accordingly. Among the thirty-eight members of PLPMA in 1973, fewer than half produced plywood or veneer, and only four specialized in these products (PLPMA 1974, 56–58). PLPMA adopted the lifting or relaxation of log export bans as its primary organization goal, which in fact only served to undermine the competitiveness of Philippine plywood exports (PLPMA 1976, 13; 1979, 2). When PLPMA was first established, its committees were organized according to legal functions (finance, marketing, etc.), not products. Vice presidents were later elected to represent producers of different products (plywood included), but there were no committees where they could discuss product development (PLPMA 1978). Three councils (including one on plywood) were established for these vice presidents in 1979, yet these councils had disappeared from PWPA's organization chart by 1980. Another indication of the unimportance of plywood in this merged association is the fact that, among the various research programs sponsored by PWPA, rarely was anything related to plywood (PWPA 1980, 10).

The unimportance of plywood on the agenda of these associations since 1960 provides a partial explanation for the fact that none of them actively pressed the government to remove or reduce the 7 percent tax imposed on logs sold locally. This tax was not a serious cost to Philippine plywood exports until Taiwan and South Korea expanded their plywood exports in the early 1960s (*Manila Daily Bulletin* 9/7/65). Since then, PMAP and PLPMA have paid only limited attention to the issue (*Republic Weekly* 2/12/71; *PDCP Monthly Economic Letter* 9/75). Nowhere in available PWPA official documents is there evidence that the association was concerned about this issue. The 7 percent tax, therefore, still exists.

Finally, neither PMAP, PLPMA, nor PWPA was able to solve the shipping problem that plagued the plywood industry throughout the decades. High freight rates made Philippine plywood exports less competitive than their Taiwanese and Korean competitors (*Manila Daily Bulletin* 3/23/65; 2/2/70). The recommendation that a producers' shipping company be built was never carried out because of the lack of member support. The most cooperative effort among plywood producers was the establishment of the Mindanao Group Port Terminal by five producers to reduce shipping costs only for themselves (*Philippine Lumberman* 3/73). The Philippine Shippers' Council was organized in 1974 by a former president of PMAP, Eduardo Cojuangco (PLPMA 1974, 8). But Cojuangco, the most notorious Marcos crony, was not interested in plywood at all. According to one PWPA official, the council in fact monopolized the Philippine shipping business and imposed extra costs on plywood and lumber exports. In 1978, when the PLPMA president laid out a reasonable plan to establish an association-owned shipping company, few members supported it (PLPMA 1978, 11–12). Since then, no similar proposal has been made.

From Corporatist State to Clientelist State

The state's cooperation with the Philippine plywood industry manifested itself differently before and after 1960. Before 1960 the state worked closely with the industry association to deal with industry-wide problems. After 1960 bureaucrats began to attend to the interests of their business clients and not to the welfare of the entire industry. The authoritarian rule and formal corporatist structure of the 1970s did not change the actual clientelist relationships between individual state officials and their business clients. The development of the Philippine plywood industry, therefore, could never get off the ground, despite its early achievements.

The state was very active in assisting the plywood industry in the 1950s. With the help of a well-organized industry association, state assistance was very effective. The existence of a corporatist state is evidenced in the fact that several government departments and their heads made the development of the plywood industry their priority.[13] The Industrial Development Center (IDC), the Commerce and Industry Department (Manuel Lim), the National Economic Council (Alfredo Montelibano), the Forest Products Research Institute, and even President Garcia and ambassador to the United States Carlos P. Romulo were very responsive to the needs of the industry, as the appearance of their names in various kinds of news and association documents shows (e.g., *Commerce* 2/59; 8/60; *Philippine Industry* 2/11/56; *Industrial Philippines* 3/60; *Manila Daily Bulletin* 7/8/55; 6/14/57; 6/19/57; 12/10/57; 2/24/58; 3/20/58; 5/27/58; 9/23/58).

Among these agencies, the IDC of the National Economic Council was the most active. IDC was co-sponsored by the Philippine Council for U.S. Aid and the U.S. International Cooperation Agency. From 1955 to 1958, it initiated an industry development program in 1955 and evenly distributed $6.5 million in loans to thirteen plywood firms (*Manila Daily Bulletin* 5/27/58; *Commerce* 2/59). IDC sponsored training programs and survey groups that sent producers to the United States (*Philippine Industry* 2/11/56; *Manila Daily Bulletin* 5/27/58) and assisted producers in exportation (*Manila Daily Bulletin* 6/14/57). When a small developmental bottleneck emerged in 1957, IDC immediately contracted with an American plywood consultant, Dawson Zaug, to formulate a long-term development program for the industry. Both production and exports of Philippine plywood picked up steam instantly (IDC 1959).

No such cooperation between the state and the industry association existed after 1960. The 1960 recession in the American housing market provided the initial shock to this cozy relationship. The change of the Philippine administration in 1961 might be another reason for the decline of state cooperation with the industry. But a more plausible explanation is that many plywood producers began to shift their attention to the logging business. Plywood producers could no longer exert consistent and strong pressure on the state for assistance. State officials began to attend to the needs of individual loggers who could provide them financial and political support. Thus, the transformation of state-business relationships from corporatism to clientelism gradually occurred.

During the 1960s the state's cooperation with the plywood industry began to decline, though some of the above-mentioned government agencies maintained contact with producers. The plywood industry was even included as a "basic industry" in the 1961 Tax Exemptions of Basic Industries Act. No other significant policies favoring the plywood industry have been formulated since, however (*Economic Research Journal* 3/71).

Furthermore, the state failed to respond promptly to a number of important demands made by the industry. First, since 1962 the state has never approved the industry's request for removing the 7 percent tax imposed on logs sold locally. The 7 percent tax gave Korean and Taiwanese plywood products an advantage in the international market because Philippine log exports to these countries were not subject to this tax.

Second, the government began to impose troublesome and expensive inspection procedures on plywood in 1964 (PMAP 1968,

Annex E, 1–2). Producers could have benefited from the inspection if it had been properly and expediently implemented.[14] But the government did not have enough qualified personnel to carry out the inspection, and long delays in sales ensued (Mendoza 1968, 43–44). At the request of producers, the inspection problem was finally resolved in 1969 when they regained responsibility for inspections (PMAP 1970, 10).

The third and most important demand of the plywood industry was a ban on log exports. Plywood producers and foreign consultants raised the issue to the government as early as 1955 (*Manila Daily Bulletin* 9/7/55). Since Philippine plywood exports were competitive even against Japanese products, the log ban was not enthusiastically pursued by plywood producers. In the 1960s, when Taiwan and Korea began to join the international plywood market, the ban on log exports to these competitors became crucial for the Philippine plywood industry. The first government order to *curb*, not ban, log exports was issued in May 1966. But the order was so vaguely worded that its implementation was totally ineffective. Furthermore, the balance-of-payments pressure in 1968 resulted in the cancellation of this ineffective order. No other similar attempt to curb log exports was proposed until 1974. The export of logs was so voluminous that local plywood and veneer producers even reported a shortage of logs for production (PMAP 1971, 10–11).

In addition to ignoring these three major demands, the state also failed to respond to plywood producers' requests to reduce red tape, lower taxes on imported materials and machinery, allow tax exemptions for exports, and provide capital and technology assistance (Mendoza 1968, 42–46). This decline in cooperation from the state came at a critical time, when Korean and Taiwanese plywood began to expand its international market share. Lacking state cooperation, the Philippine plywood industry missed the boat to prosperity in the 1960s.

Did Marcos's authoritarian development change the state's attitude toward the industry? No. On the contrary, the impact of clientelism on the plywood industry was even worse than before. Initially, the state seemed to be responsive to the needs of the plywood industry. It cut red tape in the application of tax exemptions, reduced certain taxes on packaging, reorganized the Presidential Committee on Wood Industries Development into a planning agency,[15] and promulgated the Forestry Reform Code to phase out log exports (*Manila Daily Bulletin* 7/26/72; *Philippine Lumberman* 9/73). These policies generated optimism in producers. The president of the Philippine Chamber of Wood Industries praised the declaration of martial law as the beginning of "a period of moral and social reawakening for the Filipino . . . the rebirth of a New Philippines under a New Society imbued with new ideals and values" (*Philippine Lumberman* 1/73). The president of PLPMA predicted that "business can plan more realistically, with reasonable assurance that Government policy will not be changed for the sake of political expediency or to accommodate the whims of political patronage" (*Philippine Lumberman* 3/73).

Yet politics as usual soon returned. The authoritarian state often changed its policies simply for the sake of "political expediency or to accommodate the whims of political patronage." The government imposed heavy export duties on all wood products in 1973 and added a 20 percent premium duty on non-log wood products in 1974, though some of these duties were later reduced (PDCP 1977, 154). The Presidential Committee on Wood Industries Development was established; like many other planning agencies at the time, it was simply an understaffed, underbudgeted, cosmetic agency. A Plywood Export *Control* Committee was created just before the declaration of martial law to ensure that producers did not export more than 90 percent of their products (*Philippine Lumberman* 8/73), but the committee was never heard from again.

The issue of the log ban during Marcos's rule (1965–1986) deserves special attention because of its tremendous impact on Philippine plywood exports. Marcos never had consistent policies on log bans to assist the plywood industry. Executive orders were issued in 1966 and 1967 to gradually reduce log exports, but both were suspended in 1968 and 1969 (PMAP 1971, 11). In response to the alarm produced by the disastrous flood in Central Luzon in summer 1972—and not to the plywood industry's request—the Forestry Reform Code was issued in 1974 to phase out log exports within two years. The reform, however, was suspended one year later because the government allegedly needed foreign exchange. When concessionaires illegally harvested more logs than their export quotas in 1978, Marcos ordered the release of these logs for exportation (PLPMA 1979, 7). A similar relaxation of log bans was implemented in the mid-1980s to cope with foreign exchange crises.

What was the real reason behind Marcos's ambivalent attitude toward log bans? According to an informed source, Marcos and his cronies (such as businessman Eduardo Cojuangco and former defense minister Juan P. Enrile) were either concessionaires themselves or had large investments in concessions. The Marcos family owned L.V.M. Timber, Malayan Integrated Industries, and Intercontinental Wood Processing Development Corporation (Canoy 1981, 142–43). Other cronies controlled logging companies such as Balut Island Sawmill, Liangga Bay Logging, Pamplona Redwood Veneer, Sierra Madre Wood, Southern Plywood, Taggat Industries, Veteran Woodworks, and Western Cagayan Lumber (*Manila Chronicle* 2/1/87).

Not only were these cronies able to resist bans on log exports, they were also successful in bending other government regulations. For instance, the martial law constitution (article 14, section 2) set a maximum of one hundred thousand hectares for each concession holder and limited the quantity of log exports. The National Economic Development Agency (NEDA), however, allowed exemptions for certain producers (PLPMA 1974, 5; 1975, 6). NEDA justified the exemptions on the grounds of scale economy or economic rationalization. Timber licenses were given to "fewer but larger consolidated concessions." The forest agency even waived its requirements for setting up wood-processing mills (PDCP 1977, 5). This selective implementation of the log export ban was not different from the old practice of favoritism that PCWID had criticized (PCWID 1971, 10) and hence aroused bitter resentment from those PLPMA members who had had high hopes for the authoritarian government (PLPMA 1976, 2; *Philippine Lumberman* 1/78).

The authoritarian government also failed to resolve a number of decade-old problems of the plywood industry. The 7 percent tax on logs sold locally was never reduced. After the Laurel-Langley Agreement expired in 1974, the government also failed to reach a trade agreement with the United States that would ensure that Philippine plywood exports would continue to enjoy the preferential tariff treatment that Taiwanese and Korean products enjoyed.[16] And finally, despite incessant meetings with government officials on matters of financial assistance, PLPMA did not receive any concrete cooperation from state-owned banks (PLPMA 1975, 4–6).

Conclusion

This chapter exposed the empirical problems of the developmental state theory. First, the state had little to do with the rise of Taiwan's plywood industry. During the 1950s and 1960s, when the industry registered rapid growth, the state did not formulate any effective industrial policy to assist the industry. The state's capacity, if it even existed, was not a cause for the industry's growth either, since there were few officials familiar with the production of plywood. Second, the impressive performance of the Philippine plywood industry during the 1950s was a result of close cooperation between the industry association and a state that did not fit well the characteristics of the "developmental state." Third, when the state became autonomous from industry demands, the industry began to decline. This was the case for the Philippine plywood industry after the 1960s, especially during the 1970s, and for the Taiwanese industry after the mid-1970s. Finally, the state's commitment to Taiwan's plywood industry was absent during the 1950s and 1960s, when the industry grew rapidly.

An institutional theory provides a better explanation for the performance of Taiwan's and the Philippines's plywood industries. The laissez-faire institution in Taiwan's plywood industry brought the industry to sudden prosperity in the 1960s but also led to its rapid decline in the 1980s. In the Philippine plywood industry, state corporatism created a strong potential in the 1950s. But clientelism replaced state corporatism in the 1960s and obstructed the industry's development. The authoritarian clientelism of the 1970s further suffocated the industry.

In Taiwan, plywood producers did little to combat the brutality of market forces. Before the plywood association was established in 1962, price competition was the only interaction among producers.

The prosperity of the 1950s had convinced producers that further cooperation among themselves or with the state was not necessary. In 1962, when the government ordered the industry to establish its association, producers managed to keep government control weak and association power small. During the 1960s and early 1970s the association was not well managed. It had a small budget and provided few club goods to its members. Worst of all, the association enrolled only about half of Taiwan's plywood producers, hence limiting the association's function of coordinating and providing club goods. After 1973 the association failed to coordinate its members' production as a way of keeping plywood prices above costs. TPMEA activities diminished. Unequal voting rights and conflicts between first-stage and second-stage producers further undermined the cohesion of the industry. In the 1980s, when producers again failed to collectively cope with the second oil crisis and the strategic dumping of Indonesia's corporatist plywood industry, the Taiwanese plywood industry was on the path to total destruction.

The Taiwanese state never paid much attention to the plywood industry. In the 1950s the state contributed nothing to the industry except to the lifting of controls on log imports. The further expansion of the plywood industry was capped by the autonomous state's slow reaction or indifference to the industry's demands for reducing red tape, log tariffs, and ammonia prices. At this time, Korea began to supplant Taiwan's dominance in the American plywood import market through close cooperation between its state and producers. The first oil crisis did not change the Taiwanese state's attitude toward the industry. The second oil crisis alerted the state to some extent, but the state's refusal to adopt the association's assistance proposal, stabilize ammonia supply at an internationally competitive price, and counter Indonesia's strategic dumping of plywood products drove the plywood industry, a neglected child in Taiwan's economic family, into total collapse.

By comparison, the Philippines's plywood industry could have outperformed Taiwan's and that of other Asian neighbors because of its enormous advantages over its international competitors before 1960. It had a head start and performed extremely well in the 1950s, when Japan was the only significant competitor in the international plywood market. The United States gave preferential tariff treatment to Philippine plywood exports due to the Laurel-Langley Agreement. And most important, the Philippines was the major log supplier to the plywood industries in Taiwan, South Korea, and Japan during the 1950s and 1960s. But the replacement of state corporatism in the 1950s with clientelism in the 1960s and 1970s destroyed the industry's potential.

In terms of the organization of the industry, the Plywood Manufacturers' Association of the Philippines (PMAP) was an active and cohesive industry association during the 1950s. It worked closely with government agencies for the welfare of the industry. After 1960 PMAP failed to enroll most plywood and veneer producers. Even worse, PMAP members became more interested in logging than in plywood production. By moving toward the logging business, which has traditionally been a clientelist business, PMAP no longer served as a corporatist entity for the plywood industry. In the 1970s PMAP was further merged with other loggers' associations, thus reducing the importance of plywood in the new associations' agendas. Furthermore, these formal corporatist associations, which were not well organized, either ignored or sacrificed the interests of plywood producers to maintain short-term profits in log exports.

The state's cooperation with the plywood industry shifted dramatically after 1960. State officials were very cooperative with PMAP before 1960, but after 1960 state cooperation declined. Among other burdensome taxes and red tape, the state insisted on imposing the 7 percent tax on logs sold locally, thus giving other international competitors a cost advantage. The state imposed unnecessary inspection procedures, which greatly delayed the sales of plywood. Finally, it refused the request by plywood producers to ban log exports to other international competitors. Marcos's authoritarian rule did not change the state's clientelist relationships with loggers and the state promulgated either inconsistent or ineffective policies toward the plywood industry. Because of the interests of Marcos and his cronies in forest concessions, log bans were never sincerely implemented. In the name of rationalization, Marcos cronies got larger shares of the concession pie without investing extra money in wood processing, as was required by law.

After the 1950s, lacking support from the state and from wood producers themselves, the Philippine plywood industry has never been able to compete with its counterparts in Taiwan, South Korea, and Indonesia, where either the laissez-faire institution or state corporatism contributed to the rapid growth of their plywood industries.

6

THE ELECTRONICS INDUSTRY

Foreign direct investments gave birth to the electronics industries in both Taiwan and the Philippines. While the Philippine electronics industry still suffers from the "enclave economy syndrome" that neo-Marxists have described, Taiwan's electronics industry has been transformed from a MNC-dependent assembly industry to a self-sustaining, continually upgrading locomotive for Taiwan's industrial growth in the 1980s and beyond. Unlike its textile and plywood industries, the Philippines's electronics industry was not a victim of clientelism but was rather an uncontrolled experiment under the laissez-faire institution, which led both to rapid growth and drastic decline. Taiwan's electronics industry has benefited from stable and strong state corporatism, which reaped the rewards while reducing the pains of being integrated into the world economy.

The first section compares the growth records of the two countries' electronics industries. The second section elaborates how state corporatism contributed to the rapid and consistent growth of Tai-

165

wan's electronics industry. The third section discusses the positive and negative impact of the laissez-faire institution on the Philippines's electronics industry. The last section summarizes the chapter.

The Growth Records

In both Taiwan and the Philippines, the electronics industry began as an insignificant, indigenous industry. Then foreign investments came in and totally restructured the industry, creating instant growth and wealth not only for the industry but also for the countries. The growth records of the two countries began to diverge after the initial boom, however. Taiwan's electronics industry was able to sustain its growth with continual adjustment, while the Philippines's industry exhibited wild fluctuations without significant adjustments.

Before the 1960s Taiwan's electronics industry was insignificant in scale and in export values.[1] The industry was primarily a maintenance and repair industry with some rudimentary assembly products such as cable, light bulbs, radios, and transformers.

The rapid growth of Taiwan's electronics industry began in the mid-1960s when foreign direct investments (FDIs) arrived to take advantage of Taiwan's cheap labor, a phenomenon predicted by the product cycle theory.[2] General Instrument led the foreign investment spree after 1964. Other American companies, such as Admiral, Motorola, Philco-Ford, RCA, Texas Instruments, Zenith, and the Dutch company Philips followed suit. Dozens of Japanese companies arrived, mostly in the form of joint ventures (Lin 1971, 174–76). With these new investments, Taiwan's electronic exports expanded rapidly after 1964. By 1969 the value of electronic exports had surpassed imports (TIER 1986, 46). In other words, "neocolonialism" stimulated the growth and expansion of Taiwan's electronics industry. But neocolonialism did not sustain its monopoly in the industry. With the entry of small and medium-sized enterprises owned by the Taiwanese, which contributed the most to the industry's growth (Chen 1985), the ownership structure of the industry soon changed hands. Only one decade later, local entrepreneurs had replaced FDIs as the largest investors in the industry. In 1968 the ratio of domestic capital to FDIs was one to seven (*China Times* 12/19/68); in 1978 the ratio was already three to two (*Gongs Shang Times* 3/30/80). The industry continued its strong growth in the 1970s and 1980s. Small, negative growth rates occurred in only two years (1975 and 1985), while double-digit growth rates were registered in all other years. With this strong and consistent performance, the value of electronic exports exceeded that of textile exports after 1983 and became the country's largest foreign exchange earner.

In terms of major export products, the industry began with electrical fans in 1954. Radios, black-and-white televisions, and their parts were the major export items in the 1960s. As technology and management skills improved during the 1970s, local producers began to export calculators, electronic watches, stereos, and color televisions. The technological advance of Taiwan's electronics industry was symbolized by the fact that original equipment manufacturing (OEM) was a common form of sales arrangement between local producers and foreign buyers.[3] In the 1980s the electronics industry moved further into the production of computer and communication equipment and high-tech home appliances (TIER 1986, 46–47).

Compared to Taiwan, the Philippines was not a late starter in developing its electronics industry. For instance, the local company Radiowealth was established in 1930 to assemble radio sets. Radiowealth began to produce television picture tubes in 1961. Other assemblers of transistor radio sets, televisions, and other consumer electronics for domestic consumption emerged in the mid-1960s (*Chronicle Magazine* 5/18/63). Most of these companies were owned by Filipinos.

A totally new branch of the electronics industry was introduced by the martial law regime—the semiconductor assembly industry. Two types of producers existed within this industry: local contractors and subsidiaries of multinational corporations (MNCs). Neither was closely related to other sectors of the Philippine economy, not even to producers of consumer electronics. Semiconductor producers imported their materials through consignment or parent companies and exported semi-products back to the consignor or parent companies. Local contractors started operating in the early 1970s, while the MNCs arrived after the declaration of martial law in 1972.[4]

The semiconductor industry expanded very rapidly and contributed significantly to the foreign exchange earnings of the Philippines. Before 1970 there was no record of the export of electronic parts and components (*Small Industry Journal* 1974, 9). Ten years later, however, the industry had become the largest foreign exchange earner of the nation, surpassing not only the textile and garment industries but also traditional industries such as coconut and sugar. The remarkable performance of the semiconductor industry is demonstrated by the following statistics: The share of semiconductor exports of the Philippines's total exports was only about 3 percent in 1976. It rose to 13 percent in 1981, 17 percent in 1982, and 16 percent in 1983 (*Central Bank Review* 2/85, 9). In these three years, semiconductors were also the top export product (Salgado 1985, 118). By 1983 the Philippines were alleged to have the largest number of independent semiconductor subcontractors in the world, producing about 10 to 15 percent of the world's supply (*Philippine Development* 11/83). In dollar value, the growth rates of semiconductor exports from 1981 to 1986 were 93 percent, 26 percent, 46 percent, 67 percent, −27 percent, and 8 percent.[5] The bad performance in 1985 and 1986 was due to a worldwide glut in the supply of semiconductors.

Behind this remarkable growth record, nevertheless, there was a great difference in performance between local contractors and subsidiaries of MNCs. Local contractors such as Stanford, Dynetics, and Veterans successfully led the expansion of the Philippine semiconductor industry in the early 1970s (*Business Day* 5/24/74; *Export Bulletin* 3/4/77). In 1980 local contractors exported $69 million in sales of semiconductors, four times what MNC subsidiaries exported. These MNCs immediately expanded their production and new MNCs arrived, resulting in the higher export values and growth rates of 400 percent, 26 percent, 72 percent, 103 percent, −25 percent, and 21 percent from 1981 to 1986. These MNCs' growth records exceeded that of the entire industry. In contrast, local contractors reported much lower growth rates of 10 percent, 26 percent, 17 percent, 10 percent, −33 percent, and −37 percent during the same period. The poor performance of the last two years (1985 and 1986) was associated with the fact that seven of the fifteen local contractors existing in 1984 went bankrupt in 1985 and 1986. Two of the largest local assemblers, Stanford and Dynetics, were on the bankruptcy list.[6] By 1986 the MNCs, none of which left the country in 1985 and 1986, were exporting seven times the value of local contractors' exports. In 1987 foreign subsidiaries were exporting 90 percent of the Philippines's semiconductors (SSC 1987, 1).

This difference in the export performance between MNCs and local contractors resulted in a local industry dominated by the MNCs, which established few forward and backward linkages to the local economy. Most MNCs were located in the Food Terminal Industrial Park close to the Manila International Airport, where they imported materials, parts, and even simple machine tools from their parent companies. Cheap local labor was used to process the materials in dust-free factories. Semi-products were then exported back to their parent companies, usually within a week.

How can this peculiar characteristic of the Philippine electronics industry be explained? What caused its hypergrowth? Why was there such a huge difference in performance between local contractors and MNCs? Why was local capital unable to dominate the industry gradually, as its Taiwanese counterpart did? And why does the Philippine electronics industry remain an "enclave industry"?

The answer seems to lie in the difference in institutions under which the two countries' electronics industries grew up. Because of its state corporatism, Taiwan's electronics industry benefited from and took over the dominance of foreign investments, while the laissez-faire institution allowed the Philippines's electronics industry to blossom and fade.

Taiwanese Corporatism

Organization of the Industry

The Taiwan Electric Appliances Manufacturers' Association (TEAMA) was established in October 1948. Its members included primarily repair and maintenance shops and a few producers of light bulbs, cable, and transformers from Shanghai. When the number of repair and maintenance shops grew, the government found it increasingly difficult to allocate import materials to all TEAMA members.

The government ordered a reorganization of TEAMA and established a separate association for repair and maintenance shops. Only TEAMA producers had access to import allocations (TEAMA 7/52).[7] Not many producers joined TEAMA in its early years. The association had a small staff and budget and provided few services to its members (TEAMA 1988b, 27).

The electronics industry, therefore, was not well organized before the mid-1960s. Until then, larger producers, who typically had political ties to public figures, received favorable treatment from the government in terms of loans, government procurement, and allocation of imported materials. Larger firms assembled heavy machinery and home appliances. Smaller firms, which assembled light bulbs, batteries, or radios, survived on their own capital and local sales networks. Few linkages were found between large and small producers or among all producers.

Small or large, most TEAMA members were Taiwanese. The birthplace of a producer did not create the problems of racial discrimination that it did in the textile industry. Loyalty to the new ruler and inherited wealth were more important factors in differentiating large and small producers.

After the mid-1960s TEAMA assumed an assertive role in organizing the industry. It strengthened its enrollment effort toward both foreign and domestic producers, coordinated and controlled members' production and sales, provided club goods to its members, and rationalized its organizational structure.

FDIS AND MEMBERSHIP POLICY

The Taiwanese electronics industry became organized after the arrival of FDIs in the mid-1960s. Equipped with an overwhelming advantage in capital and advanced technology, these FDIs had the potential to wipe out all local producers, large and small. TEAMA members adopted two strategies by way of response. First, they asked the government to establish that all FDI products be exported so that local producers could survive in the domestic market. Second, and more constructively, they adopted the "if-you-can't-beat-them-join-them" strategy, which included two parts: association incorporation and a local content program.

Association incorporation was TEAMA's effort to invite the FDIs to participate in association activities, though at the beginning it was more coercion than invitation. TEAMA asked the government to demand that all FDIs be TEAMA members as required by the Industry Association Law. Some FDIs tried to waive the requirement by joining an insignificant local association. The government sided with TEAMA and rejected their waiver request (TEAMA 7/67).

After the FDIs joined TEAMA, some were elected to its board of directors. William Scott, general manager of the Philco-Ford Co., was the first foreigner elected to the board of directors of any Taiwan industrial association (*Economic Daily News* 3/23/68). He represented the interests of American members. After he was summoned back by his parent company, the general manager of Admiral Corporation, a Mr. Daniel, was elected to represent FDIs. Two other Americans were also elected to the board of directors (TEAMA 1969). Foreigners maintained between two and four seats on the board of directors and the board of supervisors until the early 1980s, when local producers had levels of capital and technology comparable to those of the FDIS. The last foreign board director left in May 1983, though foreigners continued to be elected as representatives to participate in TEAMA annual meetings.

These foreign directors and supervisors were actively involved in association affairs. Scott contributed a great deal to the linkages between FDIs and local suppliers. Daniel was awarded a plaque by TEAMA for his service to the industry, an award no other TEAMA director or supervisor had ever received (TEAMA 6/76).

TEAMA did not incorporate the FDIs into the association only for social purposes. Local producers wanted to take advantage of their technology, management skills, and sales networks. TEAMA actively promoted the local content program, which established the linkage between local producers and FDIs. On the legal side, it pushed the government to regulate a minimum of 20 percent local content as a precondition for the entry and expansion of FDIs (TEAMA 1968, 26). On the private side, TEAMA conducted meetings between local producers and FDIs to solve problems of supply and demand (*Economic Daily News* 10/15/67; TEAMA 3/68). The response from the FDIs was enthusiastic. They stood to benefit from the local content program because it reduced labor and transportation costs, as long as local supplies met certain quality standards. Therefore, the FDIs began to train local technicians, provide technical know-how and management skills to suppliers, and cooperate with technical schools on internship programs.[8] They set up a timetable that would greatly increase the local content above the 20 percent requirement (*Central Daily News* 2/13/68; *Economic Daily News* 3/23/68; 8/27/68). Speaking on behalf of American members, Admiral's general manager summarized the FDIs' attitude at a TEAMA annual meeting: "We want to help the local electronics industry. . . . We, all foreign companies, will offer you assistance and suggestions, and participate in your production projects anytime you need us" (TEAMA 1969).

TEAMA further strengthened the linkage between local producers and FDIs by organizing and sending several survey groups to FDI factories. The first survey group, composed of representatives from more than fifty local producers, was organized in late 1971. The group visited seven FDIs and joint ventures that were assemblers of electronic products.[9] After the visit, the group held extensive meetings, a record of which was published in TEAMA's journals, along with demand and supply information (TEAMA 12/71). Small and medium-sized producers were the major beneficiaries of this event (TEAMA 1988b, 29). TEAMA later sponsored similar but smaller survey groups during the 1970s and 1980s (TEAMA 1/73; 3/77; 7/81).

Several production satellite systems, which connected local producers and FDIs as well as small producers and larger assemblers, emerged as a consequence of the this effort. One TEAMA director general described the essence of the program at the 1969 annual meeting:

The Western-style merger is an ideal way for the future development [of the industry]. The more appropriate and practical method in our environment, however, is to replace vertical integration with division of labor. . . . That is, larger enterprises engage in assembly, overall research, market survey, and advertisement, but avoid producing parts. Smaller enterprises produce parts and engage in specialized research, but avoid assembling final products. (TEAMA 1969, 4)

TEAMA did not target only the FDIs in its enrollment effort. It actively went after nonmember producers and prevented the loss of existing members. TEAMA systematically examined files from the Ministry of Economic Affairs, the provincial government, and private research institutions to locate new producers and nonmembers. It then sent letters, cordially asking them to join the association, with a reminder that their participation was required by law. If the letters went unanswered or the receiver refused to join, TEAMA would send a second notice, a copy of which was delivered to responsible government authorities in preparation for future legal actions (TEAMA 5/72; 1/76; 4/77; 1/80). Except for underground factories, an overwhelming majority of the newcomers were enrolled by the association. TEAMA never requested a restriction of entry; it only insisted that all new entrants join the association. This enrollment effort has been a regular and important activity of the association since the early 1970s. The association tried to put more pressure on nonmembers by other means, such as charging higher fees for issuing export licenses or refusing outright to issue such licenses. But these proposals were rejected by the government on constitutional grounds (TEAMA 3/80; 9/85).

TEAMA's enrollment effort also covered underground factories. TEAMA routinely provided the government with a list of underground factories that refused to join the association. The government would then order these factories closed (TEAMA 7/68; 4/77). This stick was used along with carrots by TEAMA to increase its membership. In addition to the various club goods discussed below, the association applied to the Provincial Police Headquarters for new producer licenses. The police headquarters, which had jurisdiction over most electronic products for national security reasons, ordered that these new licenses be issued to TEAMA members only. More than two-thirds of TEAMA members had such licenses in 1983.

The TEAMA enrollment program also aimed at preventing the

loss of existing members that attempted to establish their own associations. This part of the program was much more difficult to achieve, because TEAMA covered more products than any other industrial association while trying to keep all producers in one association. With the state's assistance, TEAMA was quite successful in controlling the proliferation of competing industrial associations. Producers of decorative light bulbs, for instance, requested withdrawal from TEAMA in 1953 and 1967 to organize their own association; the government was in accord with TEAMA's objection (TEAMA 7/67). These producers eventually established an exporters' association but were also required to stay in TEAMA (TEAMA 12/72). Some computer manufacturers organized an association in an industrial park and requested withdrawal from TEAMA, but the government denied their request (TEAMA 9/83). Although the government did not forbid the establishment of smaller, regional associations, it required that their members stay in TEAMA if they produced the same products as TEAMA members.

The only exception was the Taiwan Electric Appliances Manufacturers' Association of the Export Processing Zone (TEAMA-EPZ), which was established in 1971. Since export processing zones were subject to very different legal restrictions, the government allowed each industry to have a separate association. Nevertheless, representatives of TEAMA-EPZ and TEAMA regularly attended each other's annual meetings to discuss matters of mutual interest.

COORDINATION AND CONTROL

Since the late 1960s TEAMA has been consciously and actively promoting the technology and quality of its members' products. This association goal emerged as soon as the linkage between FDIs and local suppliers was established. The FDIs were willing to increase their local content, but local suppliers were embarrassed to discover that their products fell far below the FDIs' minimum expectations. TEAMA criticized the quality and reliability of its own members' products and was eager to improve the situation (TEAMA 1968, 26). In addition to technological cooperation with the FDIs, TEAMA asked for government assistance to establish an inspection agency exclusively for the electronics industry and to establish quality control systems in factories (TEAMA 1971, 4, 13). The United Industry Research Institute was consequently established and TEAMA members visited the institute to learn inspection procedures (TEAMA 3/72). Another inspection institute for heavy electrical machinery was established jointly by producers and the government in 1979. When electronic exports to the United States expanded immensely in the mid-1970s, TEAMA and the government declared that exports to the United States had to acquire the recognition seal of the U.S. Underwriters Laboratories (UL) as a proof of quality (TEAMA 7/77).

TEAMA provided quality control seminars to members classified by the government as low-quality factories (TEAMA 1/80). Numerous seminars on technology and management were held annually (TEAMA 1988b, 19–20). There were also small-scale quality control efforts by producers of specific products. For example, producers of electrical distributors signed a quality control agreement, with the state as arbitrator, to protect their reputation in the international market (TEAMA 11/85). TEAMA also engaged in the war against piracy of patents, which affected not only foreign companies but also large domestic producers (TEAMA 7/81; 1983, 20; 1984, 74).

To improve their technology and management, TEAMA members organized regular and irregular survey groups to visit the FDIs and foreign countries to explore investment opportunities and to keep Taiwanese producers on their toes.[10] These groups visited advanced countries such as the United States, Japan, West Germany and other European countries, as well as developing countries such as South Korea, Southeast Asian countries, and South Africa. TEAMA formed twenty-five survey groups between 1982 and 1988. To complement these groups, TEAMA sometimes sent technicians of member firms abroad for advanced training (TEAMA 1/83; 1969, 14, 20; 1988b, 18).

The association's concern for quality was also reflected in its attitude toward tariff policies. TEAMA rarely asked for an increase in tariff protection for their products, except at times of severe recession or foreign dumping, and it did not oppose the reduction in tariffs on competitive products. It did insist, however, that tariff differentials among products, parts, and materials be kept reasonable so that

Taiwanese products could compete on a fair basis. That is, the association asked the government to lower the tariffs on materials if the tariffs on parts were to be reduced, and to lower the tariffs on parts if the government intended to cut tariffs on products.

This "reasonable differential" attitude, which exposed local producers to constant but fair competition, was welcomed by the state, which was under foreign pressure to liberalize. As a result, the state approved most of TEAMA's annual proposals for tariff revisions (TEAMA 1971, 9; 2/74; 4/79; 9/87). Occasionally when conflicts arose between parts and products manufacturers, TEAMA would mediate between both groups of manufacturers before submitting its tariff proposals (TEAMA 8/77).

The "reasonable differential" represents a middle ground between free trade and protectionism. Tariff reduction on final products without proportional tariff reduction on parts and materials puts local producers at a disadvantage. Too much protection on final products, however, encourages producers' inertia and monopoly at the expense of consumers. Reasonable tariff differentials protect local producers while keeping them on their toes. Under this system, a more direct link between liberalization and growth might be observed than under a total free trade system, which sometimes destroys infant industries.

TEAMA actively coordinated its members' production and sales. Most of its coordination activities involved price agreements on, for instance, calculators, televisions, refrigerators, air conditioners, telephones, computers, and motorcycle batteries (TEAMA 1969, 13; 2/73; 9/73; 7/83; 1983, 20; 8/85). Some coordination efforts were aimed at restricting the abuse of sales pitches, such as gifts and advertisements attacking other companies (TEAMA 3/72; 2/75; 7/81).

In response to the second oil crisis, TEAMA was authorized by the government to issue export licenses and originality certificates to control export quantity and quality. It issued export licenses for televisions, stereos, lamps, telephones, and microcomputers. Unlike the textile industry, the allocation of export quotas has never been a hot issue in the electronics industry (TEAMA 4/79; 1/80; 8/80; 9/83; 10/84; 4/86).

On the import side, the association coordinated upstream and downstream producers to share unexpected costs due to currency appreciation (TEAMA 4/73). It controlled the quantity of certain imported parts (e.g., television parts) if local parts suppliers could not meet domestic demand (TEAMA 1983, 16; 1984, 10–19). TEAMA also helped producers purchase materials collectively to cut costs (TEAMA 9/73).

CLUB GOODS

The association has supplied several kinds of club goods to its members. First, since 1967 TEAMA has sponsored electronics shows in which only its members and selected foreign producers (after 1980) could participate.[11] Foreign buyers came to place orders and look for reliable suppliers. A substantial number of foreign buyers, especially large ones, came to Asia only once a year, just to visit electronics shows. The timing of Taiwan's electronics show, therefore, catered to these buyers and was held immediately after Japan's electronics show.

TEAMA closely monitored the government's procurement programs and insisted that local products be given priority. Among the major programs were the Ten Major Constructions of the 1970s, the Taiwan Electricity Company's annual procurement, and the construction of the Taibei subway system (TEAMA 1/79; 1/86). After receiving the government's shopping lists, TEAMA would notify qualified members to make a bid.

As the sole representative of the industry, the association was able to negotiate collective arrangements with other industrial associations, social groups, and foreign countries on matters of mutual interest. For instance, when the shortage of aluminum threatened the recovery of the electronics industry in 1976, TEAMA negotiated with domestic and foreign producers of aluminum to stabilize the supply and price (Chen 1976, 255). It also cooperated with toy producers to develop electronic toys, the success of which later threatened Hong Kong's reputation as the "kingdom of electronic toys" (TEAMA 3/77). Moreover, TEAMA collaborated with technology schools on internship programs, with research institutions on technology transfer, and with retailers on patent rights protection (TEAMA 2/74; 4/75; 6/76; 6/87).

After Taiwan withdrew from the United Nations in 1971 and was subsequently de-recognized by most countries, Taiwan's business associations often became the only viable legal entity in international negotiations. TEAMA took up such a role during the 1970s. In addition to dealing with the United States and Great Britain, where most Taiwanese electronic exports went, it also negotiated with the German company Telefunken to acquire its PAL patent right in order to enter the European television market (TEAMA 4/85).

Finally, TEAMA provided various legal, business, and technical services to its members. For example, in addition to issuing new members' production permits, it held regular and irregular seminars on tax rebates, finance and management for small- and medium-sized enterprises, bonded factory laws, government inspection procedures, and tax laws (TEAMA 1988b, 4–6; 4/73; 4/83; 10/84). In 1972 TEAMA established a well-equipped library that stored the product standards of Taiwan and other nations, trade and technology information, government regulations, and members' production data. The association spent about one-sixth of its annual revenue on research-related activities. It provided a free service to foreign buyers who were looking for appropriate suppliers and a free multilingual translation service to its members (TEAMA 1/85).

ASSOCIATION REVENUE AND STRUCTURE

These activities would not have been as effective if TEAMA had not been supported by large revenues and a solid organization structure. TEAMA revenues were different from those of the Taiwan Cotton Spinners' Association (TCSA) in four respects (see table 6–1). First, TEAMA revenues increased faster than TCSA revenues in the 1970s and 1980s and surpassed them after 1981. Second, growth rates of TEAMA revenues were always positive except in 1982, while TCSA had negative growth rates in 1981, 1983, and 1986. Third, large members paid proportionally more than small members in TEAMA. In TEAMA, first-level (largest) members paid more than seven times the membership fee of seventh-level (smallest) members,[12] whereas

Table 6–1
Revenues of TEAMA and TCSA
(In N.T. Dollars)

Year	TEAMA	TCSA
1966		1,112,782
1967		
1968	812,501	
1969	997,100	
1970	1,707,655	
1971	1,560,828	
1972	1,500,017	
1973	2,170,063	4,791,646
1974	2,572,952	4,890,045
1975	3,776,671	6,833,593
1976	4,523,952	7,581,465
1977	5,929,676	8,189,382
1978	6,874,514	
1979	8,585,777	9,137,725
1980	13,848,134	17,045,276
1981	19,159,998	16,984,475
1982	18,928,906	18,112,215
1983	23,522,857	17,062,986
1984	37,944,175	17,749,496
1985	39,089,174	19,283,736
1986	48,678,863	16,859,553
1987	55,826,255	

Source: TEAMA (1952–1988).

in TCSA the ratio was less than four to one. Finally, TEAMA membership fee in absolute terms was much smaller than that of TCSA. Small TEAMA members paid either N.T. $150 or N.T. $300, compared to the N.T. $1,800 and N.T. $2,700 in fees paid by their counterparts in TCSA (TCSA 1985, 60–61; TEAMA 5/81).

These differences had a number of beneficial effects on TEAMA and on the cohesion of the industry. A large and stable revenue facilitated TEAMA's operation. A lower membership fee for smaller producers encouraged their attachment to the association. Although there were seven levels of voting rights, as in the case of the plywood and textile associations, smaller members in TEAMA paid lower fees in both proportional and absolute terms. Furthermore, while the other two associations expanded their voting right differentials over the years, TEAMA started with its seven levels and continued to maintain them after 1967 (TEAMA 5/81). Smaller firms did not develop a sense of relative deprivation.

In case some members took a free ride by not submitting a membership fee, TEAMA would systematically put pressure on them by issuing reminders and warnings. If these were ignored, association privileges would be suspended. Since the membership fee was relatively low, most members complied with the association rule after receiving reminders or warnings; for example, 93 percent of TEAMA members paid their membership fees in 1982 (TEAMA 1983, 26). Those producers deprived of their association privileges had usually gone bankrupt.

In 1973 TEAMA began to accept associate members, most of whom were traders of electronic products. They paid a fee equivalent to the membership fee of a medium-level member. They enjoyed all association privileges except voting rights (TEAMA 6/73; 9/76).

Due to the increase in membership and the diversification of the industry, TEAMA's organization structure improved and became differentiated over time. In 1969 TEAMA established seven standing committees to cover the major categories of the industry: electronics, home appliances, heavy electrical machinery, electrical wire and cable, lighting, batteries, and electrical accessories. Under these seven committees were sixteen product-committees, for example, radios, electronic parts, and refrigerators (TEAMA 1969, 5). Smaller problems were resolved in these committee meetings. Larger problems, such as upstream and downstream conflicts or collective negotiations with the government, were mediated by directors general and general secretaries.

TEAMA took these standing committees seriously. One year after they were established, the annual association meeting required that these committees meet at least once every three months (TEAMA 1971, 19). Later on, while additional subcommittees were established to deal with new products, those that did not meet regularly were merged with other subcommittees. The whole committee system was revamped again in 1983 to adapt to the development of the industry. Computer, telecommunication, semiconductor, and stereo standing committees were established to replace those of wire and cable, lighting, batteries, and the old electronics committee. A total of fifty-nine subcommittees were organized under these standing committees (TEAMA 1988b, 15–17).

TEAMA established divisional offices to strengthen its local function (TEAMA 6/75). Since its headquarters was located in northern Taiwan, it placed one divisional office in central Taiwan and the other in southern Taiwan. In addition to the regular functions of the association, these local offices focused on the investigation of underground factories and the election of representatives to TEAMA's annual meetings. These offices were delegated even more power in the 1983 reorganization (TEAMA 7/83).

TEAMA had another power that other associations rarely had. Because of its large membership, it was the most important member of the National Industries Association and the largest voting bloc in the category of industry representatives of national legislative elections.[13] TEAMA garnered about one-tenth of the total votes of the industry group. In 1983 it sent one of its members to the Legislative Yuan.

The association was so well organized and effective that the Ministry of Interior Affairs always ranked it as the best performing association. The Ministry of Interior Affairs and the National Industries Association organized a number of survey groups composed of administrators from other associations to learn from TEAMA's operation (TEAMA 7/84; 11/85).

In sum, the organization of Taiwan's electronics industry has been consistently strong and cohesive due to its enrollment policy, quality control, coordination of members' production and sales, supply of club goods, large revenues, and differentiated organization structure. These factors contributed to the consistent and rapid growth of the industry.

The Cooperative State

The development of the electronics industry had not been a major concern among Taiwan's economic officials before FDIs arrived in the mid-1960s. Although it began to protect local production of radios in February 1963 in order to replace imports, the government did not have a development strategy for the industry. The institutional relationship between the state and the industry was similar to that of the plywood industry and other unimportant industries: that is, it was a laissez-faire institution.

The government embarked on the promotion of the electronics industry by offering investment incentives to FDIs. Officials in the Ministry of Economic Affairs and the Council on International Economic Cooperation and Development (CIECD) were credited by these FDIs for their active assistance in legal and financial matters (*Xinshen News* 6/16/66; 10/16/66). At the industry's initial stage (between 1964 and 1967), it was an archetypal case of state-FDI collaboration without local capital. The development of the industry was synonymous with the development of the FDIs. The industry could have degenerated into an enclave industry, as described by the neo-Marxists, had the state chosen not to respond to the demands of local producers.

Threatened by the FDIs, local producers immediately asked for government assistance. The government first responded by convening large-scale consultation meetings with producers, then cooperated with producers in formulating development plans, reducing red tape, providing reasonable protection, improving technology and quality, and strengthening TEAMA's authority. Only after intimate cooperation between the state and TEAMA had began did a significant class of indigenous industrialists emerge and expand. The following section explains these cooperation efforts.

INITIAL CONSULTATION MEETINGS

The first extensive consultation meeting on the development of the local electronics industry was held by CIECD in November 1967. TEAMA sent representatives to the meeting to formulate future development policies. The theme of the meeting was how to overhaul decade-old legal regulations on tax rebate, excessive control, and tariffs, that is, how to reduce state intervention in the market (*Central Daily News* 11/30/67).

To institutionalize producers' participation in the decision-making process, CIECD established the Committee on Electronics Industry two months after the meeting. The committee was composed of economic bureaucrats, scholars, and TEAMA's director general (*Economic Daily News* 1/13/68). It coordinated frequent meetings of economic bureaucrats and producers. For instance, CIECD held four large meetings with TEAMA members between September 1969 and September 1970. The last of these meetings was presided over by Jiang Jingguo, who was then also CIECD chairman and vice premier. TEAMA made eight major proposals concerning tariffs, tax rebates, bonded factories, red tape, and financial support; most of them were adopted immediately (TEAMA 1971, 4, 13–15).

DEVELOPMENT PLANS

Taiwan's Four-Year Plans routinely discussed the development of the electronics industry. As mentioned before, these plans served few practical purposes. Despite the fact that the fifth Four-Year Plan (1969–1972) emphasized the development of the industry, the government did not have a coherent development strategy. Before 1975 the government's assistance measures were ad hoc responses to TEAMA's demands.

Producers had requested that the state formulate a long-term, concrete development plan for the industry, like Korea's in the late 1960s (*Economic Daily News* 4/13/69). A Ten-Year Plan was formulated by the Ministry of Economic Affairs (MOE) in 1972, but was short on details (*Xinshen News* 12/31/72). The 1973 oil crisis forced the Taiwanese government to respond. In 1975 Minister of Economic Affairs Sun Yunxuan invited economic and financial officials and TEAMA representatives to revise the impractical Developmental Plan and Assistance Measures for the Electric Appliance Industry. After the new plan was implemented, Sun and TEAMA closely monitored its monthly progress (TEAMA 7/75; 3/77). This was the only development plan concerning the electronics industry that was consistently promulgated, and it worked.

In 1980 the Council for Economic Planning and Development (CEPD), the successor of the CIECD, issued another Ten-Year Development Plan for the Electronics Industry, which had in essence been manufactured in CEPD's ivory tower without the kind of concrete, practical details that marked the MOE's first Ten-Year Plan (*Gongs Shang Times* 4/5/80). Producers knew little about it beforehand and paid little attention to it afterwards; therefore, this plan died in anonymity.

The semiofficial Information Industry Institute cooperated with the Arthur D. Little Company in 1985 to formulate an industry development plan. Since the method of formulation was not disclosed, producers had little confidence in the analytical results and hence did not take the plan seriously (TEAMA 4/86).

In retrospect, the government contributed to the industry more through the measures discussed below than through development plans.[14] Among these development plans, the only plan that was effectively implemented was the one producers had consulted on beforehand.

TRADE PROTECTION

Because of its late development, Taiwan's electronics industry emerged in an environment in which protectionism began to yield to the liberalization pressure from abroad. In the 1960s, when the industry first emerged, the government maintained the protectionist legacy of the 1950s. Joint ventures were allowed to expand only if their products were exported (*Central Daily News* 6/17/63). After Taiwan's trade surplus surfaced in 1971, foreign pressure to liberalize its trade controls proved unbearable. In 1973 the Taiwanese government allowed the importation of more than two thousand items. In March 1974 it further removed the restriction on import origins; that is, it no longer discriminated against Japanese goods. The timing could not have been worse because, first, the Taiwanese electronics industry had just taken its first steps away from infancy. Second, Japan intended to dump its electronic products on other Asian countries due to American protectionism against Japanese electronic imports. And third, the prices of imported materials doubled after the oil crisis.

TEAMA's lobbying strategy focused on "reasonable tariff differentials" among products, parts, and materials so that local products had a fair chance to compete. This strategy was more acceptable to the government than an across-the-board protection measure, which would certainly invite retaliation from Taiwan's trading partners. The government made ad hoc adjustments of tariffs in 1969 in response to TEAMA's proposal and again in 1971 (TEAMA 2/69; 9/71). The major adjustment that had a far-reaching impact on the industry was made in 1974, after the restriction on import origins was removed. It took the meeting of TEAMA's director general and Premier Jiang to overcome the resistance of the Ministry of Finance (TEAMA 2/74; 7/74; 1988b, 29). The "reasonable differential" has since become the principle of TEAMA's annual proposals of tariff revision, which the government has routinely followed (e.g., TEAMA 3/81; 1982, 21; 1984, 16; 4/84; 4/86).

To protect local products from unfair competition, the government did respond to TEAMA's requests for trade barriers. Under the legislative delegation, the administration could temporarily adjust tariffs within a 50-percent range for one year without legislative approval. The government, however, used this power judiciously for fear of trade retaliation. According to available records, it did so only once: in 1975 tariffs on televisions, radios, refrigerators, air conditioners, and stereos were raised temporarily to cope with Japanese dumping.

TECHNOLOGICAL ASSISTANCE

The Taiwanese government shared with producers the concern for technological improvement and quality control. In response to a request from TEAMA, the government expanded the facilities of the MOE Xingzu United Industries Institute in order to inspect local electronic products (TEAMA 1969, 9). In 1973 this institute was merged with the Mining Industry Institute and reorganized into a semiofficial entity, the Industrial Technology and Research Institute. Over the years, the institute cooperated with TEAMA to provide quality control lessons and transfer modern technology (e.g., integrated circuits and robots) to producers (TEAMA 1/80; 1/83; 6/87; 1988b, 215). To reinforce the connection between the institute and TEAMA, an Electronics Research Center was established within the institute in 1974. The chief of the center was elected to TEAMA's board of directors and chaired the standing committee on computers (TEAMA 10/81). For heavy electrical machinery, in 1979 the government and producers invested together in an inspection and research institute—the Taiwan High Power Research and Inspection Center. Finally, the Information Industry Institute was established in 1979 to develop large- investment, slow-return electronic products (*Economic Daily News* 7/23/79).

In addition to these domestic sources of technology, the government sponsored TEAMA survey groups to FDIs and foreign countries (TEAMA 7/81; 1/83). The MOE also hired foreign consultants to assist producers with quality control (TEAMA 6/73; 3/76).

Have the government and producers always agreed on the issue of technological improvement? Not necessarily. Sometimes, the government outraced the industry's production capabilities; at other times, it fell behind. The Ministry of Finance insisted on strict standards in deducting research expenses from company taxes, while the Ministry of Economic Affairs was more lenient. Unfortunately, the Ministry of Finance was always the winner, which posed an obstacle to technological improvement (TEAMA 10/84).

Sometimes a few reckless officials jumped the gun by publishing quality standards to which most producers had little time or no capability to adapt. For example, in 1977 the Bureau of International Trade suddenly ordered that electrical exports to the United States should acquire the UL recognition prior to exportation. Many American importers at that time, however, did not ask for the UL seal. A compromise was struck between the bureau and TEAMA to extend the transition period for those companies that were not required by their American buyers to get the seal (TEAMA 7/77).

A more serious demonstration of ignorance by the government that almost destroyed a part of the industry concerned the standards on telephone exports. In 1983, without prior consultation with producers, the Bureau of National Standards and Inspection of the MOE published a set of standards on telephone exports in accordance with U.S. FCC specifications. Most producers did not have the equipment to test their products according to these standards and their parts suppliers could not adapt to the requirements either. Furthermore, none of their buyers requested such standards. The bureau was nevertheless adamant about these criteria, which threatened the very survival of telephone producers. Finally, it took Director General Jiang's personal intercession to postpone the implementation of these standards (TEAMA 7/84). Jiang later explained to producers that these standards were prematurely published by some officials who "were too eager to show off in front of their superior."

TAX AND RED TAPE REDUCTION

Burdensome taxes and excessive red tape were the major issues raised in the first two large-scale meetings between producers and officials in the late 1960s. Based on TEAMA's proposals, the Taiwanese government revamped its tax and administrative systems between 1967 and 1970 (TEAMA 1969, 9–12). TEAMA continued to push for the reduction of legal barriers in areas of bonded factory systems, tax rebate procedures, vocational training taxes, commodity taxes, issuance of export licenses, government inspection procedures, extension of customs hours, regulations on radio frequencies, property taxes, export deposits, and administrative fees (TEAMA 1971, 13; 7/71; 1/73; 8/73; 7/75; 3/76; 9/76; 9/79; 7/80; 1982, 26–27; 1/83; 4/83; 1984, 11, 16).

One major example of red tape that TEAMA was less successful in removing was the regulation that all computer accessories had to remain at customs for at least twenty-four hours before being exported. The regulation, enforced for security reasons by the Provincial Police Headquarters, caused significant delay in the sales of these time-sensitive products. Producers complained that in other developing countries where computer accessories exports were high, such as Korea, the Philippines, and Malaysia, no such regulation existed and no security problems ever occurred. Police headquarters responded that the reason security problems did not occur in Taiwan was that the regulation had worked, and besides, "how much could a one-day delay hurt business?" After TEAMA tried several times to convince police headquarters, a compromise was reached for certain computer accessories whose export required only the approval of company security personnel rather than headquarters. Additional requests to rescind the regulation were rejected (TEAMA 7/83; 11/86; 10/87; 1988, 31).

It also took TEAMA more than ten years to convince the government to provide tax incentives for the satellite system. The concept of satellite system was first formally raised in 1969 by Director General Chen. He proposed the system as a substitute for a merger as a way of economizing production. Many such systems were formed by private efforts. These systems, however, cost participating companies more taxes than integrated production. When the government adopted value-added taxes in the mid-1970s, these systems were further disadvantaged in relation to imports. Through various TEAMA lobbying efforts, the government formulated the Central Satellite Factory System in early 1983. Factories included in these systems enjoyed a tax reduction. Fourteen such systems, comprising more than two hundred firms, have been formalized since that time (TEAMA 1969, 4; 6/74; 7/80; 1988b, 210).

STRENGTHENING TEAMA'S AUTHORITY

The Taiwanese government strengthened TEAMA's influence over its members in three areas: membership policy, trade control, and government procurement.

In terms of membership policy, the government cooperated with TEAMA to keep existing members from leaving and to enroll potential members. TEAMA received support from the government to keep the producers of computers and decorative light bulbs in the association (TEAMA 12/72; 9/83). The government supported TEAMA's requests to enroll FDIs and underground factories (TEAMA 1967; 4/77). It also strengthened TEAMA's enrollment effort by giving it the authority to apply for business permits on behalf of new members (TEAMA 7/71).

The extent of the government's cooperation in enrolling underground factories, however, was limited by its resources. The abovementioned measures adopted by the central government cost little to implement. But to put direct and constant pressure on underground factories required the active involvement of local governments and police forces that were traditionally bound by local cliental interests. Both the central government and TEAMA acknowledged these limits of enrollment efforts at the local level (TEAMA 1971, 27; 1982, 6).

In the area of trade control, the Taiwanese government delegated to TEAMA the power to issue export licenses and to control imports of certain products. It authorized TEAMA to control the imports of certain television parts and stereo components (TEAMA 1983, 16; 1984, 18–19). TEAMA issued export licenses for televisions, stereos, telephones, microcomputers, lamps, and for electronic exports to Saudi Arabia (TEAMA 1/80; 9/83; 10/84; 4/86). Not all industrial or exporters' associations received the government delegation to issue export licenses, however. For example, the plywood association never got the delegation despite its repeated requests. Therefore, this trade control power strengthened TEAMA's influence over its members.[15]

Finally, the Taiwanese government responded to TEAMA's demands that government procurement should give priority to local products. Shopping lists of major procurement programs were sent to TEAMA first; then TEAMA informed qualified members (TEAMA 4/74; 3/81; 1984, 10; 6/87). Nonmembers could not receive the information except through cliental ties with government officials.

PUBLIC OFFICIALS

Unlike the textile and plywood industries, the Taiwanese electronics industry was blessed with high-level officials who were not only responsive to the industry's demands but also actively promoted its development.

Jiang Jinggou, upon taking over CIECD in 1970, let local producers join the FDI-led expansion, and revamped regulations on the industry. The director general of TEAMA and Premier Jiang agreed to the 1974 tariff revamp, which had a far-reaching impact on the industry, in a meeting intended to overcome the conservatism of the Finance Ministry.

Having been minister of economic affairs, Premier Sun Yunxuan was the chief guardian of the electronics industry. Sun had served in the Taiwan Electricity Company before becoming minister of economic affairs in 1969, and he paid special attention to the industry because of his academic and professional background in electrical engineering. After consulting with producers, the ministry reformulated the Development Plan and Assistance Measures for the Electric Appliance Industry in 1975. Sun ordered the Bureau of Industry, together with TEAMA, to monitor the monthly progress of the plan. Sometimes he presided over the monitoring meetings (TEAMA 7/75; 3/77). To maintain contact with producers, he attended TEAMA's annual meetings and received TEAMA representatives to discuss the latest problems of the industry. His swift response to TEAMA's twenty-five proposals after the 1973 oil crisis minimized damage to the industry (TEAMA 10/75).

Sun founded the Industrial Technology and Research Institute, modeled after the Korean Institute of Science and Technology. Sun's institute has been praised by producers for its technological services and technology transfer to the industry. When he was minister of economic affairs, Sun visited the Korean institute and was concerned that Taiwan's electronics industry would soon lag behind Korea's if a similar institute were not established in Taiwan. He proposed the use of government funding to establish the independent, semiofficial institute but met severe opposition from the legislature. Sun personally lobbied for the bill, and with tacit support from Premier Jiang, the bill was passed by a small margin (Yang 1989, 126–30). The very first project of the institute was the production of integrated circuits, which laid the foundation for Taiwan's exports of computers and telecommunication accessories in the 1980s.

Other officials whom producers easily recalled as having contributed to the electronics industry included Minister of Economic Affairs Li Guoding, Undersecretary Wu Meicun, and CIECD General Secretary and Minister of Economic Affairs Tao Shenyang (*Xinshen News* 4/5/67; TEAMA 1969; and my interviews with producers). Later, in 1979, Li founded the Information Industry Institute, a semiofficial organization (TEAMA 1979, 24). As all three men were former high officials of the Ministry of Economic Affairs, therefore, the ministry's Bureau of Industry and the Committee for the Development of Electronics Industry were very attentive to the demands of the industry.

The government's attention to the development of the electronics industry was further reflected in the ranks of officials who participated in TEAMA annual meetings. At the annual meetings of plywood and textile associations, participating officials were usually fourth- or fifth-ranked in their ministries. Rarely did second-ranked officials make an appearance at these meetings. In contrast, the officials who regularly showed up at TEAMA meetings were at least second-ranked, undersecretaries of various ministries and the party, especially the Ministry of Economic Affairs. Occasionally the ministers of economic affairs and of interior affairs, such as Sun Yunxuan and Zhang Guangshi of the MOE and Qiu Chuanghuan of the MOI, would join the meetings (TEAMA 1969, 1971, 1972, 1975, 1978, 1979, 1981, 1982).

In conclusion, the rapid and stable growth of Taiwan's electronics industry was due to the existence of a strong industrial association and a cooperative state. State corporatism in Taiwan not only expedited the industry's growth but also transformed the ownership structure from foreign domination to local control. In contrast, the Philippine electronics industry both benefited from the laissez-faire institution and suffered from it.

The Liberals' Showcase in the Philippines

Laissez-Faire Within the Industry

The failure of Filipino electronics producers to overcome market fluctuations seems to have been caused by their inability to organize themselves. Producers did not actively seek either political patrons or a powerful industry association to enhance their individual or collective interests.

Producers (assemblers) of consumer electronics organized the Electronics Manufacturers Association of the Philippines (EMAP) in September 1956. It was, however, a social club of larger assemblers owned by the Filipinos. Its membership policy explicitly required that 60 percent of a member company be owned by the Filipinos.

Therefore, EMAP had only nine members in 1960 (*Insurance and Finance* 11/60) and eleven in 1963 (*Chronicle Magazine* 5/18/63). Seventeen other producers organized the Philippine Chamber of Electronics Industries (PCEI) in 1963 as a competing social club.

Neither EMAP nor PCEI was an active industry association aimed at promoting the collective interests of the industry. They had no explicit organization goals, made no effort to coordinate quality standards, and did not lobby regularly for the revision of tariffs on imported materials, which were higher than those on imported products. Regardless of the existence of the associations, "individual company interests outweighed all other considerations, including the interest of the country" (*Industrial Philippines* 4/75). Then, end-product manufacturers formed the Consumer Electronics Manufacturers Association (CEMA) to wage war against the Manufacturers of Electronics Components Association (MECA), organized by components producers. CEMA had about twenty-four members in the 1970s and only nine by 1982 (Ofreneo and Habana 1987, 111, 113). The membership of MECA is unknown.

The disorganization of the electronics industry prevented it from formulating coherent policies for long-term development in the critical years of the early 1970s, when MNCs had just arrived. Local producers exerted no consistent pressure for a local content program or linkages with MNCs, as Taiwanese producers had done.

A separate group of local contractors of semiconductors emerged in the early 1970s. Some MNCs such as Telefunken and Raytheon first used these contractors to process a small quantity of microchips. After discovering the high productivity of Philippine workers, they and other MNCs began to establish their own subsidiaries to expand production and produce patent products.

Since the suppliers of materials and the buyers of semiconductors were the same foreign companies, local contractors and MNCs did not need to cooperate or compete with each other. Local contractors might compete for foreign orders which, however, were so abundant that competition was rarely a problem. Because of their specialized markets, it was not necessary for semiconductor producers to interact with local producers of consumer electronics (Lim 1985, 221). Neither side tried to correct this mismatch of supply and demand.

In 1979, sixteen local and foreign semiconductor firms located outside export processing zones (EPZ) collectively requested status as EPZ factories, in order to enjoy investment incentives. The request was not granted, but the cooperation effort led to the establishment of the first semiconductor association, the Philippine Association of Electronics Exporters (PAEE) in 1980 (*Bulletin Today* 11/ 29/79; 9/2/80). The fate of PAEE was, however, a mystery. Newspapers and the producers I interviewed never mentioned it again.

The current industry association for semiconductor producers is the Semiconductor Electronics Industry Foundation Incorporated (SEIFI). It had about twenty-two members in 1987, including all thirteen of the MNCs and most local contractors (SSC 1987). Eight producers decided not to join the association.

It is still too early to judge the success of SEIFI as an industry association. It was experimenting with a variety of activities of club goods provisions such as lobbying, drafting industry position papers, and sponsoring internships for technical students. The results were mixed because, first, SEIFI personnel were still adapting to a new organization, and second, members could not reach a consensus concerning the content or the necessity of these activities. Most members remained independent of each other, both financially and socially. "We don't even have lunch together," one manager of a large MNC told me.

Very mild clientelism existed within the industry over the years. Because of the special relationships between producers and their foreign partners, producers did not have to interact intensively with the government to solve their own problems of material supply, marketing, technology, and capital. The Philippine government had already solved most of the legal and infrastructural problems for them in the early 1970s by establishing the Food Terminal Industrial Park. A number of producers admitted privately that they still needed to give grease money to customs officials to facilitate imports and exports.[16] The burden, however, was not very costly compared to other developing countries, one experienced MNC manager said.

In sum, the Philippine electronics industry in general and the semiconductor industry in particular were very disorganized. They existed under a laissez-faire institution where even the kind of competition among producers that Milton Friedman has described rarely existed.

A Laissez-Faire State

Before the 1970s the Philippine electronics industry received little attention from the state, as its Taiwanese counterparts had before the mid-1960s. The largest amount of state revenues came from agriculture production such as coconut, sugar, and wood. In the manufacturing sector, the textile industry contributed more to state revenues, capital formation, and employment than did the Philippine electronics industry. While the Taiwanese state began to actively promote foreign direct investments in its electronics industry in the mid-1960s, the Philippine state was slow in taking advantage of the product cycle.

When the Philippines's semiconductor assembly industry began to develop in the early 1970s, the martial law government initiated a number of policies modeled after its neighboring countries to help the industry. The government facilitated the establishment of new firms and transformed the Greater Manila Terminal Food Market into a compound area for export-oriented electronics plants (*Bulletin Today* 1/1/73; 5/14/73). These policies immediately stimulated the expansion of the local industry and attracted MNCs. When MNCs arrived in the mid-1970s, the Philippine government formulated the Progressive Increase of Local Content in Electronics Manufacture Program in April 1974 and the Guidelines for the Electronics Local Content Program in January 1975 (*Industrial Philippines* 4/75). These policies, however, were not as forcefully implemented as they had been in Taiwan, for a number of reasons. First, no strong industry association existed to monitor the implementation of these policies. Second, the programs lacked implementation details. And third, the production process of semiconductors allowed little room for local producers of parts and consumer electronics to participate. Neither semiconductor producers nor these local producers exerted any effort to bridge the gap. Therefore, like many other development policies copied from abroad and imposed by Marcos's technocrats, these policies were never seriously implemented. The Progressive Export Program for Consumer Electronics Products of 1983 and the Arthur D. Little development plan contracted by the Board of Investments of 1984 faced a similar fate.

Several producers of semiconductors recalled that the Marcos government preferred the centralization of decision making. Occasional consultations with individual producers occurred, but these were more like declarations of policies than cooperative consultation meetings. Moreover, these policies were so ambiguous that most of the time producers simply ignored them.

That the government was not helpful to the electronics industry was not necessarily harmful to semiconductor producers. Before the 1985 crisis of the industry, semiconductor producers did not need much help from the government. Once the general investment incentive laws and the Food Terminal Industrial Park were put in place in the early 1970s, producers did not have to interact actively with the government except for the internal revenue department and the Manila International Airport. Producers often complained about costly delays at the airport in exporting their time-sensitive products (*Bulletin Today* 9/29/79).

In July 1982 Marcos issued Executive Order 815 to ban strikes in the semiconductor industry (Lim 1985, 221). Its effectiveness was doubtful for two reasons. First, only a few of the semiconductor companies, and even fewer of the MNCs, had unions. Second, when workers of Stanford and Dynetics, the two largest local producers, staged strikes in 1985 and 1986, the government did not enforce the order and allowed the companies to go bankrupt.

The government did not and could not provide assistance to the producers with respect to marketing, technology, quality inspection, and material supply (*Philippine Development* 11/83; *Bulletin Today* 6/18/84). Most of these problems were solved by internal markets: consignors of local contractors or MNC parent companies.

Therefore, there was a close-to-perfect laissez-faire state in the Philippine electronics industry. The state kept its hands off the industry and let the market determine how well the industry performed. The entire industry expanded rapidly, yet local producers were gradually driven out of the market by the MNCs (especially during the 1985–1986 supply glut). The industry remained relatively captive and had few backward and forward linkages to the Philippine economy.

Conclusion

Within two decades the Taiwanese electronics industry emerged from an insignificant sector of the economy in the mid-1960s, expanded rapidly during the 1970s, sailed through the turbulence of the two oil crises that wrecked the plywood and textile industries, and in 1983 finally surpassed the textile industry as the nation's largest earner of foreign exchange. What caused the strong *and* consistent performance of the electronics industry?

The applicability of the developmental state theory in this empirical comparison is again very limited. The Taiwan state became "developmental" and "committed" only after the industry revealed its growth potential and the industry association made concrete proposals to the state. The state increased its capacity in promoting industrial growth by following the industry association's blueprints and depending on its constant monitoring of policy implementation. When the state occasionally acted autonomously and established its own development agenda without consulting with the industry association, it threatened the survival of a segment of the industry. In the Philippine case, the electronics industry benefited from the nonintervention of the state. Without close cooperation between the state and industry, however, local industries could not cope with the turbulent international market.

This chapter has demonstrated that Taiwan's electronics industry was nurtured not by a developmental state but by state corporatism in which the industry was even more organized and the state even more cooperative than the state corporatism in the textile industry during the 1960s.

TEAMA made a constructive effort to establish strong and extensive linkages between local producers and FDIs when the latter first came to Taiwan in the mid-1960s. At the same time, it began to intensify efforts to enroll local producers and to keep members from leaving. TEAMA actively promoted technology and the quality of its members' products. Most notable among these measures was its insistence on "reasonable differentials" of tariff rates among products, parts, and materials to keep local producers in a healthy, competitive environment. TEAMA provided club goods to its members, such as electronics shows, government procurement opportunities, and collective bargaining with other associations. These association activities were made possible by large and stable revenues and by a highly differentiated organizational structure.

The Taiwanese state contributed to the growth of the electronics industry through effective and continual responses to its demands. The state began its promotion of the industry by convening large-scale consultation meetings with producers. A development plan was then carefully executed. The government, in response to the industry's demands, maintained reasonable tariff barriers, provided technological assistance, reduced red tape and taxes, and strengthened TEAMA's authority over its members. There were times when the government formed its own ideas about what the industry needed without first consulting producers. The resulting policy was either ignored by producers (as was the case with several long-term development plans) or almost destroyed a segment of the industry (as was the case with the regulations on the UL seal and on telephone quality standards). Finally, the industry benefited from the attention of a few high officials who were actively involved in the promotion of the industry.

In relation to the development of Taiwan's electronics industry, the Philippines has a number of interesting characteristics. Its electronics industry emerged at a similar developmental stage as Taiwan's in the mid-1960s. In the 1970s, however, the semiconductor industry replaced the traditional consumer electronics industry as the main component of the Philippine electronics industry. This new industry grew rapidly and became the major foreign exchange earner of the Philippines in the early 1980s. Despite this remarkable growth record, local assemblers of semiconductors were gradually replaced by the MNCs. The 1985–1986 worldwide glut in the supply of semiconductors wiped out half the local assemblers, including the two largest. Furthermore, the semiconductor industry developed few forward and backward linkages with other segments of the economy, resulting in a typical "enclave industry."

This chapter has argued that the peculiar attributes of the development history of the Philippine electronics industry were brought about by the existence of a laissez-faire institution within the industry. Consumer electronics producers were disorganized and divided over material and ethnic interests. This disorganization prevented them from establishing extensive linkages with the MNCs and from formulating coherent long-term development strategies. Semiconductor producers did not organize themselves because they did not see the need to. The supply of materials, technology, capital, and marketing was provided by an internal market. Furthermore, there was no need for producers to look for powerful political patrons to protect their interests. The production process had little to do with the government once basic investment incentives and infrastructural problems were solved in the early 1970s.

The Philippine state also adopted a laissez-faire attitude toward the electronics industry. Before the 1970s, the consumer electronics industry was too small to warrant state intervention. The semiconductor industry of the 1970s and 1980s, however, was too self-sufficient and complicated to allow state intervention. The state did contribute to the initial expansion of the industry by passing a number of general investment incentive laws and by establishing the Food Terminal Industrial Park. Once these policies were in place, other state-initiated industrial policies were rarely implemented or supported by producers. The rise and decline of the local semiconductor industry, therefore, was largely determined by international market forces, not by the laissez-faire state.

7

CONCLUSION

This study has proposed two theses concerning the political causes of economic development in Third World countries. First, the current explanation that the existence of a developmental state is the necessary condition for rapid economic development is theoretically and empirically invalid. Second, the institutional approach demonstrated herein provides a more accurate and rigorous explanation for the success and failure of Third World development. This chapter summarizes my empirical findings and discusses their theoretical and policy implications. Appendix 1 provides statistical tests for the market fluctuation thesis and the product cycle theory that might have explained the difference in economic performance across nations.

Relevance of the Developmental State Theory

Since the 1980s the developmental state theory has dominated both academic and policy discussions of Third World economic development. Without serious challenge the theory will continue to provide models and prescriptions to other developing countries and the former socialist countries. This study has criticized the developmental state theory from both theoretical and empirical perspectives. At the theoretical level, chapter 2 concluded that each element of the theory (autonomy, strong capacity, and developmental leadership) contains theoretical loopholes. Taken as a whole, the theory becomes inconsistent and lacks support from organization theories. At the empirical level, the national comparison of Taiwan and the Philippines in chapter 3 suggested that Taiwan's economic success was associated with a nondevelopmental state rather than a developmental state, while the Philippine failure was due to the creation of a clientelist state that happened to have the characteristics of a developmental state.

Chapters 4, 5, and 6, which are detailed analyses of the textile, plywood, and electronics industries in both countries, also rejected the developmental state theory and tended to support the opposing arguments. Table 7–1 summarizes the relationship between the developmental state theory and the growth of these industries.

If we assume that state capacity and leadership are constant across industries, then the developmental state argument can be reduced to an autonomous state argument, i.e., the existence of an autonomous state contributes to industrial growth.[1] The concept of state autonomy can be further differentiated into eight categories according to whether policy proposals help or hurt the industry, whether the business community supports them, and whether the state implements these policy proposals. For instance, statists argue that a state is autonomous when it refuses to implement interest groups' policy proposals that are detrimental to long-term industrial growth, or when it implements policies that are not supported by interest groups but are conducive to long-term economic development. Yet statists often overlook the possibility that a state can be autonomous when it refuses to implement interest groups' long-term development proposals or when it arbitrarily promulgates policies that are detrimental to industrial growth.

In general, the existence of an autonomous state tends to have either a delaying effect or a negative effect on industrial develop-

Table 7–1
Impact of State Institutions on Industrial Growth

Characteristic	Scenario 1	2	3	4	5	6	7	8
Good policy	X		X		X		X	
Bad policy		X		X		X		X
Effective implementation of policy	X			X	X			X
Nonimplementation of policy		X	X			X	X	
Support of business		X	X		X			X
Opposition to business	X			X		X	X	
Autonomy	X	X	X	X				
Nonautonomy					X	X	X	X
Impact on Industy	Positive	None	None	Negative	Positive	None	None	Negative

Note: Empirical examples:
Scenario 1: Taiwanese textile industry: importation of Pakistani yarns
Scenario 2: ?
Scenario 3: Taiwanese textile industry (1980s)
　　　　　　Taiwanese plywood industry (antidumping policy)
　　　　　　Taiwanese electronics industry (satellite system)
　　　　　　Philippine electronics industry (aid to local producers)
Scenario 4: Taiwanese textile industry (purchase of cotton for political reasons)
　　　　　　Taiwanese plywood industry (ammonia supply policy)
　　　　　　Philippine textile industry (protection of Filisyn)
Scenario 5: Taiwanese textile industy (1960s and 1970s)
　　　　　　Taiwanese electronics industry (1960s to present)
　　　　　　Philippine plywood indutry (1950s)
Scenario 6: Taiwanese electronics industry (UL and telephone policy)
Scenario 7: Philippine plywood industry (log ban)
Scenario 8: Philippine textile industry (protection?)

ment. Scenarios 1 and 2 in table 7–1 fit the theory of an autonomous state: the state initiates and implements a developmental policy that is opposed by the business community, or the state refuses to implement an antidevelopment policy that is supported by shortsighted business. With the exception of one event in Taiwan's textile industry, however, I have found no empirical evidence in any of the six industries analyzed here in support of the autonomous state theory.[2]

In scenarios 3 and 4, the existence of an autonomous state may in fact delay or hurt industrial development. Empirical evidence for such scenarios is abundant. For instance, in the 1980s the Taiwanese state declined to help the "sunset" textile industry to make industrial adjustment, refused to counter Indonesia's strategic dumping of plywood, and postponed electronics producers' repeated requests for the rationalization of the production satellite system. Before the 1980s the Taiwanese state also compelled textile producers to buy high-priced cotton from countries of diplomatic importance and required plywood producers to purchase expensive ammonia from the inefficient, state-owned fertilizer company. In the Philippines the authoritarian state protected the Filipino Synthetic Fiber Company at the expense of the development of its textile industry. It also rejected a request for assistance by Filipino semiconductor assemblers to cope with a temporary supply glut of semiconductors in 1985 and 1986. As a result, almost half of the local assemblers, including the two largest, went bankrupt.

In contrast, the existence of a nonautonomous state that is responsive to the industry's demand tends to have a positive impact on industrial growth (scenarios 5 and 6). Taiwan's textile industry in the 1960s and 1970s and electronics industry since the mid-1960s are such examples. In both cases the state promptly accepted the proposals formulated by the industry associations to reduce red tape, overcome market risks, rationalize tariff structures, consolidate cooperation among producers, and implement industrial adjustment programs. The Philippine plywood industry also had its golden days in the 1950s, when the state was responsive to the industry's developmental needs in capital supply and technological assistance.

Without prior consultation with producers, the Taiwanese government once prematurely promulgated a policy to require all electrical exports to bear the quality-recognition UL seal and to require telephone products to meet very strict international standards. Both policies could have immediately destroyed a significant segment of Taiwan's electronics industry. Through the industry association's negotiation and pressure, the government revised or postponed the policies. This case fits scenario 6 of table 7–1.

Scenarios 7 and 8 are logically consistent with the autonomous state theory and have been elaborated by Mancur Olson (1982); i.e., industrial development is delayed due to the existence of a nonautonomous state. Two events seem to support this argument. In the Philippines the state has not been able to ban log exports to promote plywood production because producers are more interested in cutting logs than in producing plywood. These loggers have been very influential in both national and local politics. In the other example, the Philippines's protection of the domestic textile industry resulted in the industry's stagnation and the garment industry's underdevelopment.

These two empirical cases, however, are subject to debate. The problem with the Philippine plywood industry is caused partially by the interest group's inertia but mainly by political-economic constraints (i.e., the clientelist relationships between loggers and local officials). The fact that Indonesian loggers made the switch to plywood production in the 1980s when sectoral corporatism emerged is a counterexample to Olson's argument. The case of the Philippine textile industry needs clarification as well. Tariff protection was supported by only a segment of the textile industry and not by the entire industry. Olson's theory is correct in explaining the fact that small groups (e.g., large textile millers) maximize their interests at the expense of a larger group (the entire textile industry). Yet this is still not the problem of interest groups per se but the problem of how interest groups are organized and how they view their long-term interests under political-economic constraints.

Consistent with the results of the national comparison, this industry-level analysis again undermines the developmental state theory. Evidence for the industry-level analysis not only reveals the lack of empirical support for the theory but also suggests that the reverse is closer to the reality: other things being equal, an autonomous state does not facilitate industrial growth but tends to delay or hurt growth. In contrast, a nonautonomous state that is responsive to corporatist business demands tends to promote industrial growth.

Institutions and Industrial Growth

In chapter 2 my theoretical arguments began with the question of how to resolve the policy and collective action problems of economic development. A developmental state has the potential of becoming a solution to these problems. But, as chapter 1 and other empirical chapters have demonstrated, the state alone cannot be a solution. Institutions, however, can make a difference. I hypothesized in chapter 2 that clientelism always leads to long-term stagnation, that the laissez-faire institution has both positive and negative impact on economic growth, and that only under state corporatism can the economy or industry grow rapidly and consistently.

In chapter 3 the national comparison of Taiwan and the Philippines revealed that Taiwan's economic success was not due to the existence of a developmental state but rather to the transition from the clientelism of the 1950s to state corporatism in the 1960s and afterwards. In contrast, the collapse of the Philippine economy in 1986 was caused by an entrenched clientelism that had been turned into a more destructive authoritarian clientelism during Marcos's rule.

In chapters 4, 5, and 6, I examined the validity of these hypotheses by comparing the textile, plywood, and electronics industries in Taiwan and the Philippines. Tables 7–2 and 7–3 summarize the results. The evidence provided in these two tables supports my hypotheses: clientelism tends to retard growth, the laissez-faire institution has both a positive and a negative impact on growth, and only under state corporatism is an industry able to grow rapidly and consistently.

Empirical cases of clientelism include Taiwan's textile industry in the 1950s, its plywood industry in the 1980s, the Philippines's textile industry, and its plywood industry after the 1950s. In all cases, the growth records of these industries were either very poor (negative or small growth rates) or fluctuated wildly.

The effects of the Chicago School's laissez-faire prescription can be observed in the cases of the Philippine electronics industry, Taiwan's textile industry in the 1980s, and its plywood industry in the 1950s and 1970s. In these cases, the industries grew rapidly. But once the international market fluctuated, those producers without government assistance or association protection were driven out of the market. The performance of the industry fluctuated accordingly.

Finally, state corporatism contributed to the remarkable growth

Table 7–2
Institutions and Industrial Growth in Taiwan

	Textile Industry	*Plywood Industry*	*Electronics Industry*
1950s			
Growth	Mild growth, then crisis	Rapid, with large fluctuations	Insignificant
Institution	Clientelism	Laissez-faire	Laissez-faire with mild clientalism
Organization of business	Disorganized	Disorganized	Disorganized
State cooperation	Clientelist	Indifferent	Indifferent
1960s to 1973[a]			
Growth	Rapid[b]	Rapid, with milder fluctuations[c]	Rapid and consistent[d]
Institution	State corporatism	Laissez-faire with mild state corporatism	State corporatism
Organization of business	Organized	Loosely organized	Strongly organized
State cooperation	Cooperative	Mildly cooperative	Very cooperative
1973 to 1979[e]			
Growth	Mild	Mild, with large fluctuations	Rapid and consistent
Institution	State corporatism in decline	Laissez-faire	State corporatism
Organization of business	Eroding cohesion	Increasingly disorganized	Strongly organized
State cooperation	Increasingly uncooperative	Uncooperative	Very cooperative
1979[e] and after			
Growth	Rapid decline	Small or negative	Rapid and consistent
Institution	Laissez-faire	Laissez-faire with mild clientelism	State corporatism
Organization of business	Loosely organized	Disorganized	Strongly organized
State cooperation	Uncooperative	Uncooperative, clientelist	Very cooperative

[a] Date of first oil crisis
[b] After 1961
[c] After 1962
[d] After 1964
[e] Date of second oil crisis

Table 7–3

Institutions and Industrial Growth in the Philippines

	Textile Industry	Plywood Industry	Electronics Industry
1950s			
Growth	Mild	Rapid	
Institution	Clientelism	State corporatism	
Organization of business	Divided	Organized	
State cooperation	Clientelist	Cooperative	
1960s			
Growth	Slow	Inconsistent, slow	
Institution	Clientelism	Clientelism	
Organization of business	Divided	Disorganized	
State cooperation	Clientelist	Clientelist	
1970s and early 1980s			
Growth	Stagnation	Inconsistent, slow	Rapid, with large fluctuations
Institution	Deepening clientelism	Clientelism	Laissez-faire
Organziation of business	Cronyistic	Disorganized	Disorganized
State cooperation	Highly clientelist	Clientelist	Indifferent

of the Philippines's plywood industry of the 1950s, Taiwan's electronics industry, and its textile industry in the 1960s and 1970s. Due to the strong cooperation between a responsive state and a well-organized industry, the growth of these industries was both rapid and consistent.

Why did state corporatism emerge in a particular industry of a country and not in other industries or other countries? The game-theoretical analysis of chapter 2 explained the difficulties of transformation from ever-present clientelism to rarely existing state corporatism. But the rise of this growth-oriented institution remains a theoretical puzzle. Due to the lack of availability of data, this study can provide only partial answers to the puzzle.

The rise of state corporatism seemed to go through the following stages: First, the state created or sponsored peak associations for political control purposes. Second, crises of economic (industrial) development occurred that provided incentives for businesses to organize themselves. Third, political entrepreneurs within business took initiative to organize a powerful association for both personal and collective interests. And finally, the state recognized and supported the authority and functions of peak associations. For instance, the Taiwan Cotton Spinners Association and the Taiwan Electric Appliances Manufacturers' Association seemed to fall into this type of institutional formation.

Some peak associations were not created by the state but by business itself. They usually started as loosely organized associations. But once they went through stages two to four, they also became corporatist associations. The Garment Business Association of the Philippines in this study and the Thai peak associations in Laothamatas's research (1992) seemed to follow this route of institutional formation.

The state apparently played an important role in institutional formation through the creation or sponsoring of these peak associations. Nevertheless, the occurrence of system-wide crises and the emergence of political entrepreneurs within business seemed to assume a more important role in the process. Without the voluntary cooperation among businesses, the state could hardly produce a strong, cohesive peak association. This seemed to be the case for Taiwan's peak associations during the 1950s, Taiwan's textile associations in the 1980s, and the Philippines's peak associations during Marcos's rule.

Theoretical and Policy Implications

Although critical of the developmental state theory, this study does not deny the importance of the state in the economy. The state, in fact, is *the* single most important economic actor in any modern economy. What is wrong with the developmental state theory is its tendency to treat the state as a "closed system" aloof from its social environment. But as organization theorists have long argued, few, if any, social organizations can be totally isolated from their social environment. The state, business associations, firms, and other economic actors have to be studied from the perspective of "open systems" (Richard Scott 1987). Figure 7–1 illustrates such a perspective that highlights the relationships among different theories of political economy.

In figure 7–1, we find that the state, intermediate organizations (such as business associations), and firms are the major actors affecting economic performance. The developmental state theory focuses exclusively on the state's internal characteristics. Clientelism describes the relationships between individual firms and state officials. The liberal economic school and the laissez-faire institution concentrate on the direct relationships between firms and economic performance. In contrast, corporatism discusses the interactions among the state, intermediate organizations, and firms (and/or labor).

The data in this figure suggest that by adopting an "open system" research design, future research can go beyond the developmental state theory and the institutional theory suggested here to provide flexible and comprehensive explanations for economic performance. There is much to gain in theoretical validity and explanatory power by *bringing the society back into* the analysis of political economy. In

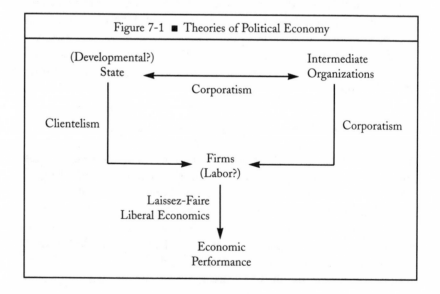

Figure 7-1 ■ Theories of Political Economy

bringing the society back in, network analyses seem to provide the most promising tool for future studies. As Winckler, along with other authors in the book he edited, has convincingly argued, "[w]ith a thousand years or more of continuous experience at dealing with states and markets, East Asian social networks are preadapted to coping with these rival political-economic forms, and quite effective at prevailing against them" (1988, 280).

At the policy level, this study suggests that Third World countries and the former socialist countries do not have to make a "hard choice" between democracy and economic development. The trade-off is probably a false issue that serves only to justify the incompetence and political ambition of authoritarian rulers. Instead, Third World countries should focus on the development of corporatist associations that are able to resolve collective action problems among their members and assist the state in formulating developmental policies. Even if the establishment of corporatist associations is difficult, there remains the second-best option of the laissez-faire institution, which provides the benefits of free market to the economy. With regard to the developmental state, the time has come to cry: Down with the state, long live the state.

APPENDIX

NOTES

REFERENCES

INDEX

Appendix

External Shocks and Industrial Performance

Two kinds of external shocks might have affected the industrial performance in developing countries, regardless of the differences in state institutions or the presence of a developmental state. The international market argument claims that the growth performance of export-oriented industries such as textiles, plywood, and electronics is simply a reflection of world market fluctuations. To test this hypothesis, I have correlated world production data with national production data. For the textile industry, I have used cotton fabrics production data from Korea, Taiwan, the Philippines, and the world (see table 4–2). For the plywood industry, I have compared Korea, Taiwan, the Philippines, Indonesia, and the world (see table 5–3). Since there is no comparable aggregate data on electronic products, the electronics industry is not included in the test.

Table A-1 reports the correlation results for the textile and plywood industries. With respect to cotton fabrics, world market fluctuations have little effect on national production. Each nation's production is also independent of other nations', which implies that these countries perform differently in the same international market environment.

Relationships between international market fluctuations and national performance in plywood production are more complicated than those in cotton fabrics production. World production has a strong and significant impact on Taiwan's and Korea's production but it has little impact on the Philippines's production. It also has a negative relationship to Indonesia's production. Since Taiwan's plywood industry has been organized under a laissez-faire institution, it is not

213

Table A-1

Market Fluctuations and Industrial Growth

	Taiwan	Philippines	Korea	Indonesia	World
Cotton Fabrics					
Taiwan	1.00				
Philippines	0.10	1.00			
Korea	−0.01	−0.17	1.00		
World	0.09	0.12	−0.06	1.00	
Plywood					
Taiwan	1.00				
Philippines	0.10	1.00			
Korea	0.17	0.13	1.00		
Indonesia	−0.59	−0.34	−0.08	1.00	
World	0.71*	0.09	0.54*	−0.43	1.00

Note: To maximize the use of available data, these statistical results are based on pair-wise regressions instead of a single correlation program that deletes cases with missing values. * $p < 0.05$. These are correlation coefficients, as explained in text.

surprising that world production has a strong and positive effect on Taiwan's performance. If my characterization of Korea's plywood industry as corporatist is correct, the Korean case may present a challenge to my institutional theory. However, what distinguishes the Korean case from Taiwan's is the fact that Korean plywood producers, through collective efforts, expanded their production in Indonesia, while their Taiwanese counterparts simply withered away. The Indonesian plywood industry, in contrast, was run by state corporatism, which overcame the effect of world market fluctuations. Correlations among national production rates again are negligible, reflecting their different performances under the same international environment. The strong yet negative impact of Indonesia's production on Taiwan's is due to the strategic dumping of Indonesian plywood on the Taiwanese market.

The second external shock that might have caused the variation in industrial performance is the product cycle. The product cycle theory (Vernon 1971) states that each new product goes through a production life cycle from birth to maturity and then to decline. One of the major causes of the cycle is the rising cost of labor and/or increasing domestic competition. When production is not cost-effi-

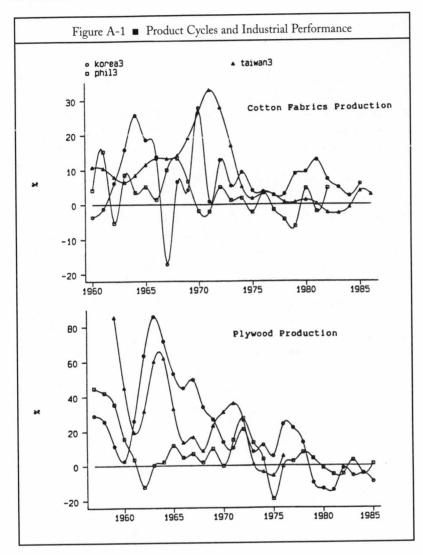

Figure A-1 ■ Product Cycles and Industrial Performance

cient in the country where the new product is introduced, production is moved abroad to cheap-labor countries to maintain competitiveness. The empirical tests of this theory are illustrated in figure A-1. To smooth out large fluctuations, data reported in the figure are three-year average rates (the average of a particular year's, its previous year's, and its next year's).

The product cycle theory explains industrial performance within each country relatively well. Taiwan's cotton fabrics production seems to fit the theory. When the plywood product cycle took effect in Taiwan, Korea, and the Philippines in the 1950s, it created an initial boom in all three countries. Then the cycle continued to run its course in the plywood industries of Taiwan and South Korea during and after the 1960s. The product cycle theory, however, is weak in explaining cross-national differences. It cannot explain why the product cycle did not run its course in Korea's textile industry and in both the Philippines's textile and plywood industries. It also fails to explain why the Korean plywood industry revitalized itself by collectively investing in Indonesia's plywood industry at the end of its product cycle while the Taiwanese plywood industry failed to do so.

These tests demonstrate further that given similar international shocks (e.g., international market fluctuations) and opportunities (e.g., product cycles), different countries or industries may react differently. The cause of their difference, therefore, must lie not at the international but at the national level.

Notes

Abbreviations

APMC	Asian Plywood Manufacturers Conference
BOI	Board of Investments
CCIS	China Credit Information Service
CEPD	Council for Economic Planning and Development
DBP	Development Bank of the Philippines
FEER	*Far Eastern Economic Review*
IDC	Industrial Development Center
ILO	International Labor Office
IMF	International Monetary Fund
OECD	Organization for Economic Cooperation and Development
PCWID	Presidential Committee on Wood Industries Development
PDCP	Private Development Corporation of the Philippines
PLPMA	Philippine Lumber and Plywood Manufacturers Association
PMAP	Plywood Manufacturers Association of the Philippines
PWPA	Philippine Wood Products Association
SSC	Systems Sciences Consult
TCSA	Taiwan Cotton Spinners Association
TEAMA	Taiwan Electric Appliance Manufacturers' Association
TPMEA	Taiwan Plywood Manufacturers & Exporters Association
TTF	Taiwan Textile Federation
USITC	U.S. International Trade Commission

217

Chapter 1. Introduction

1. Representatives of the newly industrializing countries include Singapore, Taiwan, Hong Kong, South Korea in Asia and Brazil and Mexico in Latin America. In addition to these countries, other more controversial cases can be added. Turner and McMullen (1982) add Argentina and India to the list. The OECD (1979, 18) includes Greece, Portugal, Spain, and Yugoslavia.

2. These liberal economists include Balassa (1978), Barrett and Whyte (1982), Bhagwati and Krueger (1973), Caves and Jones (1981), Hasan (1982), Keesing (1967), Little (1982), Morawetz (1977), OECD (1979), USITC (1982), and the World Bank (1980).

3. Deyo points out four problems of the strategy-centered approach: There is "substantial variation in consistency across policy instruments and over time"; strategies may be "little more than vague pronouncements"; "strategies may sometimes follow rather than precede economic trends"; and the relation between the state and strategy may be state-led or state-induced (1987a, 16–17).

4. For Marxist interpretations of Third World development, see Baumgartner and Burns (1975), Biersteker (1978), Cardoso and Falleto (1979), Chase-Dunn (1975), Chirot (1986), Dos Santos (1970), Evans (1979), Frank (1982), Galtung (1971), Gereffi (1983), Landsberg (1979), Payer (1982), Petras (1981), Sunkel (1972), Villegas (1983a), and Wallerstein (1978).

5. These criticisms are found in Andrews (1982), Barrett and Whyte (1982), Bornschier and Ballmerr-Cao (1979), Cumings (1984), Duvall, Jackson, Russett, Snidal and Sylvan (1981), Kohli (1986), Mahler (1980), and Vernon (1971).

6. Proponents have argued that a developmental state is the "essential" reason (Clough 1978, 92), the "indispensable prerequisite" (Tony Smith 1986, 57), and the "necessary precondition" (Luedde-Neurath 1988, 102) for successful economic development. Although they have correctly criticized the weaknesses in the original version of the developmental state theory, Kim and Huang (1991, 83) still accept that the state is a "partially sufficient" condition for economic growth. And Amsden (1989, 18) argues that "without a strong central authority, a necessary although not sufficient condition, little industrialization may be expected in 'backward' countries." Proponents of the statist argument include Amsden (1979), Appelbaum and Henderson (1992), Clark (1987), Clough (1978), Haggard and Moon (1983), Johnson (1982), Kohli

(1986), Gold (1981), Jones and Sakong (1980), McCord (1991), Pang (1988), Robison (1988), Tony Smith (1986), White and Wade (1988), and Haggard (1990a).

7. Smith summarizes well the autonomous state argument: "Particularistic interests of every variety must be weaker than the state, which is competent to act on behalf of what it will call the collective good" (Tony Smith 1986, 58). See also Amsden (1979), Clark (1987), Deyo (1987a), Haggard and Moon (1983), Hyun-Chin Lim (1985), and Robison (1988). For the necessity of a strong capacity state, see Gold (1981, 306), Haggard and Moon (1983, 137), Jones and Sakong (1980, 133), and White (1988, 10). For the claim of developmental leadership, see Bradford (1982), Jones and Sakong (1980, 139), and Johnson (1987, 19–31).

8. White and Wade argue that "we should make a distinction between developmentally 'rational' and 'irrational,' historically 'progressive' and 'reactionary' forms of authoritarianism, particularly considering that the former, whether socialist or capitalist, create the social and potential conditions for the emergence of more democratic and participatory institutions, a tendency we observe in all our East Asian cases" (1988, 25). Other arguments related to the committed leadership include Johnson (1987, 140), Jones and Sakong (1980, 139), Hasan (1982, 10), and Haggard and Moon (1983, 154).

9. For other criticisms of the statist view, see Almond (1988), Arnold (1989), Clark and Lemco (1988), Crone (1988), Dick (1974), Friedman (1988), Migdal (1988), Moon (1990), Lam (1990), Kim and Huang (1991). One might note that the term "developmental state" begs the question of developmental success.

10. In his statistical analysis of seventy-two developing countries in the 1960s, Dick (1974, 817–27) refutes the argument that authoritarian regimes have better economic performance than semiauthoritarian or democratic regimes.

11. For instance, Lane (1979), Levi (1981, 431–65), and Buchanan, Tollison, and Tullock (1980). Using Weberian and neo-Marxist analyses, however, we may qualify the "rent-seeking state" argument by suggesting that state leaders do not maximize rents alone but both rents and legitimacy or both rents and production taxes.

12. Lee (1991) argues that the failure of the South Korean state's automobile policy ironically led to the success of the industry. Similarly, the Korean state's success in establishing big trading companies and the Taiwanese state's failure to do so have been associated with a result that

is contrary to the policy goals: Taiwan's export growth has been stronger and more stable than Korea's (Fields 1989).

13. See Almond (1988, 853–74), Ikenberry (1986, 106, 134–37), and Zysman (1983, 297).

14. "The state's very success in building its role as a corporate actor," Rueschemeyer and Evans note, "may undercut its ability to remain autonomous and . . . effective intervention may increase the extent to which the state becomes an arena of social conflict" (1985, 49).

15. See, for instance, Brown (1982, 1–16), and Pfeffer and Salancik (1978, chap. 9).

16. Applications of this new statist approach to explaining economic adjustment in developing countries can be found in Grindle and Thomas (1991) and Nelson (1990).

17. Fransman (1986) makes a similar argument in his study of Taiwan's and Japan's successful machine tool industry. Haggard and Kaufman (1992) continue to stress the centrality of state elite preferences and state autonomy in economic adjustment.

18. George (1989) observes a stronger influence of interest groups over the Japanese state bureaucracy.

19. This sector analysis, however, seems to make arguments similar to those of the technology school of organization theories, which argues that technology determines the types of organizations. This school has been severely criticized (Mohr 1971).

20. For other similarities and differences between Taiwan and South Korea, see Lau (1986). Some scholars (e.g., Snow 1983) tend to emphasize the uniqueness of the Philippine case. As demonstrated below, however, the evidence they cite is not substantially different from that of the Asian NICs or Thailand.

Chapter 2. Institutions and Global Competitiveness

1. For an elaborate discussion of the organization problems of information processing, see Stinchcombe (1990).

2. See also the pioneering study of public administration by Stene (1940).

3. North aptly concludes that in Third World countries political and economic entrepreneurs tend to "favor activities that promote redistributive rather than productive activity, that create monopolies rather than competitive conditions, and that restrict opportunities rather than expand them. . . . The organizations that develop in this institutional

framework will become more efficient—but more efficient at making the society even more unproductive and the basic institutional structure even less conducive to productive activity. Such a path can persist because the transaction costs of the political and economic markets of those economies together with subjective models of the actors do not lead them to move incrementally toward more efficient outcomes" (1990, 9).

4. For an exemplary analysis of collective action problems in Third World countries, see Doner (1992).

5. Some scholars use the words "policy networks" (Katzenstein 1978, 308), "policy currents" (Maxfied and Nolt 1987), or "webs of contracts" (Strange 1985) to describe this analytical entity. The institutional approach of this study is different from popular institutionalism (e.g., Ikenberry 1988, Doner 1992, and Shafer 1990) or the "new economics of institutionalism" in that it attempts to go beyond description to the generation of testable, causal hypotheses.

6. See Friedman's fourteen "commandments" constructed for an ideal government in a free market economy (Friedman 1982, 35–36). In North's institutional theory of economic development (1981), the state plays complicated roles in protecting property rights.

7. The free market proponent assumes that a competitive market drives out inefficient firms and results in the survival of the fittest. The relationship between efficiency and survival may not be as clear in reality, however. Large firms tend to survive market fluctuations not because they are more efficient but because they have more organizational slack, and the financial and political capital to help them muddle through crises.

8. A similar definition of clientelism is provided by Lemarchand and Legg (1972, 151–52): "A more or less personalized, affective, and reciprocal relationship between actors, or sets of actors, commanding unequal resources and involving mutually beneficial transactions." Scott (1972, 92) defines clientelism as "a special case of dyadic (two-person) ties involving a largely instrumental friendship in which an individual of higher socioeconomic status (patron) uses his own influence and resources to provide protection or benefits, or both, for a person of lower status (client) who, for his part, reciprocates by offering general support and assistance, including personal services, to the patron."

9. As Lemarchand and Legg have argued, "where clientage networks insert themselves into a bureaucratic framework, the chances are that interpersonal relations between patrons and clients will operate at

cross purposes with, or at least independently of, the formal role relationships specified in statutory rules and regulations" (1972, 153).

10. In his study of patron-client ties in Southeast Asian countries, Scott (1972, 111–13) arrives at a similar conclusion: "A regime that is dependent on its particularistic distributive capacity is also unlikely to solve its financial dilemmas either by structural reform or by tapping new sources of revenue. . . . [It will] characteristically resort to budget deficits, especially in election years, to finance [its] networks of adherents."

11. One subtype of clientelism, namely, industrial clientelism, resembles state corporatism (Lemarchand and Legg 1972). Under this regime, interest groups establish clientage with certain officials. Since Lemarchand and Legg do not deal with the organization of the business community, the impact of state policies on business as a whole is not determined. By definition, however, industrial clientelism implies conflicts between national interests and the interests of cliental actors and state actors. By contrast, it is admissible that under state corporatism, business associations may use members' political patrons for the benefit of the whole community. The gains from this controlled clientelist practice tend to outweigh the losses to the entire business community.

12. Robison (1988) describes how the deepening of the Indonesian patronage system stimulated an initial boom of business activities in the 1970s, yet created more serious economic problems in the 1980s.

13. Exemplary research on state corporatism includes Berger (1981), Cawson (1985), Collier and Collier (1979), Malloy (1977), Robinson (1991), Schmitter (1971), Schmitter and Lehmbruch (1979), and Stepan (1978). For reasons of theoretical simplicity, labor is excluded from this study. For criticisms of the (neo) corporatism literature, see Cox and O'Sullivan (1988); their criticisms focus on the dominance and interests of the corporatist state, not the organizational traits of interest groups.

14. The administrative contract is "a structure with legitimate authority; with a manipulable incentive system; with a method for adjusting costs, quantities, and prices; with a structure for dispute resolution; and with a set of standard operating procedures [that] looks very much like a hierarchy, very little like a competitive market. Yet all these features of hierarchy are routinely obtained by contracts between firms in some sector of the economy" (tinchcombe 1990, 198). Pfeffer and Salancik's discussion of "negotiated environment" (1978, 144–80) and Laumann et al's interorganizational linkages (1978) provide a similar rationale for firms to form cooperative arrangements with each other.

15. I have defined state corporatism somewhat differently from

Schmitter, for whom corporatism is "a system of interest representation in which the constituent units are organized into a limited number of singular, compulsory, noncompetitive, hierarchically ordered and functionally differentiated categories, recognized or licensed (if not created) by the state and granted a deliberate representational monopoly within their respective categories in exchange for observing certain controls on their selection of leaders and articulation of demands and supports" (1979, 13). Later in the same article (27), he points to the information function of corporatism but not to its function of resolving collective action problems. Nor is the state's cooperation with business a vital component in his definition.

16. As Schmitter states, "In the most extreme or pure case, such corporatist policy making would involve 'private' agreements between associations that eventually receive the *pro forma* approval of parliament or executive authority—rendering them enforceable as public law and thereby making them binding on noncontracting parties, up to and including the public as a whole. These agreements are subsequently implemented through the associations themselves" (1981, 295).

17. See Deyo (1981) for Singapore's corporatism. See Moskowitz (1984), Odell (1984), and Park (1987) on South Korea's business associations (though Park regards the business associations as only executive arms of the state).

18. Scholars have occasionally referred to the corporatist features of the Hong Kong economy, for instance, Castells (1992, 65), Oshima (1987, 355), Rhee (1985, 191).

19. See Lynn and McKeown (1988), Ouchi (1984), Pempel and Tsunekawa (1979, 259) and Okimoto (1989).

20. Or, as Schmitter and Lehmbruch argue, "the more the modern state comes to serve as the indispensable and authoritative guarantor of capitalism by expanding its regulative and integrative tasks, the more it finds that it needs the professional expertise, specialized information, prior aggregation of opinion, contractual capability and deferred participatory legitimacy which only singular, hierarchically ordered, consensually led representative monopolies can provide" (1979, 27).

21. For the industrialized countries, Schmitter has concluded that "several econometric analyses of OECD data during the 1960s and 1970s consistently demonstrated that the performance of the more corporatist countries in terms of employment, inflation, and productivity was significantly better—even if little or no impact on overall growth rates was observed" (1990, 9).

22. The traditional corporatist literature, such as Collier and Collier (1979), Schmitter (1979), and Stepan (1978), assumes a strong state in state corporatism.

23. This does not mean that business associations can become political strongholds of antigovernment activities. The state may allow business associations greater economic autonomy but not necessarily greater political autonomy.

24. This assumption has been used frequently in studies of international political economy (e.g., Bornschier and Ballmerr-Cao 1979; Chu 1989; Grieco 1984, 156; Crane 1982, 93; Haggard 1985, 8; Katzenstein 1985, 37).

25. See, for example, Milner (1988).

26. For a detailed explanation of the Prisoner's Dilemma and Stag Hunt, see Hardin (1982, 22, 167).

Chapter 3. National Comparison of Taiwan and the Philippines

1. For the history of ISI in the Philippines, see Baldwin (1975), Bautista, Power, and Associates (1979), Golay (1961), Hartendorp (1961), Power and Sicat (1971), Sicat (1972), and Valdepenas (1970).

2. U.S. tariffs on Philippine exports were 20 percent lower than those imposed on other countries' products.

3. For a comparative study of the American support of the ISI strategy in the Philippines, Turkey, and Argentina, see Maxfield and Nolt (1987).

4. The 20 percent retention rate was imposed on the sales of foreign exchange in 1962 to reduce the exorbitant profits of agricultural exporters.

5. As shown by the case of the textile industry, mainlander capitalists had greater access than their Taiwanese counterparts to the mainlander-controlled government. Taiwanese capitalists, however, soon aquired similar access by hiring retired mainlander officials and party cadres as their public relations managers. Although created by the Taiwanese government in the 1950s or earlier, corporatist associations began to assume the function of interest aggregation around 1960, when problems of import substitution and rising U.S. protectionism forced producers to strengthen their only channel of interest articulation.

6. Similar arguments can be found in Ichiro Numazaki (1986).

7. The following discussion on Taiwan's textile and electronics industries will be further explored in chapters 4 and 6.

8. See an excellent study by Lam (1991b) on the rise of Taiwan's high-tech industries.

9. As Hernandez comments on the unimportance of this interim legislature, "during the six years of the interim legislature's existence it was able to pass only four substantive laws out of a total output of about 1,200 bills and resolutions" while Marcos enacted "1,935 pieces of substantive legislation, excluding unpublished and secret decrees" (1986, 269).

10. The autonomy of the Marcos state is discussed in Brillantes (1988), Hernandez (1986, 269), Canoy (1981, 89–91), Hawes (1987), Stauffer (1977, 398–400), and Timberman (1991, 81–106).

11. As Stauffer noted, "even prior to martial law, Marcos had established new central economic planning and development agencies largely free from any controls other than those he himself imposed" (1977, 397).

12. Evans (1989, 561–87) makes a similar observation about the Zairian state's autonomy from social groups but its patrimonialism with a small network of elites.

13. For detailed analysis of China's clientelist state before 1949, see Boda Chen (1949) and Dixing Xu (1947).

14. Four laws were related to business associations: the Industry Association Law (Gongyeihui Fa), Business Association Law (Shangyei Tongyei Gonghuifa), Exporters Association Law (Shuchuyei Tongyei Gonghuifa), and Trade Association Law (Shanghui Fa). Trade associations are the associations of associations, while the other three are associations of firms and/or lower-level associations.

15. The law was omnibus not only because it covered all economic activities (agriculture, mining, industry, and commerce) but also because it gave the government all the power it needed. Passed in 1938, the law authorized the Ministry of Economic Affairs, with the approval of the Executive Yuan, to take over enterprises, restrict business and labor strikes, control imports and exports, regulate price and consumption, and control production in important economic activities. Furthermore, the law was not constrained by the constitution during state-defined "emergency periods."

16. In addition to these three, large enterprises had to hire security personnel "recommended" by the party or the military. They were responsible for the security files of employees.

17. As Schmitter suggests, "capitalists when faced with a threatening disturbance in their established exchanges . . . will seek to re-

solve them by increasing the governance capacity of their sector" (1990, 21).

18. For instance, within Taiwan's diplomatic agencies stationed in the United States, there was no Taiwanese official responsible for trade promotion, as reported in late 1955 (*United Daily News* 10/15/55). The first trade promotion effort was the establishment of the Free China Trade Center in San Francisco in July 1958. It was, however, a private company (*Zhen Xin News* 7/25/58). The government began ordering its diplomatic officials to assist with trade promotion only in early 1970—a time when Taiwan's exports had already penetrated American markets (*China Times* 1/2/70).

19. Rick Doner kindly offered this challenging question to me during a telephone conversation in August 1992. For the relationship between the nature of crisis and economic adjustment in the Third World, see Nelson (1990).

20. In Taiwan, business people seem to have had more influence on industrial policies than on macroeconomic policies. The formulation of macroeconomic policies requires more extensive academic study than that of industrial policies. Therefore, the state usually consulted with economists first and then with business leaders.

21. The communist insurgency and the Mindanao independence movement were not a serious threat to Marcos in the early 1970s. The communists were not popular in the countryside because of tight patron-client relationships between landlords and peasants. Muslims constituted only 5 percent of the total population (Averch, Denton, and Koebler, 1970; Bonner 1987, 119–24).

22. Brian Fegan (1981) locates clientelist activities, which he calls "rent-capitalism," in all facets of Philippine society: primary sectors, construction, retail, the textile industry, sawmills, transportation, and even prostitution.

23. Within the Marcos government, many employees also hypocritically justified their corruption by saying it was an effort to undermine authoritarian rule (Veneracion 1988, 163).

24. For an elucidating account of Philippine local politics, see Kerkvliet (1990). He suggests, however, that in addition to clientelism, cross-class and cross-status linkages are also important factors in explaining Philippine politics.

25. In my interview, President Macapagal complained that in preparation for the 1965 election, Senate President Marcos colluded with the opposition Nationalist party to sabotage all of Macapagal's appointments

and reform bills. Macapagal had helped Marcos become president of the Senate. But it is hard to tell who betrayed whom because Macapagal had promised Marcos in 1961 that he would not seek reelection. Marcos formally turned to the Nationalist party after the Liberal party renominated Macapagal.

26. Farmers and workers did not have much organized influence on local and national politics either (Corpuz 1965, 107, 112; Wolters 1984, 196).

27. The National Federation of Sugar Cane Planters was not established until the late 1950s, when the influence of sugar producers was surpassed by ISI industrialists.

28. For a detailed study of the effect of the patronage system on the Philippines's debt problem, see Haggard (1990b).

29. One leader of the Chinese business community told me that he talked and wrote repeatedly to Marcos and the minister of trade and industry to voice the community's opposition to the eleven projects financed by foreign debts. He suggested using precious foreign loans to develop light industries instead. His suggestions were understood but never adopted. The Chinese controlled about 70 percent of the Philippine economy by then. Before martial law, Chinese opinions had significant influence on national economic policies; under an autonomous state, even Chinese business people lost their collective influence.

30. When asked by a *Fortune Magazine* reporter to explain why the cronies had enriched themselves since martial law, Imelda Marcos replied, "Well, some are smarter than others." For detailed descriptions of these Marcos cronies, see Canoy (1981) and Doherty (1982).

31. For a comprehensive study of the "ins" and "outs" after martial law was declared, see Makil (1975) and Makil, Reyes, and Koike (1983).

32. For detailed studies of the cronies and rationalization programs, see Hawes (1987), Rodriguez (1986, 163–86), and Salgado (1985).

Chapter 4. The Textile Industry

1. Taiwan's textile industry, as defined in this study, includes all textile production, ranging from upstream fiber production to downstream apparel and accessory manufacturing. This is the definition used by the Taiwan Textile Federation (TTF 1986, 11). This chapter concentrates on the cotton textile industry because it is representative of the whole industry in terms of its importance and extensive linkage with other types of textile production. In the case of the Philippines, how-

ever, a clear distinction needs to be made because its garment sector is, to a large extent, independent of its upstream spinning and weaving industries.

2. While the 1968 agreement allowed only a 5 percent increase, the 1974 agreement had a 60 percent increase of quotas, the 1975 Multifiber Agreement increased quotas by 19 percent, and the 1978 agreement increased various quotas from 14 to 64 percent (*Manila Daily Bulletin* 7/5/67; *Bulletin Today* 7/27/78).

3. Most research on Taiwan's textile industry reported that there were about twenty thousand spindles and two thousand looms during Japanese rule. More than half of these machines, however, were either destroyed by the American bombardment or melted down by the Japanese to produce weaponry.

4. A similar scheme was implemented in China during the anti-Japanese war. The policy, called "exchanging cotton with yarn, exchanging yarn with fabrics" (Ihua Huansha, Isha Huanbu), resulted in oligopoly. Small and medium-sized enterprises were driven out of the market, because only the influential few had access to these arrangements (Xu 1947, 104).

5. In 1948, 205 Taiwanese textile producers, including spinners, weavers, garment makers, etc., organized the Taiwan Machinery Cotton Textile Industry Association. The association was disbanded by the government after 1949 and merged with other GMD-sponsored industry associations.

6. A number of official proposals to merge the three public enterprises that had been subsidized illegally by public banks never materialized due to the great political influence of these three companies (*United Daily News* 1/9/59; 10/3/62). One of the companies, Taibei Textile, was reorganized by a competent manager who was later forced to resign because he purged a few political influentials from the company (*United Daily News* 9/13/62). Despite the fact that the government bailed out these three public enterprises in 1961, all three were sold to private entrepreneurs between the late 1960s and early 1970s (*Economic Daily News* 7/12/67; Lin 1978, 50).

7. Unlike the situation in the Philippines, imported textiles were never a serious threat to Taiwanese producers, who grew up in a protectionist environment of high tariffs and strict quantitative import controls. The producers, therefore, did not propose increased protectionism as a solution to their crisis.

8. As one major producer recalled, "export profits were not larger

than domestic sales. But after the collapse of the domestic market, we had to export" (*Central Daily News* 8/8/71).

9. The Taiwanese government, to some extent, had tolerated the proliferation of underground factories. Industrial associations and local police departments usually knew where these factories were. But according to the Chinese moral code of "thou shalt not cut off the livelihood of others," very few associations actively requested the government to shut down these factories.

10. *Gonglun News* 3/4/63; *Zhengxin News* 4/29/63; 11/8/66; *United Daily News* 3/9/67; and *Economic Daily News* 12/19/67; 8/13/69.

11. There were only three mergers in 1976 (TCSA 1978, 1).

12. The Ministry of Economic Affairs and CUSA each had a textile committee. The Central Trust Bureau and the Provincial Government's police division had supervisory power over the industry (Li and Chen 1987, 272; Ni 1985, 197). The Administrative Yuan's Economic Stabilization Board also had a committee (the second committee) in charge of the development of the textile industry. The Central Bank, the FETCC, and the Ministry of Finance all had jurisdiction over the industry.

13. The ministry convened six formal, regular meetings with producers between February 1959 and October 1960 (*Central Daily News* 2/1/59; *Xing Sheng News* 10/5/60).

14. The Working Committee proposal was dropped, however, in a meeting with producers (*United Daily News* 7/25/62).

15. See chapter 3 for the political cause of the FETCC's dissolution.

16. One can argue that the purchase of American cotton is a lobbying expense because American cotton growers act as the political guardian of Taiwan's textile exports. This argument is only partially true, because American cotton growers are not more effective and active lobbyists than are retailers. Cotton growers also supply cotton to American textile producers who oppose textile imports.

17. For instance, Luciano Millan, a former congressman, was the TMAP executive secretary in the 1960s. Former BOI governor Hermenegildo Zayco became president of the TMAP after the 1986 revolution.

18. The TMAP membership ranged between twelve (in 1956) and twenty-four (in 1988), while the total number of millers was about one hundred in the 1960s and more than two hundred in the 1970s and 1980s (*Manila Daily Bulletin* 8/10/57; 8/11/61).

19. Some garment or remnant producers imported brand-new textile materials disguised as rags or used clothing, which were under a lower

tariff rate. Some government agencies also imported a large quantity of textiles under the Japanese reparation program (*Manila Daily Bulletin* 7/8/63; 12/18/64; 3/11/68).

20. For instance, the six-point program proposed by the TMAP in 1961 was all about protection and financing and nothing about exports (*Chronicle Yearbook* 1961, 134). The only exception was the TMAP president's proposal, reported in 1963, which fell on deaf ears among both government officials and TMAP members (*Manila Daily Bulletin* 1/1/63).

21. By contrast, producers of knitted textiles never complained about smuggling. The price of domestic knitted textiles was more or less the same as the international price. The profit of smuggling, therefore, was marginal. Ironically, the TMAP's protectionism encouraged smuggling.

22. P. L. Lim was also a vice president of the TMAP, but his political influence was not derived from this position.

23. Some integrated mills were allowed to import various kinds of textiles to make final finished products (e.g., garments) for export. They did not, however, process these imported textiles. Instead, they sold them to the black market for a larger and immediate profit, and bribed customs officials to fill out false export receipts to be used in the application for imported textiles.

24. In 1962 and 1963, for instance, remnant imports from the United States and Japan were undervalued by one-third to one-half (*Industrial Philippines* 4/64).

25. The other, to no one's surprise, was Dewey Dee's Continental Manufacturing Company.

26. "Dollar salting" refers to the practice whereby exporters underdeclare their dollar earnings to the Central Bank in order to sell dollars on the black market at a higher exchange rate. This practice was not uncommon in South Korea and Taiwan, where the governments could not eliminate the black market and had in fact deliberately tolerated the practice to encourage exports.

27. The tripartite dialogue was instituted within three industries in the 1970s: garments, electronics, and pharmaceutical.

Chapter 5. The Plywood Industry

1. In the 1980s the Korean plywood industry had the worst performance among the three in terms of production growth rates. I do not have data to evaluate whether this performance was related to institu-

tional transformation. There is one important distinction, however, between the performance records of Taiwan and Korea in the 1980s. Both countries suffered from the high price of logs and Indonesia's rising production of plywood. While the decline of the Taiwanese plywood industry during this period was associated with the bankruptcy of its producers, in Korea it was associated with the fact that major Korean producers began to relocate their mills to Indonesia and later helped Indonesia become the kingdom of plywood (APMC 1983, 42). In this sense, the Korean plywood industry was revitalized in Indonesia.

2. Signs of state corporatism in the Malaysian plywood industry emerged in the mid-1970s (APMC 1984, 66–67).

3. Veneer is an intermediate product between logs and plywood. Logs are first peeled or sliced into very thin sheets. With simple cutting and fixing, wood sheets become veneer. Stacking a few layers of veneer, adding glue, hot pressed, and then fixing them slightly produces a piece of unfinished plywood. Manufacturers can process the unfinished plywood further by adding a layer of high-quality wood, metal sheet, or other decorative colors or materials.

4. In 1959 the president of the Plywood Manufacturers' Association of the Philippines (PMAP) claimed that "the quality improvement of Philippine plywood is now surpassing that of Japanese plywood" (*Insurance and Finance* 4/59).

5. TPMEA proceedings published before 1970 do not have page numbers.

6. As Schmitter notes, "much of the resistance to corporatization comes from existing interest associations that prize their organizational autonomy and defend their traditionally pluralistic ways of operating" (1981, 313).

7. Plywood producers had criticized the bureau's opposition to log imports as irrational because the logs they imported were a species not grown in Taiwan. Although there were some substitutions between different species of logs, the direct conflict of interest was not severe.

8. As noted earlier, the export boom was also due to the fact that around this time American plywood importers established links with Taiwanese producers.

9. In 1962 the government, in coordination with the GMD, inspected the TPMEA to "understand its mobilization capability for the military recovery of the mainland" (TPMEA 1963).

10. In 1964 one report found that most of the plywood mills did not own concessions (*Manila Daily Bulletin* 4/6/64). But most PMAP mem-

bers had concessions. One can infer, therefore, that the PMAP failed to enroll nonconcession plywood producers.

11. A Confederation of Forest Industry Associations was established by producers in 1977. It was also "welcomed by the government" for its alleged purpose of representing all wood industries (PLPMA 1978, 2–3). It was not very active, however.

12. According to my respondents, there were serious complaints from PLPMA members (especially from plywood producers) about the merger of the PLPMA and the PCWI. Because of the government's insistence, however, the merger proceeded despite the opposition.

13. Because of its macroeconomic concerns, the Central Bank was not particularly responsive to the industry's demands. Its decontrol of foreign exchange in 1960 helped plywood exports, but cannot be credited with a deliberate industrial policy (*Manila Daily Bulletin* 2/7/59; 9/12/59; 6/2/60).

14. In Japan and Taiwan the inspection was performed by producers themselves; the governments were not involved.

15. The committee was created at the suggestion of wood producers, including the PMAP (PMAP 1970, 22).

16. Before 1974 Philippine plywood exports paid only 40 percent of the lowest tariff rate. After 1974 it paid the full amount, i.e., 20 percent of the FOB value, while Taiwanese and Korean plywood paid only 10 percent of the FOB value (PLPMA 1979, 22).

Chapter 6. The Electronics Industry

1. The Taiwanese electronics industry includes electrical machinery, home appliances, and electronics. This is the formal definition adopted by the Taiwan Electrical Appliances Manufacturers' Association.

2. In the mid-1960s Taiwan's wage rates, including those of technicians and assembly line workers, were about one-tenth of American wage rates. At that time, Japanese wages were on the rise and the United States began to restrict Japanese electronics exports (*Zhen Xin News* 1/9/66; *Economic Daily News* 12/8/70). These foreign investments opened a huge job market to Taiwanese women (*Central Daily News* 9/11/68).

3. The term "OEM" means that the local manufacturer has to produce goods that meet the exact specifications supplied by the foreign buyer. "Original equipment" implies that the commodity has estab-

lished its reputation and market. The buyer wants to keep the market but also to shift to foreign producers to save production costs.

4. In 1974 Intel was the first MNC to establish a semiconductor subsidiary in the Philippines.

5. These figures were calculated from Board of Investments (BOI) records reported in SSC (1987). The growth rates of Philippine semiconductor *and* electronics exports from 1978 to 1986 were 104 percent, 63 percent, 63 percent, 25 percent, 19 percent, 5 percent, 26 percent, −20 percent, and −13 percent (SEIFI 1987).

6. According to one source, Stanford Microsystems was the largest subcontractor in the Far East (*Bulletin Today* 7/16/84). It employed seventy-five hundred persons and produced 2.5 million units per day.

7. References to TEAMA sources are to a 45-volume set of TEAMA internal documents and proceedings, which I collected during my field research. Internal documents will be referred to by date; proceedings, by year and page number.

8. Local producers complained that the FDIs competed with them for local technicians (*Economic Daily News* 10/17/67; 10/4/71). The FDIs' effort to train local technicians might have been a response to these complaints.

9. The seven FDIs and joint ventures were Motorola, General Instrument, Admiral Overseas, RCA, Philco-Ford, Zenith, and Shenbao (a joint venture with Sony and Sharp).

10. Korea has been Taiwan's major competitor in industrial exports. Each country has paid close attention to what happened in the other. TEAMA organizes annual survey groups to Japan and Korea and reports of these survey groups are distributed to its members (TEAMA 4/77; 3/78; 3/80). TEAMA began to organize such survey groups in 1972, following Korea's efforts (TEAMA 7/72). One of the interesting and beneficial aspects of this mutual attention is that producers in both countries have used these survey reports to push their governments to adopt more favorable policies toward the electronics industry.

11. Between 1968 and 1972 CIECD was the planner of electronics shows. After 1973 TEAMA took over the planning.

12. When membership fees were adjusted in 1976, the burden was placed on larger firms. Smaller firms continued to pay the old fee (TEAMA 6/76).

13. According to the Taiwan constitution, professional groups such as industry, trade, education, agriculture, and fishing may nominate

their representatives into national legislatures, separately from those elected by ordinary citizens.

14. As Lam (1991a) argues, Taiwan's state planning to promote its electronics industry was ad hoc until the late 1970s. The state lagged behind the industry's development due to officials' shortsightness.

15. The practice of issuing export licenses is somewhat confusing in this case. Based on the fact that TEAMA once asked the government to approve a higher fee for issuing licenses to nonmembers, and further, to deny export licenses to nonmembers, there were apparently some nonmember producers who had been allowed to export (TEAMA 3/80; 9/85). According to the association law, however, all producers were to join TEAMA if their products fell within the jurisdiction of the association. Further study needs to be done to determine whether there were cliental factors at work.

16. As one producer said, "the government was corrupt but efficient."

Chapter 7. Conclusion

1. Arnold's research (1989) on the state-industry relationship in Taiwan's automobile industry suggests that state capacity and leadership may not be constant across industries. The developmental state at the macro level may be antidevelopment at the industry level.

2. The Taiwanese state once allowed some imports of Pakistani cotton yarns to force the textile industry to reduce yarn prices for its downstream factories. The link between the Taiwanese textile industry and its downstream producers was thus consolidated. Since the Philippine state did not discipline its textile industry as the Taiwanese state did, one can cite this incident as a supporting case. This is, nevertheless, controversial because the Taiwanese state, under pressure from downstream producers, was mainly considering the survival of downstream producers and not the long-term linkage between upstream and downstream production. The state, therefore, was at best "relatively autonomous," and the linkage was an unintended consequence.

References

Newspapers

Chinese

Central Daily News
China Times
Economic Daily News
Gonglun News
Minzhong Daily News
Taiwan News
United Daily News
Xinshen News
Zhengxin News (predecessor of *China Times*)

English

Asian Wall Street Journal
Business Day
Manila Bulletin (April 1986 to present; it was called *Manila Daily Bulletin* from 1938 to September 1972, and *Bulletin Today* from October 1972 to April 1986)

Books and Articles

Aggarwal, Vinod K. 1985. *Liberal Protectionism: The International Politics of Organized Textile Trade*. Berkeley: University of California Press.

Aguilar, Carmencita T. 1981. Philippine Development Policies and U.S. Development Assistance. Paper submitted to the 2d International Philippine Studies Conference, University of Hawaii.

Ahn, Choong Yong. 1986. Economic Development of South Korea, 1945–1985. *Korea and World Affairs* 10(1): 91–117.

Alburo, Florian, and Geoffrey Shepherd. 1985. Trade Liberalization

Experience in the Philippines, 1960–84. Philippine Institute for Development Studies Working Paper No. 86–01.

Allison, Graham T. 1971. *Essence of Decision: Explaining the Cuban Missile Crisis*. Boston: Little, Brown.

Almond, Gabriel A. 1988. The Return to the State. *American Political Science Review* 82(3): 853–74.

Amsden, Alice H. 1979. Taiwan's Economic History. *Modern China* 5(3): 341–80.

_____. 1989. *Asia's Next Giant: South Korea and Late Industrialization*. New York: Oxford University Press.

Andrews, Bruce. 1982. The Political Economy of World Capitalism. *International Organization* 36(1): 135–63.

Appelbaum, Richard P., and Jeffrey Henderson, eds. 1992. *States and Development in the Asian Pacific Rim*. Newbury Park, CA: Sage.

Arnold, Walter. 1989. Bureaucratic Politics, State Capacity, and Taiwan's Automobile Industrial Policy. *Modern China* 15(2): 178–214.

Asian Development Bank. 1987. Loan, Technical Assistance and Private Sector Operations Approvals. Manila: Asian Development Bank.

Asian Plywood Manufacturers Conference (APMC). 1984. *Proceedings of the 8th Asian Plywood Manufacturers Conference*. Manila: PWPA.

Averch, H. A., F. H. Denton, and J. E. Koehler. 1970. *A Crisis of Ambiguity: Political and Economic Development in the Philippines*. Report prepared for the Agency for International Development. Santa Monica, CA: Rand Corporation.

Balassa, Bela. 1978. Development Strategy and the Six Year Plan in the Republic of China. Manuscript.

_____. 1984. The Policy Experience of Twelve Less Developed Countries, 1973–1979. In *Comparative Development Perspectives*, ed. Gustav Ranis and Cynthia T. Morris. Boulder: Westview Press.

Baldwin, Robert E. 1975. *The Philippines*. New York: Columbia University Press.

Barrett, Richard E., and Martin King Whyte. 1982. Dependency Theory and Taiwan. *American Journal of Sociology* 87(4): 1064–89.

Baumgartner, T., and T. R. Burns. 1975. The Structuring of International Economic Relations. *International Studies*, 19(2): 126–59.

Bautista, Romeo M., John H. Power, and Associates. 1979. *Industrial Promotion Policies in the Philippines*. Manila: Philippine Institute for Development Studies.

Bello, Walden, David Kinley, and Elaine Elinson. 1982. *Development*

Debacle: The World Bank in the Philippines. San Francisco: Institute for Food and Development Policy.

Berger, Suzanne, ed. 1981. *Organizing Interests in Western Europe: Pluralism, Corporatism, and the Transformation of Politics.* Cambridge: Cambridge University Press.

Bhagwati, Jagdish N., and Anne O. Krueger. 1973. Exchange Control, Liberalization, and Economic Development. *American Economic Review* 63(2): 419–27.

Biersteker, Thomas J. 1978. *Distortion or Development? Contending Perspectives on the Multinational Corporation.* Cambridge: MIT Press.

Board of Investments (BOI), the Republic of the Philippines. 1972. The Garment Industry—1972. Manila: BOI.

Bonner, Raymond. 1987. *Waltzing with A Dictator: The Marcoses and the Making of American Policy.* New York: Times Books.

Bornschier, Volker, and Thanh-Huyen Ballmerr-Cao. 1979. Income Inequality. *American Sociological Review* 44(June): 487–506.

Bradford, Colin I., Jr. 1982. The Rise of the NICs as Exporters on a Global Scale. In *The Newly Industrializing Countries: Trade and Adjustment,* ed. Louis Turner and Neil McMullen. London: George Allen & Unwin.

———. 1986. East Asian "Models." In *Development Strategies Reconsidered,* ed. John P. Lewis and Valeriana Kallab. Washington, D.C.: Overseas Development Council.

Brillantes, Alex B., Jr. 1988. The Executive. In *Government and Politics of the Philippines,* ed. Raul P. De Guzman and Mila A. Reforma. Singapore: Oxford University Press.

Broad, Robin. 1988. *Unequal Alliance, 1979–1986: The World Bank, the International Monetary Fund, and the Philippines.* Quezon City, the Philippines: Ateneo De Manila University Press.

Brown, M. Craig. 1982. Administrative Succession and Organizational Performance. *Administrative Science Quarterly* 27 (March): 1–16.

Buchanan, James, Robert D. Tollison, and Gordon Tullock, eds. 1980. *Toward a Theory of the Rent-Seeking Society.* College Station: Texas A&M University Press.

Buffington, Sidney L. 1957. Third Quarterly Report to Industrial Development Center and United States Operation Mission to the Philippines on Development of the Textile Industry in the Philippines. Manuscript.

Burns, Tom, and G. M. Stalker. 1961. *The Management of Innovation.* London: Tavistock Publications.

Cai, Zhongkuen. 1983. Taiwan Diqu Mianfang Gongye Jingying Chengzhang Zhi Yanjiu [A study of the growth of Taiwan's cotton textile industry]. Master's thesis. Danjiang University.

Canoy, Reuben R. 1981. *The Counterfeit Revolution: The Philippines from Martial Law to the Aquino Assassination*. Manila: Philippine Editions.

Cardoso, Fernando Henrique, and Enzo Faletto. 1979. *Dependency and Development in Latin America*. Trans. Marjory Mattingly Urquidi. Berkeley: University of California Press.

Carino, Ledivina V., ed. 1986. *Bureaucratic Corruption in Asia: Causes, Consequences and Controls*. Quezon City, the Philippines: JMC Press.

Carroll, John J., S.J. 1965. *The Filipino Manufacturing Entrepreneur: Agent and Product of Change*. Ithaca: Cornell University Press.

Castells, Manuel. 1992. Four Asian Tigers with a Dragon Head. In *States and Development in the Asian Pacific Rim*, ed. Richard P. Appelbaum and Jeffrey Henderson. Newbury Park, CA: Sage.

Castro, Amado A. 1965. Philippine-American Tariff and Trade Relations, 1898–1954. *Philippine Economic Journal* 4: 29–56.

_____. 1971. *A Survey of Philippine Economic Development, 1946–1970*. Kyoto, Japan: Center for Southeast Asian Studies.

Caves, Richard E., and Ronald W. Jones. 1981. *World Trade and Payments: An Introduction*. 3d ed. Boston: Little, Brown.

Cawson, Alan, ed. 1985. *Organized Interests and the State: Studies in Meso-Corporatism*. Beverly Hills, CA: Sage.

Chalmers, Douglas A. 1977. The Politicized State in Latin America. In *Authoritarianism and Corporatism in Latin America*, ed. James M. Malloy. Pittsburgh: University of Pittsburgh Press.

Chase-Dunn, Christopher. 1975. The Effects of International Economic Dependence on Development and Inequality. *American Sociological Review* 40(December): 720–38.

Chen, Boda. 1949. *Zhongguo Sida Jiazu* [China's four big families]. Huadong Xinhua Shudian.

Chen, Cheng. 1961. *Taiwan Tudi Gaige Jiyao* [Gist of Taiwan's Land Reform]. Taibei: Taiwan Zhonghua Shuju.

Chen, Maobang. 1976. Taiwanqu Diangong Qicai Gongye Xiankuang [The current situation of Taiwan's electronics industry]. In *Zhonghua Minguo Gongye Fazhan Gaikuang*. Taibei: National Industry Association.

Chen, Mingtong. 1991. Weiquan Zhentixia Taiwan Difang Zhenzhi Jingying De Liudong 1945–86 [The mobility of local political elite under an authoritarian regime]. Ph.D. diss., National Taiwan University.

Chen, Zhaonan. 1985. Taiwan Diqu Dianzi Changshang Zhi Jiaru Tuichu U Chengzhang [The entry, exit, and growth of electronics firms in Taiwan]. *Jingji Luenwen* 13: 47–90.

China Credit Information Service (CCIS). 1976. *Business Groups in Taiwan*. Taibei: China Credit Information Service.

Chirot, Daniel. 1986. *Social Change in the Modern Era*. Orlando, FL: Harcourt Brace Jovanovich.

Chou, Tein-chen. 1985. The Pattern and Strategy of Industrialization in Taiwan. *Developing Economies* 23(2): 138–58.

Chu, Yun-han. 1989. State Structure and Economic Adjustment of the East Asian Newly Industrializing Countries. *International Organization* 43(4): 647–72.

Clark, Cal. 1987. The Taiwan Exception. *International Studies Quarterly* 31: 327–56.

Clark, Cal, and Jonathan Lemco. 1988. The Strong State and Development. *Journal of Developing Societies* 4: 1–8.

Clough, Ralph N. 1978. *Island China*. Cambridge: Harvard University Press.

Cole, Allan B. 1967. Political Roles of Taiwanese Enterprisers. *Asian Survey* 7: 645–54.

Collier, Ruth Berins, and David Collier. 1979. Inducements Versus Constraints: Disaggregating "Corporatism." *American Political Science Review* 73: 967–86.

Comisso, Ellen. 1986. Introduction: State Structures, Political Processes, and Collective Choice in CMEA States. In *Power, Purpose, and Collective Choice: Economic Strategy in Socialist States*, ed. Ellen Comisso and Laura D'Andrea Tyson. Ithaca: Cornell University Press.

Corpuz, Onofre D. 1965. *The Philippines*. Englewood Cliffs, NJ: Prentice-Hall.

Council for Economic Planning and Development (CEPD). 1987. *Taiwan Statistical Data Book*. Taibei: CEPD.

Cox, Andrew, and Noel O'Sullivan, eds. 1988. *The Corporate State: Corporatism and the State Tradition in Western Europe*. Cambridge: Edward Elgar.

Crane, George T. 1982. The Taiwanese Ascent. In *Ascent and Decline in the World-System*, ed. Edward Friedman. Beverly Hills, CA: Sage.

Crone, Donald K. 1988. State, Social Elites, and Government Capacity in Southeast Asia. *World Politics* 40(2): 252–68.

Cuaderno, M. 1952. The Bell Trade Act and the Philippine Economy. *Pacific Affairs* 25: 323–33.

Cuaderno, Miguel, Sr. 1961[?]. *Problems of Economic Development (The Philippines—A Case Study)*. Manila: N.P.

Cumings, Bruce. 1984. The Origins and Development of the Northeast Asian Political Economy. *International Organization* 38(1): 1–40.

De Dios, Emmanuel S., ed. 1984. *An Analysis of the Philippine Economic Crisis*. Quezon City, the Philippines: University of the Philippines Press.

De Guzman, Raul P., and Mila A. Reforma, eds. 1988. *Government and Politics of the Philippines*. Singapore: Oxford University Press.

Development Bank of the Philippines (DBP). 1975. The Prospects of the Philippine Garments Industry. Manila: DBP.

Deyo, Frederic C. 1981. *Dependent Development and Industrial Order*. New York: Praeger.

———. 1987b. Coalitions, Institutions, and Linkage Sequencing— Toward a Strategic Capacity Model of East Asian Development. In *The Political Economy of the New Asian Industrialism*, ed. Frederic C. Deyo. Ithaca: Cornell University Press.

Deyo, Frederic C., ed. 1987a. *The Political Economy of the New Asian Industrialism*. Ithaca: Cornell University Press.

Dick, G. William. 1974. Authoritarian Versus Nonauthoritarian Approaches to Economic Development. *Journal of Political Economy* 817–27.

Di Palma, Giuseppe. 1980. The Available State. In *Italy in Transition: Conflict and Consensus*, ed. Peter Lange and Sidney Tarrow. London: Frank Cass.

Doherty, John F. 1982. Who Controls the Philippine Economy. In *Cronies and Enemies: The Current Philippine Scene*, ed. Belinda Aquino. Occasional Paper No. 5. Philippine Studies Program, University of Hawaii.

Doner, Richard F. 1991. *Driving a Bargain: Automobile Industrialization and Japanese Firms in Southeast Asia*. Berkeley: University of California Press.

———. 1992. Limits of State Strength. *World Politics* 44(3): 398–431.

Doronila, Amando. 1985. The Transformation of Patron-Client Relations and Its Political Consequences in Postwar Philippines. *Journal of Southeast Asian Studies* 16: 99–116.

Dos Santos, Theotonio. 1970. The Structure of Dependence. *American Economic Review* 60(2): 231–36.

Duvall, Raymond, Steven Jackson, Bruce M. Russett, Duncan Snidal, and David Sylvan. 1981. A Formal Model of 'Dependencia Theory'. In *From National Development to Global Community: Essays in Honor of Karl W. Deutsch*, ed. Richard L. Merritt and Bruce M. Russett. London: George Allen & Unwin.

Edwards, George C., III. 1980. *Implementing Public Policy*. Washington, DC: Congressional Quarterly Press.

Evans, Peter. 1979. *Dependent Development: The Alliance of Multinational, State, and Local Capital in Brazil*. Princeton: Princeton University Press.

_____. 1987. Class, State, and Dependence in East Asia. In *The Political Economy of the New Asian Industrialism*, ed. Frederic C. Deyo. Ithaca: Cornell University Press.

_____. 1989. Predatory, Developmental, and Other Apparatuses. *Sociological Forum* 4(4): 561–87.

Far Eastern Economic Review (FEER). Various issues.

Fegan, Brian. 1981. Rent-Capitalism in the Philippines. The Philippines in the Third World Papers, Series No. 25. Third World Studies Center, University of the Philippiens.

Fewsmith, Joseph. 1980. The Emergence of Authoritarian-Corporatist Rule in Republic China: The Changing Pattern of Business Association in Shanghai. Ph.D. diss., University of Chicago.

Fields, Karl J. 1989. Trading Companies in South Korea and Taiwan. *Asian Survey* 29(11): 1073–89.

Frank, Andre Gunder. 1982. Asia's Exclusive Models. *Far Eastern Economic Review* 25: 22–23.

Fransman, Martin. 1986. International Competitiveness, Technical Change and the State. *World Development* 14(12): 1375–96.

Friedman, David. 1988. *The Misunderstood Miracle: Industrial Development and Political Change in Japan*. Ithaca: Cornell University Press.

Friedman, Milton. 1982. *Capitalism and Freedom*. 2d ed. Chicago: University of Chicago Press.

Galenson, Walter, ed. 1979. *Economic Growth and Structural Change in Taiwan: The Postwar Experience of the Republic of China*. Ithaca: Cornell University Press.

Galtung, Johan. 1971. A Structural Theory of Imperialism. *Journal of Peace Research* 8(2): 81–117.

Gates, Hill. 1979. Dependency and the Part-time Proletariat in Taiwan. *Modern China* 5: 381–408.

George, Aurelia. 1989. Japanese Interest Group Behaviour. In *Dynamic and Immobilist Politics in Japan*, ed. J. A. A. Stockwin, Alan Rix, Aurelia George, James Horne, Daiichi Ito, and Martin Collick. Honolulu: University of Hawaii Press.

Gereffi, Gary. 1983. *The Pharmaceutical Industry and Dependency in the Third World*. Princeton: Princeton University Press.

Gereffi, Gary, and Donald L. Wyman, eds. 1990. *Manufacturing Miracles: Paths of Industrialization in Latin America and East Asia*. Princeton: Princeton University Press.

Gerschenkron, Alexander. 1962. *Economic Backwardness in Historical Perspective: A Book of Essays*. Cambridge: Harvard University Press.

Golay, Frank H. 1961. *The Philippines: Public Policy and National Economic Development*. Ithaca: Cornell University Press.

———. 1965. Obstacles to Philippine Economic Planning. *Philippine Economic Journal* 4(2): 284–309.

Gold, Thomas B. 1981. *Dependent Development in Taiwan*. Ph.D. diss., Harvard University.

———. 1986. *State and Society in the Taiwan Miracle*. New York: M.E. Sharpe.

Goldstein, Judith. 1986. The Political Economy of Trade. *American Political Science Review* 80(1): 161–84.

Granovetter, Mark. 1985. Economic Action and Social Structure: The Problem of Embeddedness. *American Journal of Sociology* 91(3): 481–510.

Greenhalgh, Susan. 1988. Families and Networks in Taiwan's Economic Development. In *Contending Approaches to the Political Economy of Taiwan*, ed. Edwin A. Winckler and Susan Greenhalgh. Armonk, NY: M.E. Sharpe.

Gregor, A. James, Maria Hsia Chang, and Andrew B. Zimmerman. 1981. *Ideology and Development: Sun Yat-sen and the Economic History of Taiwan*. Berkeley: University of California Press.

Grieco, Joseph M. 1984. *Between Dependency and Autonomy: India's Experience with the International Computer Industry*. Berkeley: University of California Press.

Grindle, Merilee S., and John W. Thomas. 1991. *Public Choices and Policy Change: The Political Economy of Reform in Developing Countries*. Baltimore: Johns Hopkins University Press.

Haggard, Stephan. 1990a. *Pathways from the Periphery: The Politics of*

Growth in the Newly Industrializing Countries. Ithaca: Cornell University Press.

———. 1990b. The Political Economy of the Philippine Debt Crisis. In *Economic Crisis and Policy Choice: The Politics of Adjustment in the Third World*, ed. Joan M. Nelson. Princeton: Princeton University Press.

Haggard, Stephan, and Chung-in Moon. 1983. The South Korean State in the International Economy. In *The Antinomies of Interdependence: National Welfare and the International Division of Labor*, ed. John Gerard Ruggie. New York: Columbia University Press.

Haggard, Stephan, and Robert R. Kaufman, eds. 1992. *The Politics of Economic Adjustment: International Constraints, Distributive Conflicts, and the State*. Princeton: Princeton University Press.

Haggard, Stephan, Byung-kook Kim, and Chung-in Moon. 1991. The Transition to Export-led Growth in South Korea. *Journal of Asian Studies*, 50 (4, November): 850–73.

Hamilton, Clive. 1983. Capitalist Industrialization in East Asia's Four Little Tigers. *Journal of Contemporary Asia* 13: 35–73.

———. 1986. *Capitalist Industrialization in Korea*. Boulder: Westview Press.

Hamilton, Gary G., and Nicole Woolsey Biggart. 1988. Market, Culture, and Authority. *American Journal of Sociology* 94 (Supplement, July): S52–94.

Hannan, Michael T., and John Freeman. 1977. The Population Ecology of Organizations. *American Journal of Sociology* 82: 929–64.

Hardin, Russell. 1982. *Collective Action*. Baltimore: Johns Hopkins University Press.

Hartendorp, A. V. H. 1961. *History of Industry and Trade of the Philippines: The Magsaysay Administration*. Manila: Philippine Education Company.

Hasan, Parvez. 1982. Growth and Structural Adjustment in East Asia. World Bank Staff Working Papers, No. 529. Washington, D.C.: World Bank.

Hawes, Gary. 1987. *The Philippine State and the Marcos Regime: The Politics of Export*. Ithaca: Cornell University Press.

Hayek, F. A. 1933. The Trend of Economic Thinking. *Economica* (May).

Hernandez, Carolina G. 1986. Political Institution Building in the Philippines. In *Asian Political Institutionalization*, ed. Rober A. Scalapino, Seizaburo Sato, and Jusfu Wanandi. Berkeley: Institute of East Asian Studies, University of California.

Ho, Samuel P. S. 1978. *Economic Development of Taiwan, 1860–1970*. New Haven: Yale University Press.

Hsiao, Hsin-huang Michael. 1981. *Government Agricultural Strategies in Taiwan and South Korea: A Macrosociological Assessment*. Taibei: Academia Sinica.

Hu, Dunyu. 1969. *Zai Fazhanzhong De Taiwan Jinji* [Taiwan's economy in development]. Taibei: Taiwan Zhonghua Shuju.

Huntington, Samuel P. 1968. *Political Order in Changing Societies*. New Haven: Yale University Press.

_____. 1988. One Soul at A Time. *American Political Science Review* 82(1): 3–10.

Hutchcroft, Paul D. 1992. The Political Foundations of Booty Capitalism in the Philippines. Paper delivered at the annual meeting of the Political Science Association, Chicago, Illinois.

IBON Databank. 1983. *The Philippine Financial System*. Metro Manila: IBON Databank Phi.

Ikenberry, G. John. 1986. The Irony of State Strength. *International Organization* 40(1): 105–37.

_____. 1988. Conclusion: An Institutional Approach to American Foreign Economic Policy. *International Organization* 42(1): 220–43.

Industrial Development Center (IDC), National Economic Council, the Republic of the Philippines. 1959. *Plywood and Veneer Industry in the Philippines*. Manila: IDC.

International Labor Office (ILO). 1974. *Sharing in Development: A Programme of Employment, Equity and Growth for the Philippines*. Geneva: International Labor Office.

International Monetary Fund (IMF). 1987. *International Financial Statistics Yearbook*. Washington, D.C.: IMF.

Jacoby, Neil H. 1966. *U.S. Aid to Taiwan: A Study of Foreign Aid, Self-Help, and Development*. New York: Praeger.

Jiang, Dixian. 1988. Wushinianlai Mianfangzhiye Jianku U Zijiu Zhi Jiantao Ji Lizheng [Reviews and examples of the cotton textile industry's hardship and self-help in the past fifty years]. In *Zhongguo Fangzhi Xuehui Chengli Wushi Zhounian Jinian Zhuankan*, ed. Zhongguo Fangzhi Xuehui. Taibei: Zhongguo Fangzhi Xuehui.

Jo, Sung-hwan. 1981. Overseas Direct Investment by South Korean Firms. In *Multinationals from Developing Countries*, ed. Krishna Kumar and Maxwell G. McLeord. Lexington, MA: Lexington Books.

Johnson, Chalmers. 1982. *MITI and the Japanese Miracle: The Growth of Industrial Policy, 1925–1975*. Stanford: Stanford University Press.

_____. 1986. The Nonsocialist NICs. In *Power, Purpose, and Collective Choice: Economic Strategy in Socialist States*, ed. Ellen Comisso and Laura D'Andrea Tyson. Ithaca: Cornell University Press.

_____. 1987. Political Institutions and Economic Performance. In *The Political Economy of the New Asian Industrialism*, ed. Frederic C. Deyo. Ithaca: Cornell University Press.

Jones, Leroy P., and Il Sakong. 1980. *Government, Business, and Entrepreneurship in Economic Development: The Korean Case*. Cambridge: Harvard University Press.

Katzenstein, Peter J., ed. 1978. *Between Power and Plenty: Foreign Economic Policies of Advanced Industrial States*. Madison: University of Wisconsin Press.

_____. 1985. *Small States in World Markets: Industrial Policy in Europe*. Ithaca: Cornell University Press.

Kaufman, Robert R. 1977. Corporatism, Clientelism, and Partisan Conflict. In *Authoritarianism and Corporatism in Latin America*, ed. James M. Malloy. Pittsburgh: University of Pittsburgh Press.

Keesing, D. B. 1967. Outward-Looking Policies and Economic Development. *Economic Journal* 77(306): 303-20.

Keohane, Robert O., and Joseph S. Nye. 1977. *Power and Interdependence: World Politics in Transition*. Boston: Little, Brown.

Kerkvliet, Benedict J. Tria. 1990. *Everyday Politics in the Philippines: Class and Status Relations in a Central Luzon Village*. Berkeley: University of California Press.

Kim, Jeong-Hyun, and Chi Huang. 1991. Dynamics of State Strength and Policy Choices. *Pacific Focus* 6(2): 83–108.

Kim, Kyong-Dong, ed. 1987. *Dependency Issues in Korean Development: Comparative Perspectives*. Seoul: Seoul National University Press.

Kohli, Atul, ed. 1986. *The State and Development in the Third World*. Princeton: Princeton University Press.

Koo, Hagen. 1986. The Political Economy of Industrialization in South Korea and Taiwan. *Korea and World Affairs* 10(1): 148–80.

Kuang, Bihua. 1987. *Taiwan Fuhao Liezhuan* [Biographies of Taiwan's millionaires]. Taibei: Guangjiaojing.

Kuo, Shirley W. Y., Gustav Ranis, and John C. H. Fei. 1981. *The Taiwan Success Story: Rapid Growth with Improved Distribution in the Republic of China, 1952–1979*. Boulder: Westview Press.

Lake, David A. 1992. Powerful Pacifists. *American Political Science Review* 86(1): 24–37.

Lam, Danny K. K. 1990. Independent Economic Sectors and Economic

Growth in Hong Kong and Taiwan. *International Studies Notes* 15(1): 28–34.

_____. 1991a. The Myth of State Led Industrialization. Presented at the Annual Meeting of the American Political Science Association, Washington, D.C.

_____. 1991b. Explaining Economic Development: A Case Study of State Policies Towards the Computer and Electronics Industry in Taiwan (1960–80). Diss. Carleton University, Ottawa, Ontario.

Lande, Carl H. 1965. *Leaders, Factions, and Parties: The Structure of Philippine Politics.* Monograph Series No. 6, Southeast Asia Studies, Yale University. Detroit, MI: Cellar Book.

_____. 1977. The Dyadic Basis of Clientelism. In *Friends, Followers, and Factions: A Reader in Political Clientelism,* ed. Steffen W. Schmidt, James C. Scott, Carl Lande, and Laura Guasti. Berkeley: University of California Press.

Landgrebe, Justus G., and Jacques Brussier. 1964. Study of the Philippine Wood Products Industry and Financial Analysis of the Plywood Industry. Manila: World Bank Resident Mission.

Landgrebe, J. G. 1966. The Philippine Textile and Timber Trades. *Philippine Economic Journal* (1st semester).

Landsberg, Martin. 1979. Export-led Industrialization in the Third World. *Review of Radical Political Economics* 11(4): 50–63.

Lane, Frederic C. 1979. *Profits from Power: Readings in Protection Rent and Violence-controlling Enterprises.* Albany: State University of New York Press.

Laothamatas, Anek. 1988. Business and Politics in Thailand. *Asian Survey* 28(4): 451–70.

_____. 1992. *Business Associations and the New Political Economy of Thailand: From Bureaucratic Polity to Liberal Corporatism.* Boulder: Westview Press.

Lau, Lawrence J., ed. 1986. *Models of Development: A Comparative Study of Economic Growth in South Korea and Taiwan.* San Francisco: Institute for Contemporary Studies.

Laumann, Edward O., Joseph Galaskiewicz, and Peter V. Marsden. 1978. Community Structure as Interorganizational Linkages. *Annual Review of Sociology* 4: 455–84.

Laumann, Edward O., and David Knoke. 1987. *The Organizational State: Social Choice in National Policy Domains.* Madison: University of Wisconsin Press.

Lee, Naeyoung. 1991. The Politics of Industrial Restructuring: The

Case of the South Korean Auto Industry. Paper delivered at the Annual Meeting of the Midwest Political Science Association, Chicago, Illinois.

Lehmbruch, Gerhard. 1979. Consociational Democracy. In *Trends Toward Corporatist Intermediation*, ed. Philippe C. Schmitter and Gerhard Lehmbruch. Beverly Hills, CA: Sage.

Leibenstein, Harvey. 1976. *Beyond Economic Man: A New Foundation for Microeconomics*. Cambridge: Harvard University Press.

Lemarchand, Rene, and Keith Legg. 1972. Political Clientelism and Development. *Comparative Politics* 4(2): 149–78.

Levi, Margaret. 1981. The Predatory Theory of Rule. *Politics and Society* 10: 431–65.

Li, Guoding. 1957. How Industrialization Could Help Improve Taiwan's Balance of Payments. *Industry of Free China*, 7(2) 8–16.

_____. 1959. A Review of the Economic Situation in Taiwan in 1958. *Industry of Free China* 11(3): 2–21.

_____. 1977. *Taiwan Jingji Kuaisu Chengzhang De Jingyan* [Taiwan's experience of rapid economic growth]. Taibei: Zhengzhong.

_____. 1985a. *Li Guoding Xiansheng Zengsong Ziliao Yingben: Meiyuan U Daikuan Lei*. [Xeroxed data donated by Mr. Li Guoding: U.S. Aid and Loan]. Retained by the Institute of the Three People's Principles, National Taiwan University. [This series of collections does not have page numbers.]

_____. 1985b. *Li Guoding Xiansheng Zengsong Ziliao Yingben: Gongye Fazhan Lei (1)*. [Xeroxed data donated by Mr. Li Guoding: industrial development]. Retained by the Institute of the Three People's Principles, National Taiwan University.

_____. 1985c. *Li Guoding Xiansheng Zengsong Ziliao Yingben: Jingji Fazhan (10)* [Xeroxed data donated by Mr. Li Guoding: economic development]. Retained by the Institute of the Three People's Principles, National Taiwan University,

Li, Guoding, and Chen Muzai. 1987. *Woguo Jingji Fazhan Celue Zongluen* [Out country's development strategies]. Vol. 1. Taibei: Lianjing.

Li, Huiqing. 1985. Woguo Fangzhiping Chukou Peie Wenti Zhi Yanjiu. [A Study of Our Country's Textile Export Quotas]. Master Thesis. Zhenzhi University.

Lim, Hyun-Chin. 1985. *Dependent Development in Korea 1963–1979*. Seoul: Seoul National University Press.

Lim, Manuel T., ed. 1985. *Industry Analysis for Business Policy and Planning*. Manila: Sinag-Tala.

Lin, Bangchong. 1969. Taiwan Mianfangzhi Gongye Fazhan Zhi Yanjiu [A study of the development of Taiwan's cotton textile industry]. *Taiwan Yinhang Jikan* 20(2): 76–125.

Lin, Rongfang. 1971. Taiwan Dianzi Gongye Zhi Qiaowaizi [Foreign investments in Taiwan's electronics industry]. *Taiwan Yinhang Jikan* 22: 172–78.

Lin, Zonghua. 1978[?]. *Ziyou Zhongguo Mianfangzhi Gongye Zhi Yanjiu* [A study of free China's cotton textile industry]. Taibei: N.P.

Little, Ian M. D. 1982. *Economic Development: Theory, Policy, and International Relations.* New York: Basic Books.

Liu, Fengwen. 1980. *Waihui Maoyi Zhengce U Maoyi Kuozhan* [Foreign trade policy and trade development]. Taibei: Lianjing.

Luedde-Neurath, Richard. 1988. State Intervention and Export-oriented Development in South Korea. In *Developmental States in East Asia*, ed. Gordon White. New York: St. Martin's Press.

Lynn, Leonard H., and Timothy J. McKeown. 1988. *Organizing Business: Trade Associations in America and Japan.* Washington, D.C.: American Enterprise Institute for Public Policy Research.

Macapagal, Diosdado. 1968. *A Stone for the Edifice: Memoirs of a President.* Quezon City, the Philippines: Mac Publishing House.

Machado, K. G. 1975. From Traditional Faction to Machine. *Journal of Asian Studies* 33(4): 523–47.

Mahler, Vincent A. 1980. *Dependency Approaches to International Political Economy: A Cross-National Study.* New York: Columbia University Press.

Makil, Perla Q. 1975. *Mobility by Decree: The Rise and Fall of Philippine Influentials Since Martial Law.* Quezon City, the Philippines: Ateneo de Manila University Press.

Makil, Perla Q., Leonora A. Reyes, and Kenji Koike. 1983. *Philippines Business Leaders.* Tokyo: Institute of Developing Economies.

Malloy, James M., ed. 1977. *Authoritarianism and Corporatism in Latin America.* Pittsburgh: University of Pittsburgh Press.

Marcos, Ferdinand E. 1970. National Discipline, State of the Nation Message. Manila: Department of Public Information.

———. 1973. *Notes on the New Society of the Philippines.* Manila: Office of Media Affairs.

———. 1983. *Revolution from the Center.* Hong Kong: Raya Books.

Maxfield, Sylvia, and James H. Nolt. 1987. Protectionism and the Internationalization of Capital. Manuscript.

McCord, William. 1991. *The Dawn of the Pacific Century: Implications for Three Worlds of Development*. New Brunswick, NJ: Transaction.

Mendoza, Luningning S. 1968. The Plywood Industry in the Philippines. Master's thesis. College of Business Administration, University of the Philippines.

Meyer, John W., and Brian Rowan. 1977. Institutionalized Organizations: Formal Structure as Myth and Ceremony. *American Journal of Sociology* 83: 340–63.

Migdal, Joel S. 1988. *Strong Societies and Weak States: State-Society Relations and State Capabilities in the Third World*. Princeton: Princeton University Press.

Milne, Stephen. 1983. Corporatism in the ASEAN Countries. *Contemporary Southeast Asia* 5: 172–84.

Milner, Helen V. 1988. *Resisting Protectionism: Global Industries and the Politics of International Trade*. Princeton: Princeton University Press.

Miranda, Felipe B. 1986. The Political Economy of ASEAN Development: The Philippines Under Marcos. Manuscript.

Moon, Chung-in. 1990. Beyond Statism. *International Studies Notes* 15(1): 24–27, 34.

Morawetz, David. 1977. *Twenty-five Years of Economic Development 1950 to 1975*. Washington, D.C.: World Bank.

_____. 1981. *Why the Emperor's New Clothes Are Not Made in Colombia: A Case Study in Latin American and East Asian Manufactured Exports*. New York: Oxford University Press.

Moskowitz, Karl, ed. 1984. *From Patron to Partner: The Development of U.S.-Korean Business and Trade Relations*. Lexington, MA: Lexington Books.

Myint, H. 1982. Comparative Analysis of Taiwan's Economic Development with Other Countries. *Academia Economic Papers* 10(1): 15–37.

Nakamura, Takafusa. 1981. *The Postwar Japanese Economy: Its Development and Structure*. Trans. Jacqueline Kaminski. Tokyo: University of Tokyo Press.

Nelson, Joan M., ed. 1990. *Economic Crisis and Policy Choice: The Politics of Adjustment in the Third World*. Princeton: Princeton University Press.

Nelson, Richard R., and Sidney G. Winter. 1982. *An Evolutionary Theory of Economic Change*. Cambridge: Harvard University Press.

North, Douglass C. 1981. *Structure and Change in Economic History*. New York: W. W. Norton.

_____. 1990. *Institutions, Institutional Change and Economic Performance.* Cambridge: Cambridge University Press.

Nowak, Thomas C., and Kay A. Snyder. 1974. Clientelist Politics in the Philippines. *American Political Science Review* 68(3): 1147–70.

Numazaki, Ichiro. 1986. Networks of Taiwanese Big Business. *Modern China* 12(4): 487–534.

O'Connor, David C. 1988. Microelectronics-Based Innovations: Strategic Implications for Selected Industries in the Second-Tier Newly Industrializing Countries (NICs) of Southeast Asia. Report prepared for the OECD Development Center.

O'Connor, James. 1973. *The Fiscal Crisis of the State.* New York: St. Martin's Press.

Odell, John S. 1984. Growing Trade and Growing Conflict Between the Republic of Korea and the United States. In *From Patron to Partner: The Development of U.S.-Korean Business and Trade Relations*, ed. Karl Moskowitz. Lexington, MA: Lexington Books.

Ofreneo, Rene E., and Esther P. Habana. 1987. *The Employment Crisis and the World Bank's Adjustment Program.* Quezon City, the Philippines: University of the Philippines.

Okimoto, Daniel I. 1989. *Between MITI and the Market: Japanese Industrial Policy for High Technology.* Stanford: Stanford University Press.

Olson, Mancur. 1982. *The Rise and Decline of Nations: Economic Growth, Stagflation, and Social Rigidities.* New Haven: Yale University Press.

Organization for Economic Cooperation and Development (OECD). 1979. *The Impact of the Newly Industrialising Countries: On Production and Trade in Manufactures.* Paris: OECD.

Oshima, Harry T. 1987. *Economic Growth in Monsoon Asia: A Comparative Study.* Tokyo: University of Tokyo Press.

Ouchi, William G. 1984. *The M-Form Society: How American Teamwork Can Recapture the Competitive Edge.* Reading, MA: Addison-Wesley.

Pang, Chien-Kuo. 1988. The State and Economic Transformation. Ph.D. diss., Brown University.

Park, Chung Hee. 1979. *Korea Reborn: A Model for Development.* Englewood Cliffs, NJ: Prentice-Hall.

Park, Moon Kyu. 1987. Interest Representation in South Korea. *Asian Survey* 27(8): 903–17.

Payer, Cheryl. 1982. *The World Bank: A Critical Analysis.* New York: Monthly Review Press.

Pempel, T. J., and Keiichi Tsunekawa. 1979. Corporatism Without

Labor? In *Trends Toward Corporatist Intermediation*, ed. Philippe C. Schmitter and Gerhard Lehmbruch. Beverly Hills, CA: Sage.

Petras, James F. 1981. *Class, State, and Power in the Third World: With Case Studies on Class Conflict in Latin America*. Montclair: Allanheld, Osmun.

Pfeffer, Jeffrey, and Gerald R. Salancik. 1978. *The External Control of Organizations: A Resource Dependence Perspective*. New York: Harper & Row.

Philippine Lumber and Plywood Manufacturers Association (PLPMA). 1974–.

1976, 1978, 1979. *Annual Report*. Manila: PLPMA.

Philippine Wood Products Association (PWPA). 1980–1987. *Annual Report*. Manila: PWPA.

Plywood Manufacturers Association of the Philippines (PMAP). 1968. Status of the Veneer and Plywood Industry in the Philippines. Position paper in regard to the inclusion of the veneer and plywood industry in the investments priorities plan under R.A. No. 5186 "Investments Incentives Act."

———. 1970, 1971. *Annual Report*. Manila: PMAP.

Porter, Michael E. 1990. The Competitive Advantages of Nations. *Harvard Buisness Review* (2): 73–93.

Poulantzas, Nicos. 1973. *Political Power and Social Classes*. Trans. Timothy O'Hagan. London: NLB and Sheed & Ward.

Presidential Committee on Wood Industries Development (PCWID). 1971. Philippine Forestry and Wood Industries Development. Report of the PCWID.

Private Development Corporation of the Philippines (PDCP). 1974. Studies on Philippine Industries: Number 10—Textile Industry. Manila: PDCP.

———. 1977. Studies on Philippine Industries: Number 16—The Wood Industry (Updated). Manila: PDCP.

Przeworski, Adam. 1985. *Capitalism and Social Democracy*. Cambridge: Cambridge University Press.

Przeworski, Adam, and Henry Teune. 1970. *The Logic of Comparative Social Inquiry*. New York: John Wiley.

Qu, Jinzhou. 1964. Taiwan Zhi Dueiri Maoyi [Taiwan's trade with Japan]. *Taiwan Yinhang Jikan* 15(3): 41–84.

Ramiro, Rolando R. 1965. A Survey of Some Attitudes Toward Current Governmental Policies Affecting Business and Industry. *Philippine Review of Business and Economics* 2(1): 26–33.

Rhee, Yung Whee. 1985. *Instruments for Export Policy and Administration: Lessons from the East Asian Experience.* World Bank Staff Working Papers No. 725. Washington, D.C.: World Bank.

Robinson, Pearl T. 1991. Niger: Anatomy of a Neotraditional Corporatist State. *Comparative Politics* 24(1): 1–20.

Robison, Richard. 1988. Authoritarian States, Capital-Owning Classes, and the Politics of Newly Industrializing Countries. *World Politics* 41: 52–74.

Rodriguez, Filemon C. 1986. *The Marcos Regime: Rape of the Nation.* Quezon City, the Philippines: MOED Press.

Rudolph, Lloyd, and Suanne H. Rudolph. 1988[?]. Centrist Politics, Class Politics and the Indian State as Third Actor. Manuscript.

Rueschemeyer, Dietrich, and Peter B. Evans. 1985. The State and Economic Transformation. In *Bringing the State Back in*, ed. Peter B. Evans, Dietrich Rueschemeyer, and Theda Skocpol. Cambridge: Cambridge University Press.

Salgado, Pedro V. O.P. 1985. *The Philippine Economy: History and Analysis.* Quezon City, the Philippines: R.P. Garcia.

Schmitter, Philippe C. 1971. *Interest Conflict and Political Change in Brazil.* Stanford: Stanford University Press.

———. 1979. Still the Century of Corporatism? In *Trends Toward Corporatist Intermediation*, ed. Philippe C. Schmitter and Gerhard Lehmbruch. Beverly Hills, CA: Sage.

———. 1981. Interest Intermediation and Regime Governability in Contemporary Western Europe and North America. In *Organizing Interests in Western Europe: Pluralism, Corporatism, and the Transformation of Politics*, ed. Suzanne Berger. Cambridge: Cambridge University Press.

———. 1990. Sectors in Modern Capitalism. In *Labor Relations and Economic Performance*, ed. Renato Brunetta and Carlo Dell' Aringa. New York: MacMillan.

Schmitter, Philippe C., and Gerhard Lehmbruch, eds. 1979. *Trends Toward Corporatist Intermediation.* Beverly Hills, CA: Sage.

Schumpeter, Joseph A. 1934. *The Theory of Economic Development: An Inquiry into Profits, Capital, Credit, Interest, and the Business Cycle.* Trans. Redvers Opie. New Brunswick, NJ: Transaction Books.

Scott, James C. 1972. Patron-Client Politics and Political Change in Southeast Asia. *American Political Science Review* 66(1): 91–113.

Scott, W. Richard. 1987. *Organizations: Rational, Natural, and Open Systems.* 2d ed. Englewood, NJ: Prentice-Hall.

Senghaas, Dieter. 1985. *The European Experience: A Historical Critique of Development Theory*. Trans. K. H. Kimmig. Dover, NH: Berg Publishers.

Shafer, Michael D. 1990. Sectors, States and Social Forces. *Comparative Politics* 22(2): 127–50.

Shalom, Stephen Rosskamm. 1981. *The United States and the Philippines: A Study of Neocolonialism*. Philadelphia: Institute for the Study of Human Issues.

Shen, Yunlong. 1972. *Yin Zhongrong Xiansheng Nianpu* [Biography of Yin Zhongrong]. Taibei: Zhuanji Wenxue.

Sicat, Gerardo P. 1972. *Economic Policy and Philippine Development*. Quezon City: University of the Philippines Press.

Smith, Adam. 1976 [1904]. *The Wealth of Nations*. Chicago: University of Chicago Press.

Smith, Tony. 1986. The Underdevelopment of Development Literature. In *The State and Development in the Third World*, ed. Atul Kohli. Princeton: Princeton University Press.

Snow, Robert T. 1983. The Bourgeois Opposition to Export-Oriented Industrialization in the Philippines. Third World Studies Papers Series No. 39. Third World Studies Center, University of the Philippines.

Stauffer, Robert B. 1977. Philippine Corporatism. *Asian Survey* 17(4): 393–407.

Stene, Edwin O. 1940. Public Administration. *American Political Science Review* 34: 1124–37.

Stepan, Alfred. 1978. *The State and Society: Peru in Comparative Perspective*. Princeton: Princeton University Press.

Stinchcombe, Arthur L. 1990. *Information and Organizations*. Berkeley: University of California Press.

Strange, Susan. 1985. Protection and World Politics. *International Organization* 39(2): 233–60.

Sunkel, Osvaldo. 1972. Big Business and "Dependencia." *Foreign Affairs* (April): 517–31.

Sussman, Gerald, David O'Connor, and Charles Lindsey. 1984. The Political Economy of a Dying Dictatorship. *Philippine Research Bulletin*, Summer: 1–7.

Systems Sciences Consult (SSC). 1987. Electronics Sector: Part 1 of the Program. Progress report submitted to the Department of Trade and Industry and Board of Investments, the Government of the Philippines.

Tai, Hung-Chao. 1974. *Land Reform and Politics: A Comparative Analysis.* Berkeley: University of California Press.

Tai, Hung-Chao, ed. 1989. *Confucianism and Economic Development: An Oriental Alternative?* Washington, D.C.: Washington Institute Press.

Taiwan Cotton Spinners Association (TCSA). 1951–1966. Internal documents. My collection.

Taiwan Cotton Spinners Association. 1972–1987. *Taiwanqu Mianfang Gongye Tongye Gonghui Huiyuan Daibiao Dahui Shouce.* [TCSA proceedings.] Taibei: TCSA.

Taiwan Electric Appliance Manufacturers Association (TEAMA). 1952–1988. Internal documents and proceedings. 45 volumes. My collection. [When unnumbered, reference by date.] Taibei: TEAMA.

———. 1988. *Taiwanqu Diangong Qicai Gongye Tongye Gonghui Sishi Zhounian Jinian Tekan* [A special edition for the fortieth anniversary of TEAMA]. Taibei: TEAMA.

———. 1989–1991. Proceedings of the Annual Meeting. Taibei: TEAMA.

Taiwan Plywood Manufacturers & Exporters Association (TPMEA). 1962–1991. *Taiwanqu Heban Zhizao Shuchuye Tongye Gonghui Huiyuan Daibiao Dahui Shouce* [TPMEA proceedings]. Taibei: TPMEA.

Taiwan Textile Federation (TTF). 1980. *Statistics on Taiwan Textile and Apparel Industries.* Taibei: TTF Weekly.

———. 1986. *Statistics on Taiwan Textile and Apparel Industries.* Taibei: TTF Weekly.

———. 1987. *Textile Year Book 1987.* Taibei: TTF.

Talingdan, Arsenio P. ed. 1966. *Public Administration and Management in the Philippines.* Quezon City, the Philippines: Phoenix Press.

Tancangco, Luzviminda G. 1988. The Electoral System and Political Parties in the Philippines. In *Government and Politics of the Philippines,* ed. Raul P. De Guzman and Mila A. Reforma. Singapore: Oxford University Press.

Timberman, David G. 1991. *A Changeless Land: Continuity and Change in Philippine Politics.* New York: M.E. Sharpe.

Turner, Louis, and Neil McMullen, eds. 1982. *The Newly Industrializing Countries: Trade and Adjustment.* London: George Allen & Unwin.

U.S. International Trade Commission (USITC). 1982. *Emerging Textile-Exporting Countries.* Washington D.C.: U.S. International Trade Commission.

Valdepenas, Vicente B., Jr. 1970. *The Protection and Development of Philippine Manufacturing.* Manila: Ateneo de Manila University Press.

Veneracion, Jaime B. 1988. *Merit or Patronage: A History of the Philippine Civil Service*. Quezon City, the Philippines: Great Books Trading.

Vernon, Raymond. 1971. *Sovereignty at Bay: The Multinational Spread of U.S. Enterprises*. New York: Basic Books.

Villegas, Edberto M. 1983a. Japanese Capitalism and the Asian Development Bank. Third World Studies Papers Series No. 38. Third World Studies Center, University of the Philippines.

_____. 1983b. *Studies in Philippine Political Economy*. Manila: Silangan.

Vogel, Ezra F. 1985. *Comeback: Case by Case Building the Resurgence of American Business*. New York: Simon and Schuster.

Wade, Robert. 1988. State Intervention in 'Outward-looking' Development. In *Developmental States in East Asia*, ed. Gordon White. New York: St. Martin's Press.

_____. 1990a. Industrial Policy in East Asia. In *Manufacturing Miracles: Paths of Industrialization in Latin America and East Asia*, ed. Gary Gereffi and Donald L. Wyman. Princeton: Princeton University Press.

_____. 1990b. *Governing the Market: Economic Theory and the Role of Government in East Asian Industrialization*. Princeton: Princeton University Press.

Wallerstein, Immanuel. 1978. *The Capitalist World-economy*. Cambridge: Cambridge University Press.

Wang, Kejing. 1987. *Taiwan Mingjian Chanyie Sishi Nian* [Taiwan's private industries in the past forty years]. Taibei: Zili Wanbao.

Wang, Zuorong. 1967. *Tai Wan Jin Ji Fa Zhan Zhi Lu* [The road of Taiwan's economic development]. Taibei: N.P.

Wen, Boxian. 1966. *Zhonghua Minguo Gongshang Fadian* [Industrial and commerce laws of the Repubic of China]. Taibei: Zhongguo Gongshang.

White, Gordon, ed. 1988. *Developmental States in East Asia*. New York: St. Martin's Press.

White, Gordon, and Robert Wade. 1988. Developmental States and Markets in East Asia. In *Developmental States in East Asia*, ed. Gordon White. New York: St. Martin's Press.

Winckler, Edwin A. 1988. Globalist, Statist, and Network Paradigms in East Asia. In *Contending Approaches to the Political Economy of Taiwan*, ed. Edwin A. Winckler and Susan Greenhalgh. Armonk, NJ: M.E. Sharpe.

Wolters, Willem. 1984. *Politics, Patronage and Class Conflict in Central Luzon*. Quezon City, the Philippines: New Day.

Wong, Siu-lun. Modernization and Chinese Cultural Traditions in Hong Kong. 1989. In *Confucianism and Economic Development: An Oriental Alternative?* ed. Hung-Chao Tai. Washington, D.C.: Washington Institute Press.

Woodward, Joan. 1980. *Industrial Organization: Theory and Practice.* 2nd ed. New York: Oxford University Press.

World Bank. 1976. *The Philippines: Priorities and Prospects for Development.* Washington, D.C.: World Bank.

———. 1980. *Philippines: Industrial Development Strategy and Policies.* Washington, D.C.: World Bank.

———. 1987a. *Philippines: A Framework for Economic Recovery.* Washington, D.C.: World Bank.

———. 1987b. *World Development Report 1987.* Washington, D.C.: World Bank.

———. 1988. *World Development Report 1988.* Washington, D.C.: World Bank.

Wu, Yuan-li. 1985. *Becoming An Industrialized Nation: ROC's Development on Taiwan.* New York: Praeger.

Wurfel, David. 1979. The Changing Relationship Between Political and Economic Elites in the Philippines. In *Poverty and Social Change in Southeast Asia*, ed. Ozay Mehnet. Ottawa: University of Ottawa Press.

Xu, Boyuan. 1969. *Waimaohui Shisi Nian* [The past forty years of the Foreign Exchange and Trade Control Committee]. Taibei: Foreign Exchange and Trade Control Committee.

Xu, Dixing. 1947. *Guanliao Ziben Luen* [On bureaucratic capitalism]. Hong Kong: Nanyiang.

Yang, Aili. 1989. *Sun Yunxuan Zhuan* [Biography of Sun Yunxuan]. Taibei: Tianxia Zazhi.

Ye, Wanan. 1970. Taiwan Jingji Jianshe Jihua Zi Neirong U Bianzhi [The content and formulation of Taiwan's economic development plans]. *Taiwan Yinhang Jikan* 21: 1–35.

Ye, Zhongbo. 1970. Taiwan Jingji Jianshe Jihua Zhi Zhixing U Chengguo [The implementation and outcomes of Taiwan's economic development plans]. *Taiwan Yinhang Jikan* 21: 36–56.

Yen, Yonghuang. 1976. Taiwan Heban Gongye Fazhan Zhi Shizheng Yanjiu [An empirical study of the development of Taiwan's plywood industry]. *Taiwan Yinhang Jikan* 27: 111–35.

Yin, Zhongrong. 1959a. A Retrospect on "Adverse Trend in Taiwan's Industrial Development." *Industry of Free China*, 11: 2–10.

_____. 1959b. A Review of Existing Foreign Exchange and Trade Control Policy and Technique. *Industry of Free China*, 12: 2–21.

Yu, Zongxian, ed. 1975a. *Essays on Taiwan's Money and Finance*. Taipei: Lianjing.

Yu, Zongxian, ed. 1975b. *Essays on Taiwan's Agricultural Development*. Taipei: Lianjing.

Zeigler, Harmon. 1988. *Pluralism, Corporatism, and Confucianism: Political Association and Conflict Regulation in the United States, Europe, and Taiwan*. Philadelphia: Temple University Press.

Zhang, Zonghan. 1980. *Guangfuqian Taiwan Zi Gongyehua* [Taiwan's industrialization before retrocession]. Taibei: Lianjing.

Zhou, Zhen. 1973. Taiwan Heban Waixiao Uqi Wenti Zhi Tantao [A study of the exportation and problems of Taiwan's plywood]. *Taiwan Yinhang Jikan* 24: 83–114.

Zysman, John. 1983. *Governments, Markets, and Growth: Financial Systems and the Politics of Industrial Change*. Ithaca: Cornell University Press.

Index

Agencies: international, 6, 8, 28–29, 84; state, 42, 81, 115–18, 119–20

Agricultural sectors, 56; in Taiwan, 53–54, 145, 147

Aid, foreign. *See* U.S. aid

Ammonia supplies, for plywood industry, 145–46, 147

Asia, corporatism in, 39

Association for Exporters, 72

Authoritarianism, 12, 219*n8;* and economic development, 4, 219*n10;* in the Philippines, 79–85, 123, 159; in Taiwan, 60, 73. *See also* Clientelism, authoritarian

Autonomous state, 219*n7,* 220*n14;* in developmental state concept, 10–11, 12–13, 200–03; the Philippines as, 64–65, 74, 123–24; Taiwan as, 59–60, 105, 110, 148–49

Bailouts, government: of Marcos cronies, 83, 85; in Taiwan textile industry, 93, 97

Balance-of-payments pressure: caused by export-led industrialization strategy, 7; effect on Philippine plywood industry, 158

Balassa, Bela, 7, 8, 42

Bankruptcies: in semiconductor industry, 168–69; in textile industry, 93, 97

Banks, lack of cooperation of, 161

Bataan Export Processing Zone, 59

Bataan nuclear power plant, corruption in, 81

Bell Mission, 57, 58

Black market, 58, 116, 230*nn23, 26;* in Taiwan, 54, 104, 147

Bonded factories, in Taiwan plywood industry, 142, 144, 146

Brazil, liberal economics in, 8

Bureaucracy, 11, 13–14, 65; under clientelism, 34, 79–81; limitations of, 28–31, 61, 75–76. *See also* Red tape

Bureau of Industry, 107

Bureau of International Trade (BIT), 107

Business associations, 23, 224*n23;* and clientelism, 33, 39, 67–68, 78, 85; and corporatism, 35–39, 206–07, 209, 222*n11;* functions of, 17–18, 42–43, 71–73, 178; in game models of economic institutions, 46; growth of, 69–70, 73–74, 97–98; in laissez-faire system, 31. *See also* Industry associations

Business community, 72; confidence of, 33, 35; under corporatism, 36, 38; ethnicity of Philippine, 81, 227*n29*

Business sectors, 56, 73; under clientelism, 67, 78

Capacity, state, 33–34; in developmental state concept, 11, 13

Capital: of foreign direct investments, 170–71; of Taiwan, 54

Capital-intensive projects, 58, 81

Capitalism, 223*n20;* booty, 80; in dependency theory, 9–10, 30

Capitalists, 85; state's autonomy from, 10, 13, 59–60, 65

Central Bank, and Filipino textile industry, 116

Centralization, in developmental state concept, 13–14, 60, 65

China, 4, 54–55, 68

259